11·35
2.

Rebellion, Revolution, and Armed Force

STUDIES IN SOCIAL DISCONTINUITY

Under The Consulting Editorship of:

CHARLES TILLY   EDWARD SHORTER
University of Michigan   *University of Toronto*

William A. Christian, Jr. Person and God in a Spanish Valley

Joel Samaha. Law and Order in Historical Perspective: The Case of Elizabethan Essex

John W. Cole and Eric R. Wolf. The Hidden Frontier: Ecology and Ethnicity in an Alpine Valley

Immanuel Wallerstein. The Modern World-System: Capitalist Agriculture and the Origins of the European World-Economy in the Sixteenth Century

John R. Gillis. Youth and History: Tradition and Change in European Age Relations 1770 – Present

D. E. H. Russell. Rebellion, Revolution, and Armed Force: A Comparative Study of Fifteen Countries with Special Emphasis on Cuba and South Africa

In preparation

Kristian Hvidt. Flight to America: The Social Background of 300,000 Danish Emigrants

Rebellion, Revolution, and Armed Force

A Comparative Study of Fifteen Countries with Special Emphasis on Cuba and South Africa

D. E. H. Russell

Division of Social Science
Mills College
Oakland, California

Academic Press, Inc.   New York San Francisco London

A Subsidiary of Harcourt Brace Jovanovich, Publishers

ACADEMIC PRESS, INC.
111 Fifth Avenue, New York, New York 10003

United Kingdom Edition published by
ACADEMIC PRESS, INC. (LONDON) LTD.
24/28 Oval Road, London NW1

Library of Congress Cataloging in Publication Data

Russell, D. E. H.
     Rebellion, revolution, and armed force.

     (Studies in social discontinuity)
     Bibliography: p.
     1.   Revolutions.   2.   Revolutions—Case studies.
3.   Armed forces—Political activity.   I.   Title.
II.   Series.
HM281.R86   301.5′92   74-7205
ISBN 0−13−785745−1

To those who are struggling for a more just South Africa

... few attempts seem to have been made to assemble the historical facts of various revolutions in an endeavor to deduce from them whether there be any general laws which govern the practical conduct of a revolutionary outbreak and account for its success or failure.

K. C. CHORLEY, *Armies and the Art of Revolution*

To determine whether revolutions are governed by constant laws, there is only one method: we must compare one with the other the greatest possible number of revolutions . . . and we must see whether between these phenomena so far apart in time and space there can be discovered similarities and dissimilarities which are constant.

G. SALVEMINI, *Historian and Scientist; An Essay on the Nature of History and the Social Sciences*

Contents

Preface

The study on the role of armed forces in rebellion, presented in the second half of this volume, was written originally as my doctoral dissertation.[1] While these chapters have since been revised to include the most recent scholarly data, in those cases where the data were already considerable and of good quality, the analyses were not redone. However, for many cases where new data on the behavior of the armed forces were available, they were incorporated into the case studies.

In contrast to the original study, the scope of the book has been greatly broadened. General questions relating to oppression are raised and discussed, the literature on rebellion and revolution is critically evaluated, the cases of Cuba and, particularly, South Africa are analyzed in detail, and finally, the implications of the findings and analyses are presented, especially as they relate to foreign policy toward South Africa.

A number of people have been very helpful in different ways throughout the course of this study. Most of all I wish to thank Charles Tilly for

[1]D. E. H. Russell, A comparative study of the relation between the loyalty of armed forces and the outcome of mass rebellion in the twentieth century. Unpublished doctoral dissertation, Harvard University, 1970.

his ready and sound advice on many occasions. He was particularly helpful in the early phases of the research, and then again later in his suggestions as to how I might transform my dissertation into a more readable
and, hopefully, a more significant book. Aside from his personal advice,
which has been considerable, I found his own work most useful when it
came to designing and carrying out my study: first, because of his insis-
tence on the need to try to measure political upheaval, while at the same
time do justice to the data; and second, because of his unusual ability
to do work that is guided by important theoretical considerations, as well
as highly sophisticated methodology. These exemplary attributes, combined with his personal encouragement and advice, have been invaluable
to me.

Next, I want to thank Kenneth Carstens for the many informative
comments and useful suggestions he made after reading an earlier draft of
of the book, particularly on the South African material. I followed many
of his suggestions and incorporated some of his information. I am also
very grateful for his encouragement and enthusiasm for the book, in spite
of its depressing conclusions, and for his helping me to go against the
usual scholarly tradition in clearly expressing my view in favor of intervention in support of black Africans in South Africa. I believe scholarship
should inform people's politics, even when it leads to regrettable conclusions. I also believe that political concern should not make scholarship suspect. Kenneth Carstens helped me to be more true to these views.

I would like to thank Maria Leslie for going through the Spanish sources
for the cases of Cuba (1912, 1959), Brazil (1930), and Bolivia (1952).
Although there was very little specific information on the behavior of the
armed forces in these rebellions in the Spanish sources, it was important
that this material be examined. (Since these sources were so unhelpful,
however, most of them have not been included in the selected bibliography.)

I am very grateful to Arlene Daniels for her willingness to make extensive editorial suggestions on the first half of the book at a time that was
very inconvenient for her. I also want to thank Jack Fremont for his suggestions on the style of the Introduction and Chapter One; and Laurie
Tempkin and Linda Wong for their help in the arduous task of locating
books and articles at the University of California library at Berkeley.

Finally, I am very grateful to Phyillis Pacin for her incredible ability to
decipher my handwriting and for her careful typing of the final manuscript.

I also want to thank the Center of International Studies at Princeton
University for a Research Associateship during the academic year 1967—
1968, which gave me time to research the study presented in this volume.
And, I would like to thank Mills College for a grant to help me cover
typing costs.

Credits

Pages 7 and 15: From Tilly, Charles, and James Rule. 1965. *Measuring political upheaval*. Princeton, New Jersey: Center of International Studies, Princeton University Research Monograph No. 19

Page 14: From Johnson, Chalmers A. 1966. *Revolutionary change*. Boston: Little, Brown, pp. 32, 91. Copyright © 1966 by Little, Brown and Company. Reprinted by permission.

Page 17: From Draper, Theodore. 1962. *Castro's revolution. Myths and realities*. New York: Praeger.

Pages 32 and 35: From van den Berghe, Pierre L. 1965. *South Africa: A study in conflict*. Middletown, Connecticut: Wesleyan University Press. Copyright © 1965 by Weslyan University Press. Reprinted by permission of the publisher.

Page 34: From Bunting, Brian. 1964. *The rise of the South African reich*. London: Penguin.

Pages 43, 52, and 82: From Adam, Heribert (Ed.) 1971. *South Africa: Sociological perspectives*. London and New York: Oxford University Press. Reprinted by permission of the publisher.

Page 61: From Chorley, Katherine. 1943. *Armies and the art of revolution*. London: Faber and Faber.

Page 88: From Chapelle, Dickey. 1962. *How Castro won*. In F. M. Osana (Ed.), *Modern guerilla war: Fighting communist movements 1941–1961*. New York: Free Press. Originally published in the Marine Corps Gazette, February 1960. Copyright 1960 by the Marine Corps Association.

Pages 92–95: From *Afghanistan*, by W. K. Fraser-Tytler, revised by Sir M. C. Gillet. Published 1967 by Oxford University Press and reproduced by permission of the publisher.

Pages 96–98:   From Swire, Joseph. 1929. *Albania: The rise of a kingdom*. London: Unwin Bros., Ltd.

Pages 100–101:   From *Hispanic American Report*, Vol. 5, No. 4. (May, 1952) pp. 34–35. Reproduced by permission of the Center for Latin American Studies, Stanford University.

Pages 104–106:   From *Politics in Brazil, 1930–1964: An experiment in democracy*, by Thomas E. Skidmore. Copyright © 1967 by Oxford University Press, Inc. Reprinted by permission.

Pages 106 and 107:   From Bello, José M. 1966. *A history of modern Brazil, 1899–1964*, Transl. by J. L. Taylor. Stanford, California: Stanford University Press.

Pages 109–111:   From *China*. Reprinted by permission, ©. *Encyclopaedia Britannica*, 1967.

Page 114:   From Gittings, John. 1967. *The role of the Chinese army*. London and New York: Oxford University Press.

Pages 115–116,   From Lieuwen, Edwin. 1958. *Arms and politics in Latin America*.
119, and 124   New York: Praeger.

Page 120:   From Goldenberg, Boris. 1965. *The Cuban revolution and Latin America*. New York: Praeger.

Pages 121–123:   From Cline, Howard F. 1963. *The United States and Mexico*. Cambridge, Massachusetts: Harvard University Press.

Pages 126–127:   From Hasluck, Eugene L. 1938. *Foreign affairs, 1919–1937*. Cambridge, England: Cambridge University Press.

Pages 128–129:   From Hall, Daniel G. E. 1960. *Burma*, 3rd ed. London: Hutchinson.

Pages 129–130:   From Trager, Frank N. 1954. *Burma: Land of golden pagodas*. New York: Foreign Policy Association.

Pages 132–134:   From *Columbia* by W. O. Galbraith. Published 1966 by Oxford University Press under the auspices of the Royal Institute of International Affairs.

Pages 136–137:   From Russell H. Fitzgibbon, *Cuba and the United States, 1900–1935* [1935]. New York: Russell & Russell, 1964.

Pages 138–139:   From *New International Yearbook: A compendium of the world's affairs*, 1933. New York: Funk & Wagnalls.

Pages 140–141:   From Hughes, Serge. 1967. *The fall and rise of modern Italy*. New York: Macmillan. Copyright©1967 by Serge Hughes.

Pages 142–143:   From *New International Yearbook: A compendium of the world's affairs*, 1934. New York: Funk & Wagnalls.

Introduction

I grew interested in the subject of rebellion when I finally became convinced that the radical social change so desperately needed in South Africa—the country of my birth—could not be achieved through traditional political channels. I found Leo Kuper's (1960, p. 94) conclusion that the whites in South Africa would not be converted by the voluntary suffering entailed by passive resistance intellectually compelling; and I found it a confirmation of my own experiences, particularly in peaceful demonstrations. I accepted Kuper's view that whites could resist conversion because they so strongly believe in the rightness of white domination. Most white South Africans really do not see the "nonwhites" (that is, all peoples with skins darker than their own) as fellow human beings, and consequently are unmoved by the involuntary suffering intrinsic to the black experience in South Africa.[1] Indeed, this suffering is directly related to the benefits the whites receive in a system they have created. Here is what seems to me to be the key reason for the probable ineffectiveness of nonviolent

[1]A rather personal illustration of this is provided by the experience of my brother. He is a white Anglican priest who works in a black African resettlement location in South Africa. As a means of protesting the insufficiency of the government pensions and rations for black

1

means in the South African situation: The whites have too much to lose by a breakdown of a caste system that reserves for them virtually all the power, money, and high-status positions available in the nation. And since the whites in South Africa are no different from any other entrenched group that enjoys a monopoly of privilege and power, they cannot be expected to voluntarily relinquish their position.

However, seeing the futility of a nonviolent strategy and the need for a violent rebellion is one thing. Organizing rebellion is quite another, for it is necessary that a rebellion not only happen, but that it succeed. But is a successful rebellion possible in South Africa? While Kuper's analysis leads to the conclusion that nonviolent methods cannot work against oppressors like white South Africans, it might just as well be true that violent methods will not work either. Many people optimistically believe that if social change is desperately needed and morally justified, it will, or at least *can,* happen. Yet is this notion realistic, both in the South African situation, and in general? What determines the success or failure of a rebellion? Why do some rebellions succeed in overthrowing the regime that is trying to suppress them, while others fail? And more specifically, what is the relationship between regime oppressiveness and the outcome of rebellion? In seeking an answer to these questions, one finds the literature on rebellion, revolution, and related phenomena of extraordinarily little help.

First, it seems that nearly all students of this subject have been preoccupied with the *causes* of rebellion or revolution. The question of what determines the *outcome* has been virtually ignored. Eckstein (1965) makes this point nicely:

> ...almost nothing careful and systematic has been written about the long-run social effects of internal wars .... Little more is available on the determinants of success or failure in internal wars .... But in regard to etiology, to "causes," we are absolutely inundated with print [p. 136].[2]

The profusion of material on etiology not withstanding, there is little agreement on the question of causes. Eckstein (pp. 143–144) lists 21 of the conditions that students of "internal war" (as he calls it) have regarded as causes;

Africans, he recently tried to live for 6 months on $6.37 a month. This is the amount on which African pensioners are expected to live; those receiving rations or maintenance grants receive half this amount. Over and over again whites were appalled at the level of deprivation this involved for him. Since what he experienced was commonplace for black Africans, it is obvious that the horror of living on this inadequate amount was only brought home to many of them because it was a white who was suffering.

[2]Eckstein includes both rebellions and revolutions in his more general category of "internal war."

several of these are quite incompatible. (An evaluation of some of the most widely held of these theories is undertaken in Chapter Three.)

A second imbalance in the literature is the pronounced focus on causes or preconditions as they relate to rebels. The notion that there might also be *regime* preconditions is much less developed. Even when social structural factors are considered important, these factors tend to be regarded as relevant to the rebels, rather than to the regime. For example, it is much more likely that the effect of industrialization on rebel organization and militancy will be considered, than its effect on the coercive capacity or efficient organization of the regime.

This particular type of narrow focus is especially evident in the way armed forces are usually discussed. On the one hand, their importance is widely acknowledged in frequent assertions such as Lenin's that: "No revolution of the masses can triumph without the help of a portion of the armed forces that sustained the old regime ... [Lieuwen 1961, p. 134]." On the other hand, closer examination of this common view shows that it rarely goes beyond lip service; for, in fact, the role or potential role of the armed forces in revolutions is not usually seen as deserving of detailed study, and the behavior of the armed forces is seldom used as an explanation of the outcome of particular rebellions.

A third criticism of the literature is that the theories have been developed largely from analyses of successful cases. Unsuccessful cases and situations in which no revolution has occurred have been virtually ignored. Brinton (1952, p. 22) refers to the "abortive" revolution as if it were a distinct type having nothing in common with a successful revolution. It may be, however, that many of the generalizations that have been made about successful revolutions apply to unsuccessful revolutions, too.

Fourth, it is disappointing to find so little agreement about many issues in this field. Rebellions and revolutions have interested people for centuries, but we really *know* very little about them. Theories and generalizations abound, but rigorous, systematic studies are practically nonexistent. Millions of people have given their lives in support of theories, but few have been willing to do the difficult and often tedious work necessary to establish their theories by the test of science, rather than combat. Until there are more volunteers for this safer, but less dramatic, undertaking, we will continue to *know* little about rebellion and revolution, though we will still be inundated with theories and convictions about them, many of which will be incompatible.

One reason for the chaotic state of the field is that theorists are apt to arrive at their theories and generalizations ex post facto, on the basis of a detailed knowledge of only one or two cases. There is an urgent need for rigorously and systematically conducted studies of many cases that can provide solid tests of the more important theories of rebellion and revolution.

Unfortunately, then, the literature provided me with no satisfactory answers to questions concerning the determinants of the outcome of rebellion, especially as these might apply to the South African situation. The literature was equally unhelpful in throwing light on more specific questions regarding the relationship between regime oppressiveness and the outcome of rebellion. Can regimes and/or their agents of social control, if very oppressive, succeed in suppressing rebellions? Or, on the contrary, does extreme oppression necessarily sow the seeds of its own destruction? And most specifically, can the South African regime maintain its system of injustice and exploitation, or can a rebellion against it succeed? These are the questions explored in this book.

Gurr (1970b; this view is also expressed on p. 238) expresses a widely held view that: "The regime that responds to their [the rebels'] demands only with suppression will intensify their hostility, and is thus likely to speed its own destruction [p. 358]." And again: "No pattern of coercive control, however intense and consistent, is likely to deter permanently all enraged men from violence, except genocide [p. 358]." But is this optimistic view justified? Or is it possible for a sizable proportion of the members of a society to be coerced into living within a system they would desperately like to change? It is difficult to devise a study to answer this question. After all, we cannot assume that people who do not rebel are satisfied with the society in which they live. Nor, as Goode (1972) points out, can we "deduce from observing the use of a low amount of force that all or most subordinates approve the system, or share its values [p. 518]." (Note that Goode is referring to a low amount of force on the part of the rulers.) Studying actual cases of rebellion is the best way to get at this question, since rebellions, at least large-scale ones, are unambiguous indications that many members of a society are dissatisfied, want change, and are actually mobilized against the government and its agents to try to effect change.

If Gurr's widely accepted view, that oppression and coercion cannot work, turns out to be incorrect, the major assumption of the value-consensus school of sociology will be undermined—that is, to quote Dahrendorf (1959), that "every functioning social structure is based on a consensus of values among its members [p. 161]." Moreover, the optimists who believe that "good" must necessarily triumph in the end, will be proven wrong. It would be comforting indeed to find that an oppressive and unresponsive regime is likely to bring about its own destruction: but if this is not the case, it is important for scholars, as well as rebels, to know it.

These are some of the questions that are explored in this book. They are important questions for active and armchair rebels, scholars of rebellion and revolution, those interested in the particular fate of South Africa, humanists concerned with issues of justice, those interested in the factors relevant to achieving radical social change, and policy makers who would like their policies to be based on sound assumptions. I believe this book should also interest sociologists who work in the areas of conflict, social change, and social movements, and those who are concerned with the validity of the value-consensus versus coercion theories. Dahrendorf (1959) has observed that " . . . there is today a considerable need for reorienting sociological analysis to problems of change, conflict, and coercion in social structures, and especially in those of total societies [p. xi]." This book certainly fits all these stipulations. It also satisfies Goode's (1972) plea, in his presidential address to the American Sociological Association, that sociology face up to the great importance of force in human society.

From a methodological point of view, this book should interest comparativists, particularly those who work with historical data, or who believe in the importance of quantitative analysis. And I hope this study will speak to all, sociologists and nonsociologists alike, who believe that phenomena such as rebellion and revolution should be subjected to rigorous methods of research. My hope is that we will start to accumulate scientific knowledge about rebellion and revolution in order to go beyond the current situation in which intuition, knowledge of one or two cases, and wishful thinking, are the bases for our views.

CHAPTER SURVEY

Chapter One is an examination of the relevant literature on rebellion and revolution. In it I make explicit the bases for my bald statements of dissatisfaction with this literature.

In Chapters Two and Three, I discuss the issues of major concern in the context of two different countries. The successful Cuban rebellion of 1958–1959 has often been cited as proof that oppressive policies backfire and ultimately defeat the regimes that use them, and that even the strongest army can be overcome by a resolute band of rebels. Yet the South African regime has been very oppressive for many years without being disturbed by a substantial rebellion. These two cases bring the question of the relationship between oppression and the outcome of rebellion into clear view. They also provide good illustrations of where and why analysts of rebellion and revolution seem to have gone astray. Moreover, the South African case offers me the opportunity to go beyond ex post facto analysis, to put my conclusions on the line by making a definite prediction about whether or not a successful rebellion can occur there.

The role of the armed forces is also examined. Specifically, is Lenin's assertion correct—can a revolution not succeed without the assistance of part of the armed forces? Fourteen cases of successful and unsuccessful rebellions, drawn from different countries and different points in time, are the basis for testing Lenin's theory.

To engage in a rigorous comparative study of this magnitude requires very careful definition of the phenomenon under investigation (in this case, mass rebellion); it requires a method of case selection that is maximally unbiased; and it requires the development of various measures of the variables to be compared across cases. Chapter Four deals with the concept of rebellion and considers its relationship to revolution. The reasons for differentiating these two concepts are discussed, a typology of rebellion is developed, and a detailed rationale for my definition of mass rebellion is given. Chapter Five describes the method used for selecting the seven cases of successful and seven cases of unsuccessful rebellion. Data sources are also discussed in this chapter, and the procedure for operationalizing the variables to be compared is presented. Chapter Seven analyzes each of the seven successful rebellions. Chapter Eight examines each of the unsuccessful cases.

The results of these case studies are summarized and analyzed in Chapter Six, prior to the case-study presentations, to avoid their getting lost in all the data. The theoretical and practical implications of the study are also discussed in Chapter Six.

A final word. It is probably clear by now that my use of the term rebellion is similar to the common use of the term revolution. As I have noted above, the distinction between these concepts is examined in Chapter Four. For now, suffice it to say that *rebellion* is defined as a form of violent power struggle in which the overthrow of the regime is threatened by means that include violence. In a successful rebellion, overthrow is achieved, whereas it is not achieved in an unsuccessful rebellion. A successful *revolution* may be said to have occurred when substantial social change follows a rebellion; and a revolution is regarded as unsuccessful when little social change results therefrom.

1

The Ancien Regime,
Its Armed Forces,
and the Outcome of Rebellion:
The Wisdom of the Past

In 1965, Eckstein pointed out that: "The existing literature concentrates very largely on the rebels, treating internal war as due mainly to changes in the non-elite strata of society to which no adequate adjustment is made by the elite. [1965, p. 145]." This analysis applies to some of the classical scholars, as well as to many contemporary sociologists and historians. Tilly (1964a, b), for example, while acknowledging the importance of the regime in understanding political upheaval,[1] focuses his analysis on "the revolutionary crowd (1964a, p. 100, and b) ." (However, his most recent,

---

[1]For example, Tilly and Rule wrote in 1965:

> Consider another problem in establishing the relationship between particular social changes and political upheaval; if the investigator considers only these two sets of variables, he will certainly fail, for the capacity of the society or its caretakers to repress or dissipate open conflict always stands between them . . . . Weak governments can exist in a variety of conditions of social change; the weakness of the government surely affects the frequency, intensity, shape, and success of violent conflict [p. 24].

unpublished work reveals that this is no longer the case (see Tilly, 1974); Rudé (1959, 1964) also concentrates on the rebels, as do many other contemporary historians of the French Revolution of 1789 [see Tilly (1964a) for an analysis of the works of several of these authors]. Hobsbawm (1959) exemplifies this focus too, in his studies of the British working movements and of "primitive rebels."

Other scholars who are less historically oriented also concentrate on the rebels. Davies (1962, 1969), for example, considers the "state of mind" of the masses as the key variable in whether a revolution will occur or not. And Gurr (1965, 1968, 1970b), while he at least regards the regime as an important "intervening variable," is basically in agreement with Davies's emphasis on the people's "state of mind." With the exception of Le Bon,[2] social–psychological analyses of rebellion, revolution, and mass movements, also tend to ignore the regime for the rebels. Hoffer (1951), for example, as the title of his book, *The True Believer*, indicates, focuses on the mass-movement participant to the exclusion of the regime or the overall social context within which movements occur. This point applies as well to the work of Ellwood (1905–1906), Hopkins (1938), Riezler (1943), and Cantril (1941). Smelser (1963) is exceptional in his emphasis on the importance of the structural context, particularly the regime and its agents of social control, in the origin, development, and outcome of social movements.

These scholars, who ignore the role of the regime and its agents in the revolutionary process, would have the blessing of Marx, for whom revolution is a matter of historical inevitability. At a certain stage in economic development, the factory provides a place for the development of solidarity among the workers, a sense of consciousness of exploitation, and an organizational base for action. Meanwhile, there is an inevitable trend toward increasing exploitation by the capitalists of a growing army of the proletariat. The capitalist regime tries to "resist" the revolution, but the polarization inherent in this stage of capitalism depletes the capitalists' numbers, and their efforts are doomed. There is no shortage of potential revolutionary leaders to fill the places of those arrested and killed. Brutal suppression can only increase the solidarity and consciousness of the workers.[3]

To the extent that the assumptions and theories of Marx permeate our

[2]Gustave Le Bon (1913) wrote, for example, that "The great revolutions have usually commenced from the top, not from the bottom. . .[p. 29]." And again, "It has been very justly said that governments are not overthrown, but that they commit suicide [p. 54]." However, this point of view is less apparent in his better-known work, *The Crowd: A Study of the Popular Mind*.

[3]This is an area where Mao (1967) is in absolute agreement. "In the final analysis, their [the reactionaries] persecution of the revolutionary people only serves to accelerate the people's revolutions on a broader and more intense scale [p. 41]."

thinking today, it is no wonder that there has been so little work on the determinants of success and failure of rebellions and revolutions, and on the role of the regime and the armed forces. Why examine the forces of suppression if they are ultimately useless?

Weber also ignored the regime and armed forces in his discussion of revolutionary change.[4] In times of distress, he theorized, charismatic leaders arise who express and explain the distress, then direct their followers toward a revolutionary "solution" of their discontent.[5] However, Weber failed to discuss the role of hostile and repressive regimes, or friendly and permissive ones in the causes, outcomes, or types of revolutionary movements. Nor did he consider the case in which the regime imprisons any potential charismatic figure. It is true that there are many examples where charisma survives both the imprisonment and death of a leader (Jesus Christ is the most obvious example), but this argument does not adequately come to terms with the possibility that repressive regimes may pose serious, if not insurmountable, obstacles to charismatic leaders.

The fact that Marx and Weber underestimated the importance of the ancien regime and its agents of social control in the occurrence and outcome of rebellion and revolution has, no doubt, contributed to the contemporary scholarly neglect of these topics. Military variables, in particular, are very unpopular with most historians and sociologists who study rebellion and revolution. As McAlister (1957) amusingly observes: "Historians did not like armies because they spoiled history. Their military functions were rather contemptuously relegated to military history and their dimly perceived extramilitary role in society was swept under the rug [p. 582]. " Janowitz (1968), who has contributed so much to the recent development of the field of military sociology, explains the paucity of research on internal and external war as being due to "the intellectual posture of sociology. The discipline," he observes, "has failed to develop a realistic understanding of social structure which would include the military establishment and the role of force [p. 17]."

There are at least four more reasons for the scholarly neglect of the ancien regimes and their armed forces. First, given the great interest in the causes of political upheaval, the focus on rebels has proven to be a very fruitful

[4]As Stanislav Andreski (1968) points out, Weber is one of the very few classical sociologists "who appreciated the importance of military factors in shaping societies [p. 1]." However, this does not apply to Weber's (1947) analysis of revolutionary change and charismatic authority, where the regime, together with the social–structural context, is given little attention.

[5]"Revolutionary" in the sense of "break with an established order." See Weber (1963, p. xxxv). The "distress," in Weber's (Gerth & Mills, 1958) conception, includes practically everything: "psychic, physical, economic, ethical, religious, [and] political distress [p. 245]."

way of studying them, as well as an effective way of replacing myths with facts regarding the social composition of rebellious movements. If it is not the poor who rebel, then the cause cannot be poverty. If the rebels are involved in continuing social and political organizations, then a great increase in the number of "uprooted" people cannot cause rebellion or revolution. These are findings that were brought to light by very careful analyses of exactly who rebelled during the French Revolution of 1789 (see Tilly, 1964a). This approach to research became very popular, particularly with students of the French Revolution, after Brinton's (1930) classic study, *The Jacobins,* showed how wrong were most people's assumptions about the rebels in the French Revolution.

Second, many theorists of social change and social conflict are concerned with long-term, rather than short-term, change and conflict. Given this perspective, particular leaders or regimes become relatively unimportant. For example, Barrington Moore or Talcott Parsons may not consider it very important if a rebellion is delayed 50 years or so; what matters to them is the route to modernization represented, or the long-run consequences.[6] In addition, the Marxist view that political institutions are determined by economic structures has become quite commonly accepted, if in a somewhat milder form than Marx presented. These reformulations hold that political institutions cannot really alter society in a fundamental way. Where Marx emphasized economic variables, Parsons emphasizes values and religion; but few sociologists treat political variables as critical.[7] Students of totalitarianism have a great appreciation for the impact of regimes on society, and naturally enough, political scientists stress political factors in social conflict, but within sociology, the polity is more often viewed as a dependent variable.

The third reason for the current neglect of ancien regimes is ideological. Rebels, both the active and armchair variety, do not want to believe that rebellions and revolutions can be prevented by regimes or armies. They prefer to think that oppressive regimes can be overthrown if the rebels do the right things (as do I). Indeed, it is often regarded as reactionary even to stress the importance of the regime and armed forces. However I believe that a real understanding is served neither by reactionary nor radical wishes.

[6]Goode's (1972) perspective here comes closer to mine. He points out

the cruel fact that a human being lives but a short time, while . . .conquests and tyrannies may last for centuries. To say that they are ineffective because they will ultimately fail to impose their social and cultural systems, ignores the truth that temporarily they do so; and 'temporarily' may well outlast the life of an individual [p. 509].

[7]David Snyder and Tilly (1972) are exceptional in arguing that "the principal, immediate causes of collective violence are political [p. 520]," not economic.

In explaining why sociologists have resisted the study of the military, Janowitz (1968) suggests another important ideological factor: while "sociology has flourished in societies in which there is a strong liberal tradition [p. 17]," this tradition "has served as a barrier to a sociology of the military, for the liberal tradition has in general sought to handle the problem of military institutions by denial [pp. 17–18]."[8] In other words, sociology has played ostrich, rather than confront the importance of the military.

Fourth, sociologists who subscribe to the "integration theory" (see the Introduction) often believe that a regime represents the people's choice. Johnson (1966), for example, writes: "Sociological value theory explicitly rejects the notion that social cooperation is coerced [p. 132]." If people cannot be coerced, then studies of regimes and armed forces, ordinarily seen as the agents of coercion, become much less important in studying rebellion. In any case, whatever the reasons underlying the neglect of the study of ancien regimes and military institutions, the sociology of revolution suffers greatly for it.

Very little work has also been done on the determinants of the outcome of rebellion and related phenomena. Andreski (1968) points out that "the question why a revolution took place must be split into two: first, why did the rebellion occur, and second, why did it succeed [p. 158]?"[9] He goes on to say that "it must not be assumed that there is a simple relation between the incidence of rebellions and their success [p. 158]." Unfortunately, this caution has been heeded but rarely. In fact, Stinchcombe (1965) argues:

> . . . a sociological theory of revolution ought not to expect to be able to tell who will win in a revolutionary situation, but to tell that there will be a fight with unlimited means . . . . Explaining who won, and why, is primarily a problem of military science, not of social science [p. 170].

---

[8]Similarly, Goode (1972) argues that "The systematic study of force . . . has been singularly neglected in the history of social thought [p. 508]." He observes:

> We sociologists have neglected such an examination because we share a long humanistic tradition whose biases deny the ultimate importance of force. We have been taught to believe in man's unconquerable soul, his often mute but always staunch resistance to tyranny . . . . [We] continue to feel, whatever the evidence before our eyes, that somehow human beings do resist force and force threat over time, and that man's will to freedom not only endures, but prevails [p. 509].

[9]Others have made the same point: see Eckstein (1965, p. 136); Johnson (1964, pp. 17–18); and Chorley (1943, p. 11). In fact, Chorley has contributed many useful ideas on the determinants of the outcome of revolutions, particularly the sociomilitary determinants. Her pioneer work in this area has not received the attention it deserves. Unfortunately, however, her comparative analysis is in the historical tradition, rather than in a systematic sociological one.

This is easier to assert than to demonstrate, since work to substantiate or refute such a hypothesis has not yet been done. I believe the results of this study contribute to a refutation of Stinchcombe's point of view.

While there have been few systematic, empirical studies of regime variables in the context of revolution, many classical and contemporary scholars *have* stressed the importance of the regime and its armed forces in the revolutionary process [notably Mosca (1939), Pareto (1935), Chorley (1943), Janos (1964), Andreski (1968), Finer (1962), Edwards (1927), Brinton (1952), Kornhauser (1959, 1966), Smelser (1963), and Eckstein (1965)[10]]. Moreover, contemporary scholars other than Tilly and Gurr have at least acknowledged their importance [for example, Sorokin (1925), Gottschalk (1944), Johnson (1964, 1966), and Stone (1966)], as have revolutionaries like Lenin (Connor, 1968) and Trotsky (1959). However, the notion of "regime variables," like "rebel variables," is amorphous; and there is no consensus on which aspects of regimes are crucial. Finally, where the importance of the regime or the armed forces is recognized, rarely does either variable figure in the analysis of revolution. In light of my concern in this volume with the role of the armed forces in rebellions, I consider below the inadequacy of the literature on this particular topic.

Both Lenin and Le Bon assert the importance of the armed forces in revolution, but do not incorporate its role into their analyses. I have already noted Lenin's claim that "no revolution of the masses can triumph without the help of a portion of the armed forces that sustained the old regime ... [Lieuwen, 1961, p. 134]." Yet when Lenin (Connor, 1968, pp. 151–157) explained how the March 1917 overthrow of the Russian regime was achieved, he said nothing about armed forces. Similarly, Le Bon (1913) insists that, "It is obvious that revolutions have never taken place, and will never take place, save with the aid of an important faction of the army [p. 29].[11] Nevertheless, his analysis focuses largely on "the crowd," and he fails to deal with the important question of what determines whether a faction of the army will "aid" or not.

Smelser,[12] Brinton,[13] Chorley,[14] and Calvert[15] agree with Lenin and Le Bon in their emphasis on the behavior of the armed forces. And in the main these authors, particularly Chorley, go beyond merely asserting the key role of armed forces in the outcome of rebellions. Andreski (1968), too, once subscribed to this view; for example in *Military Organization and Society*, he argued that, "so long as the government retains the loyalty

[10]It is the first six of these authors who place the greatest emphasis on the importance of the regime and its armed forces.

of the armed forces, no revolt can succeed [p. 71]." He (Andreski, 1967) now argues that the Cuban rebellion of 1958–1959 disproves this generalization. Interestingly, Andreski believes it used to be "the best-founded sociological principle in this field [p. 247]."

Leiden and Schmitt (1968), on the other hand, believe that ". . .the view (held by such writers as Gustave Le Bon and Katherine C. Chorley) that no revolution can be consummated without the army's support cannot be substantiated [p. 25]." Though Leiden and Schmitt fail to develop and substantiate *their* position, apparently their viewpoint is widely accepted in the literature.

Che Guevara's (1961, p. 1) and Mao's (1963) belief, a belief shared by Hobsbawm (1965), Debray (1967), and C. Wright Mills (1960),

---

[11]Elsewhere, Le Bon (1913) makes a similar assertion: "A revolution cannot be effected without the assistance or at least the neutrality of the army, but it often happens that the movement commences without it [p. 52]."

[12]Smelser (1963) agrees with Le Bon's (1913, p. 52) statement regarding the crucial role of the armed forces. He quotes precisely the passage from Le Bon, quoted in note 11, then expands on it:

> This aid may originate from the failure of the ruling classes to call out the troops; from the refusal of the troops to fight the revolutionaries, either by standing idly by, by fraternizing with the revolutionaries, or by actively assisting the revolutionaries [p. 372].

[13]Brinton (1952) writes that:

> No government has ever fallen before revolutionists until it has lost control over its armed forces or lost the ability to use them effectively; and conversely that no revolutionists have ever succeeded until they have got a predominance of effective armed force on their side [pp. 94–95].

[14]Chorley (1943) provides much data to support her conclusion that:

> The rule then emerges clearly that governments of the *status quo* which are in full control of their armed forces and are in a position to use them to full effect have a decisive superiority which no rebel force can hope to overcome [p. 20].

[15]According to Peter Calvert (1970):

> Now, in normal cases, the amount of force disposed of by the army is so disproportionately large compared with any force that may be levied and deployed against it that a revolution is possible only if it has been alienated from the pre-revolutionary regime, and impossible if it is uncompromisingly opposed to change. This is well known. . . [p. 118].

The only documentation of these views offered by Calvert is the citation of an article on 'Strategy' by a colonel for the thirteenth edition of the *Encyclopaedia Britannica*.

that "Popular forces can win a war against the army,"[16] has almost become a truism, albeit a truism incompatible with the view that no rebellion can succeed without some defection on the part of the armed forces. Incompatible, that is, unless such defection is assumed. Pettee (1938), for example, asserts that, "It is probable that the army never fails to join a revolution where all other factors are present, and never fails to oppose it when the other conditions of success are not satisfied [p. 105]." While this view is highly deserving of investigation, it is not an acceptable assumption without substantive evidence. And neither Pettee nor anyone else has yet provided such evidence.

From this brief review of the literature, it is evident that many scholars and revolutionaries hold diametrically opposed views on the importance of the role of the armed forces in revolution. Other authors appear to subscribe to both these views simultaneously. Johnson (1966), for example, in his well-known book, *Revolutionary Change*, argues:

> Such superior force may delay the eruption of violence; nevertheless, a division of labor maintained by Cossacks is no longer a community of value-sharers, and in such a situation (e.g., South Africa today), revolution is endemic and, *ceteris paribus,* an insurrection is inevitable [p. 32].

On the other hand, he later argues in the same volume:

> So long as the leaders can still use the army successfully to coerce social interaction, the system will continue to persist. However, the power deflation will approach maximum proportions, producing a "police state" (e.g., South Africa today) [p. 91].

Surprisingly, Johnson's inconsistency on this issue is not unusual—and, in fact, it is common for both views to be embraced at the same time. When a particular event such as the Cuban rebellion of 1959 occurs, it is seen as substantiating the belief that oppression cannot last indefinitely.

---

[16]For example, Hobsbawm (1965) writes:

> When. . .a guerrilla war has become genuinely national and nation-wide, and has expelled the official administration from wide stretches of the countryside, the chance of defeating it are zero [p. 36]. [The] number of Goliaths who have been felled by Davids with slingshots is now very impressive: the Japanese in China, the Germans in wartime Yugoslavia, the British in Israel, the French in Indo-China and Algeria [p. 33].

It should be noted that in every case Hobsbawm mentions, a second power is involved, making it either an anticolonial rebellion or a rebellion against a foreign occupation. C. Wright Mills (1960) expresses essentially the same view when generalizing from the Cuban case:

> It is a moment of military truth. That truth is that guerrilla bands, led by determined men, with peasants alongside them, and a mountain nearby, can defeat organized battalions of the tyrants equipped with everything up to the atom bomb [p. 114].

(Finally, "the pot must boil over.") However, a situation such as the suppression of the Hungarian rebellion by the Russians in 1956 is seen as substantiating the view that coercion works. ("Who could win against such odds?!") What is unusual about Johnson's two statements is that he cites the very same case—South Africa—in support of both views. Of course, it is possible that in certain conditions, one view is true, and in other conditions, the other holds. But the debate rarely reaches such sophisticated heights, much less becomes subject to empirical verification. As Tilly and Rule (1965) have observed:

> Considering the importance of the phenomenon, the literature concerned with the measurement of internal political violence is remarkably weak. Innumerable writers have offered theories of conflict and coercion, but almost all are so abstract that they do not concern themselves with the immediate problems of classifying such events and quantifying their occurrence [p. 28].

2

Oppression and Rebellion:
A Comparison of Cuba and South Africa

In Cuba, on 1 January 1959, rebels finally achieved the overthrow of the Batista regime. In South Africa, while there has been considerable unrest, particularly during the 1950s and early 1960s, no attempt has been made to overthrow the regime by violent means (at least not on a significant enough scale even to approach the notion of mass rebellion used in this study). *Mass rebellion* is defined as a form of violent power struggle, which occurs within an autonomous political system, in which the rebels are largely from the masses, and in which the overthrow of the regime is threatened by means that include violence. The criterion of threat requires the rebellion be fairly large scale (exactly how large will be spelled out later).[1]

Why was it possible for a mass rebellion to succeed in Cuba, whereas in South Africa there has not been even an unsuccessful mass rebellion?

In seeking an answer to this question, it is interesting to examine the reasons given for the success of the Cuban rebellion by analysts of the Cuban case. Draper's (1962) position on this topic is one quite commonly

[1]Rebellions initiated by the military may be both threatening and small in scale, but these kinds of rebellions are not included in this study.

16

taken. First he poses the question: "How could such a small band 'defeat' Batista's army of over 40,000?" He then replies:

> The answer is that it did not defeat Batista's army in any military sense. It succeeded in making Batista destroy himself. . . . The army and secret police struck back blindly, indiscriminately, senselessly. The students, blamed as the main troublemakers, were their chief victims. It became safer for young men to take to the hills than to walk in the streets. The orgy of murders, tortures, and brutalities sent tremors of fear and horror through the entire Cuban people and especially the middle-class parents of the middle-class students. This universal revulsion in the last six months of Batista's rule penetrated and permeated his own army and made it incapable of carrying out the offensive it launched in May against Castro's hideout [p. 14].
>
> The forces at Batista's disposal were to the very end so superior in numbers that only a vast popular revulsion can account for Batista's debacle. Batista's Chief of Staff, General Francisco Tabernilla, came much closer to the truth[2] when he was asked whether the army could have successfully resisted Castro's march on Havana. "It could," he replied, "but not for a long time, because by that time, the people of Cuba were already against the regime of Batista, and *there is no army, once the people get up in arms, that can suppress it* [Draper, 1962, p. 42; italics added].

Draper's view that Batista's oppressive tactics backfired is widely held [see Thomas (1971, pp. 959, 967, 975), MacGaffey and Barnett (1965, pp. 162–163), Huberman and Sweezy (1960, p. 59), Freeman (1963, p. 76), Brennan (1959, p. 172), and Goldenberg (1965)]. Many also share Draper's acceptance of General Tabernilla's view that once "the people" get up in arms, no army can suppress them. Mills (1960), for example, in *Listen Yankee!* asserts: "It is a moment of military truth. That truth is that guerrilla bands, led by determined men, with peasants alongside them, and a mountain nearby, can defeat organized battalions of the tyrants equipped with everything up to the atom bomb [p. 114]."

The very name, Ché Guevara, now conjures up the image of an oppressed people successfully taking up arms. As Leites and Wolf (1970) point out, the notion that "insurgent conflicts, unlike other conflicts, or to a greater extent—is a struggle for the hearts and minds of the people, a political rather than a military conflict [p. 4]" is pervasive. Yet if this view is correct, why does it not apply in South Africa where the vast majority of the people are extremely oppressed by a minority group that resorts to harsh and brutal methods of suppression and repression,[3] and where the situation has steadily deteriorated over the past two decades? Why is it

---

[2]Closer to the truth, Draper means, than the view that the rebels' victory was a military one.

[3]"Repression" refers to policies aimed at preventing resistance from occurring; "suppression" refers to policies aimed at discouraging the continuation or repetition of resistance when it occurs.

that the Cuban case at least seems consistent with the view that oppressiveness sows the seeds of its own destruction, whereas the South African case
does not?

One possible answer is that the Cuban regime was more oppressive than
is the South African regime, or that the nature of the oppressiveness differs
in important ways. Another possibility is that the "causes," or preconditions,
of rebellion were present in Cuba, but are not in South Africa. A third
answer may be that the unusual racist character of the South African situation
sets it apart from Cuba and most other cases, so that South Africa becomes
the exception to the general laws of rebellion. All of these possibilities
have to be considered.

The first task must be to clarify the term, "oppressive." To this end,
it seems useful to differentiate among four dimensions of regime oppressiveness.

1. *Political structure:* If people's political rights are severely restricted,
   then the political structure will be considered highly oppressive.
2. *Regime unity:* Where the regime personnel are united in their policies
   toward the oppressed, particularly with regard to the suppression
   of resistance, the regime will be viewed as oppressive.
3. *Coercion resources:* When the armed forces of the regime have
   considerable resources in terms of size, arms, and equipment, then
   the regime is able to be more oppressive than if these resources are
   low.
4. *Regime and armed force willingness to coerce:* If the regime and its
   agents of social control are willing to use the coercive resources
   available to them in the face of challenge from the oppressed, then
   the regime will be regarded as highly oppressive.

Hence, a highly oppressive regime can be defined as one which has the
resources to coerce (3), is willing to use them (4), is united in its policies
toward the oppressed (2), and allows both its law-abiding and rebellious
citizens few rights (1).

By these criteria, then, how oppressive was the regime in Cuba prior
to the rebels' victory at the end of 1958? Before presenting the data to
answer this question, I must briefly indicate its inadequacy.

The information required for a thorough evaluation of the political
structure is particularly unsatisfactory. Interest in the political structure has
been much greater for the postrebellion period than for the period prior to
1959. So, for example, the report on Cuba of the International Commission
of Jurists (1962) has very little to say about the rule of law when Batista was

in power. There are also at this time, few first-rate scholarly works on the rebellion itself. Yet, hopefully, the sources are not so poor that the conclusions to be drawn are invalidated.

CUBA

Oppressiveness of the Cuban Regime

Political Structure

Batista was no newcomer to the business of ruling the country when he executed his coup d'etat, with the help of a faction of the army, in 1952. He had been a sergeant in the army 20 years earlier; and he had led an army revolt in 1933, known as the "Sergeants Revolt," soon after which he emerged as the power behind the government. Batista ruled as Army Chief of Staff, 1934–1940, and was one of the drafters and promoters of the liberal constitution of 1940. Ironically, it was the restoration of this same constitution that later became one of Castro's major goals.

After the adoption of the 1940 constitution, General Batista was elected President, and his semimilitary regime ruled for the next 4 years. Free presidential elections were held after his first 4-year term was over in 1944, and again in 1948. In 1949, hungry for presidential power once more, Batista formed a new political party and announced his candidacy for the next election. As the time for the election approached, he realized his chances of winning the Presidency were very low, so he staged an almost bloodless coup on 10 March 1952, proclaiming himself President.

In the month following the coup, Batista adopted a new constitutional code in which freedom of speech, of assembly, and of the press could be suspended by Presidential decrees at any time for periods of 45 days. He promised that there would be new elections 18 months later, but until that time, he decreed, all political parties and the old Congress would be suspended, the Premiership and Vice-Premiership would be abolished, and strikes would be prohibited. Batista would rule with the help of his loyal supporters. An 80-member Advisory Council was created to make suggestions on legislation. The law-making powers, however, remained with Batista and his Cabinet. "The people and I are the dictators [in Thomas, 1971, p. 790]" he declared, though few could have believed him. Many of the leaders of the dissolved political parties fled into exile "to escape prosecution or persecution [in Macgaffey and Barnett, 1965, p. 153]."

In 1953, a law was passed that provided severe penalties "for any disre-
spectful attack on the government, effectively stifling criticism of the regime
[Ibid., p. 134]." Nevertheless, many restrictions were eased in 1954,
when Batista prepared to stage an election in which he would be the only
Presidential candidate. Since the election was not free, however, it was
largely boycotted by the opposition parties. In any case, after the inaugura-
tion in 1955, Batista did restore the 1940 constitution. This gesture notwithstanding, there were repeated efforts to oust him from power by force;
consequently, much of the time he governed by "state of siege."

In effect, then, the essential constitutional clauses were suspended, and
Batista's "control of Congress was virtually complete [Ibid.]." In 1958,
another rigged election was held, but as in 1955, the election aroused
little popular interest [Ibid., p. 148]." During the last years of Batista's
rule, urgency courts, established during an earlier dictatorship, came into
frequent use. They were supposed to provide speedy trials when constitutional guarantees were suspended and there were a large number of arrests
to be processed, but in fact they were often used to support the arbitrary
exercise of police powers[Ibid., p. 139].

Most authorities agree that without the support of the army and police
force, Batista could not have remained in power. He was helped by the
fact that he had done much to strengthen these forces during his earlier
rule. After the "Sergeants Revolt," in 1933, Batista, the International Commission of Jurists (1962) reports, turned the army into "his own personal instrument, dismissing the career officers and replacing them by his own men
[p. 47]." Similarly, in 1952, Batista raised the pay of the army, filled the
senior posts with men on whose loyalty he could count, and reorganized
the army so as to make the government secure. In fact, many of his strongest
supporters in the army were promoted by him from sergeant to officer status
in 1933 (Macgaffey and Barnett, 1965, p. 146); and it was in the army
that Batista's regime found its most willing ally in corruption (International-
Commission of Jurists, 1962, p. 48).

The police force was reorganized in similar fashion, the new chief
announcing openings for 2000 more men and promising new motorcycles,
cars, and weapons for all in the force (Thomas, 1971, p. 791). It appears,
according to Thomas (1971), that the rank and file of both the police and
the army accepted Batista's new regime "with satisfaction [pp. 791–
792]." And, Macgaffey and Barnett (1965) state that throughout his rule,
the top military personnel, as well as the Cabinet, "served at the will of
President Batista [p. 135]."

Thus, as in any real dictatorship, the political rights of the law-abiding
Cuban citizen were limited, and the right to oppose the regime through
institutional channels was likewise severely curtailed. What about the rights

of individuals who opposed the regime violently? Since the leaders of Castro's 26 July Movement trace the beginning of the revolution to their attack on the Moncada and Bayamo barracks, the way in which Castro and his 162 followers were created on that occasion is next examined.

Arms were collected, and the plan was to attack and take over the Moncada fortress, a small military post at Bayamo, a radio station, and a hospital on 26 July 1953. The more modest purpose of the attack was to capture an arsenal to arm the group and also perhaps other anti-Batista volunteers. This would be the first step in building a revolutionary movement. But Thomas (1971, p. 828) suggests that there was also a more ambitious hope—that this attack might actually spark off a popular uprising in the whole province.

The attack ended disastrously, with many of the group gunned down or rounded up afterward and killed. Others were arrested, and some of them tortured. According to Thomas, "the savagery of the repression exceeded normal expectations [p. 840]." Batista reacted with great alarm: he suspended Constitutional guarantees and put the army on the alert throughout the island, and "hundreds of people were detained [p. 839]." Castro and 31 of his followers were tried under the following article:

> A penalty of imprisonment of from three to ten years shall be imposed upon the perpetrator of any act aimed at bringing about an armed uprising against the constitutional powers of the State. The penalty shall be imprisonment for from five to twenty years, in case the insurrection actually be carried into effect [in Macgaffey and Barnett, 1965, p. 276].

Castro received a 15-year sentence, his brother Raúl, 13, and the other rebels received lesser terms (Thomas, 1971, p. 843). In fact, all of the group spent less than 2 years in jail, being released in a general political amnesty in 1955.

This event reveals two contradictory characteristics that are relevant in evaluating the oppressiveness of the Cuban political structure. On the one hand, the laws were not *that* punitive; a sentence of 15 years for leading a violent revolutionary attack is a far more lenient sentence than is meted out in many dictatorships. The release of the rebels after only 2 years in prison is also lenient. Similarly, Goldenberg reports (1965), a relatively mild "punishment" was meted out to Senator Pelayo Cuervo Navarro, who said on television in 1953 that "Batista must be overthrown by force [p. 147]." The senator was arrested, but he was released shortly afterward. On the other hand, Batista's mobilization of the whole army and his suspension of constitutional guarantees constitute a rather extreme reaction to the attack on Moncada barracks. So does the brutality of the police toward the rebels, which, according to Thomas (1971, p. 841), was sanctioned by Batista.

Despite this inconsistency, it seems that Cuba should be regarded as highly oppressive, since the laws protective of people's rights were so often suspended; moreover, there was little concern on the part of Batista and his supporters for keeping police behavior within the law. The political structure was in fact one in which there were very few restraints on Batista and his henchmen, and clearly, Batista's claim that "the people" were dictators along with him is completely unsupportable.

Regime Unity

The word, dictatorship, is usually used of the Cuban regime since, from 1952 to 1958, it was more or less Batista's personal creation and subject to his will. Yet the dimension of regime unity does not make a great deal of sense when applied to a dictatorship, for how can one person be at odds with himself? It is true that near the end, despite his attempts to purge the disloyal, Batista lost the support of the armed forces. But it does not seem appropriate to regard this as indicative of "regime disunity," since the willingness of the armed forces to coerce the rebels is a separate dimension of analysis.

Under this dimension, then, the regime may be regarded as united, one of the strengths of a dictatorship being precisely that it cannot be subject to disunity.

Coercion Resources

It is certainly possible to devise an absolute measure of the size of a regime's coercion resources, and in fact this has been done by some comparativists. [For example, Andreski (1968) developed the concept of a military potential ratio (MPR), which is the ratio of persons in the army to the total population.] But the fact remains that resources are also relative, dependent upon the size of the resources available to the opponents. In this respect, Cuba is often seen as a David-and-Goliath situation. "There they were," writes Brennan (1959), "twelve men—with less than two hundred rounds of ammunition—against an army, navy, and airforce of thousands [p. 113]." How valid is this romantic picture?

Estimates of the size of Batista's armed forces vary. According to Brennan (p. 68), there were 21,000 in the army in 1953, at the time of the (generally acknowledged) first incident of the rebellion. By May 1958, this figure had increased to 29,000 (p. 225), with a police force of 7,000 (p. 203). Huberman and Sweezy (1960, p. 56) estimate that by this same date, there were 30,000 men in the army, navy, and airforce. Draper (1962, p. 14) and

Thomas (1971, p. 941) give a figure of 40,000 for the army, while Sartre (1961) claims 50,000 soldiers when Batista was "at the pinnacle of his power [p. 16]." Phillips (1960) says that when Batista fled the country he left behind "the largest army he had ever controlled [p. 394],"— 46,000 soldiers, which included 15,000 new recruits.

Assuming there is some validity to these figures, Batista had 7,000 police and 29,000–50,000 soldiers at his command. What about the strength of the opposition?

Thomas (1971, p. 901) claims that not only did very few of Castro's followers survive the attempt to reach the Sierra Maestra mountains from their training base in Mexico (there were only 15 of them), but the number of armed guerrillas never grew substantially. In the early summer months of 1958, 1½ years after Castro and his men reached the Sierra, and only 6 months before the defeat of the regime, Castro's whole armed force consisted of only 180 men (Goldenberg, 1965, p. 162). Although there were other rebel forces not under Castro's command, Goldenberg reports that there were not "more than 1,000 men in all the different fighting groups in June–July 1958 [p. 162]." It was only after 31 December 1958, when Castro's success was assured, that thousands joined him. [In Goldenberg (1965, p. 159), the number of fighters is said to have risen to 40,000.] Before this point, "reliable sources say that on the day of victory the whole Castro army consisted of 803 men, which together with all other groups made up a force of 1,000 to 1,500 [*Ibid.*]." Sources vary on the figures, but it is clear that, in terms of numbers, the David-and-Goliath image is appropriate.

The rebels have always maintained that the United States supplied Batista with all the military equipment he needed; and some authors agree that by the time the United States embargo was called on 14 March 1958, Batista had all the arms he required (for example, Brennan, 1959, p. 67.) Other sources claim that the embargo was never fully implemented (for example, Huberman and Sweezy, 1960, p. 66); or that it was futile, because Batista had access to British arms suppliers [for example, Sartre (1961, p. 16) and Draper (1962, p. 39)]. According to Thomas (1971, p. 985), the effect of the embargo was chiefly psychological, though he says elsewhere that the arms available at the end of the struggle were inferior and outdated. Yet Phillips (1960) claims that the embargo had a decisive impact: "During the months that followed [the embargo] his [Batista's] agents had considerable difficulty in finding arms. Eventually they did, but it was too late by then [pp. 351–352]."

Disturbing as are such varied assessments in the literature, all accounts of actual engagements confirm Draper's (1962, p. 42) conclusion that Batista's forces were, to the very end, far superior in both numbers and weapons to the rebels. Arms were a major problem for Castro from the start of the rebellion—the most important source of munitions was Batista's forces themselves—and only in the last 6 or so months of fighting was much military equipment actually captured.

In considering the coercion resources of the regime, the focus so far has been on the army rather than the police, and on the guerrillas in the countryside rather than the city rebels. This is due to the inadequacy of the sources: first, no figures are available on the number of rebels in the cities, other than vague statements, such as Macgaffey and Barnett's (1965), that "thousands of Cubans participated actively in the movements against Batista [p. 283]." Second, it is difficult to decide who in fact was a rebel; there are so many different levels of support and participation. While accurate figures on the dead, wounded, and arrested might provide a basis for an estimate of urban rebels, none exists. And although several sources claim 20,000 were killed, not only does this appear to be a myth (see Goldenberg, 1965, p. 144), but so many accounts emphasize the arbitrariness of much police action, that the identity of a corpse as a rebel is simply uncertain. Also, the figure cited above does not reveal on which side the casualty was fighting. Thus, I can only suggest that were figures available, the number of urban rebels would not come anywhere near the number of men under Batista's command, nor would they have had a comparable arms supply. It is relevant to note at this point that 20% of the regime's budget was "absorbed" by the military (Macgaffey and Barnett, 1965).

Batista's armed forces are frequently described as "rotten to the core." (See Thomas, 1971.) Since appointments and promotion were not based on military merit, but on politics, family connections, and personal likes and dislikes, and since corruption and high living were commonplace, it is, therefore, not surprising that both army and police were reputed to be inefficient, undisciplined, lazy, with a very low esprit de corps (Thomas, 1971; Brennan, 1959, p. 14). Furthermore, soldiers were not trained for guerrilla warfare, and this was at least a contributory factor to the ludicrous performance of the army in the Sierra Maestra (Thomas, 1971). Yet had the armed forces been really determined to preserve Batista's regime, presumably some of these qualities would have been rectified—which is to say that characteristics like inefficiency and laziness are perhaps a direct function of motivation to coerce, and are but loosely related to resources.

Hence, despite the inefficiency and inappropriate training of Batista's forces, it seems reasonable to regard the regime's resources for coercion as considerable, particularly when compared with those of the rebels. This brings us to a fuller consideration of the motivation to suppress the rebels.

Regime and Armed Force Willingness to Coerce

Batista's willingness to use all available means of coercion to suppress the rebellion is one of the most widely accepted aspects of the Cuban case (see Macgaffey and Barnett, 1965). Again and again he is reported to have "suppressed all opposition ruthlessly" and relied on the "use of terror and violence [p. 33]." Arbitrary police executions, arrests, and torture were commonplace. Goldenberg (1965), for example, writes that "many people were assassinated or became victims of the terror. The police tortured and murdered, the army competed with the police, and pro-Batista armed bands...vied with both...[p. 144]." And elsewhere, Goldenberg (1965) states that: "Terror ruled the country. Torture became an everyday event, corpses of young people appeared in the streets and in the plains bodies could be seen hanging from trees [p. 159]." Similar descriptions appear in many accounts, some of which go into great detail about specific cases of brutality; most of them emphasize the innocence of many victims. For example, Freeman (1963) has this to say: "Batista's police assumed that because the majority of the rebels were students or ex-students, all students were suspect. Police arrested students indiscriminately, and sometimes in their zeal to uncover rebels tortured them indescribably, hoping to turn something up [p. 74]." The two quotations from Draper at the beginning of this chapter are in the same vein.

It does not seem justified to interpret such brutal behavior as merely counter-terroristic, since, according to Thomas (1971), the rebels did not engage in arbitrary violence, and "there appear to have been no instance of torture by them [p. 968]." Thomas explains the brutality toward Castro and his fellow attackers of the Moncada barracks as due in part to Batista's men having "a real interest in serving the regime," and hence feeling personally threatened by the rebels. He further suggests that the soldiers and police were poor and ill-educated, and so felt all the more hostile toward a revolt led by members of the middle class (p. 841). But "it is also clear," Thomas asserts, "that they would not have so acted had it not been for their presumption that their superior officers would not cause them to bear responsibility for their actions [*Ibid.*]." Therefore, it seems that the behavior of the police and army reflected Batista's willingness to use whatever means necessary to stay in power. But it is also a reflection of the willingness of the armed forces to coerce. Nevertheless, most sources agree that while Batista remained willing to use all means of coercion, the armed forces did not.

Even before Castro's "invasion" in 1956, a group of younger officers, known as the *Puros,* headed by Colonel Ramón Barquin, attempted a coup.

Their plans were betrayed, and so nothing came of them (Thomas, 1971, p. 884). Another group of army officers also tried to foment disorder in order to justify a coup that would establish a totalitarian regime (*Ibid.*, p. 885). Neither group had any connection with Castro or other civilian rebel groups, but these incidents clearly indicate unwillingness among a small minority of the armed forces to support Batista.

Though Castro had earlier condemned the notion of armed-force collaboration against Batista, a section of the navy, in cooperation with the 26 July Movement, as well as other rebel groups, actually tried to overthrow the regime on 6 September 1957 (*Ibid.*, p. 961). Apparently, Thomas says, "the 26 July Movement had had for some months a following among the younger officers of the navy. . .[*Ibid.*]." The day before the attack was scheduled, the naval officers in Havana tried to postpone the action. This attempt was successful in Santiago and Mariel, but not Cienfuegos. Even so, the rebels managed to take over Cienfuegos, including the naval and police stations there—for only a morning. Thomas estimates that about 400 rebels took part in the revolt, and about 300 were killed. "It was the largest action in the civil war so far [p. 964]."

However, it is generally agreed (see Macgaffey & Barnett, 1965) that "the majority [of the armed forces] remained loyal until Batista's increasing reliance on repressive force and his appointment of officers willing to use extreme brutality brought about a gradual loss of military as well as civilian support [pp. 162–163]." Since the Cuban rebellion was one of the seven cases drawn in the random sample of successful rebellions, a detailed analysis of the behavior of the armed forces substantiating this conclusion is presented in Chapter Seven.

Summary and Conclusions

It seems clear that the political structure of Batista's regime was highly-oppressive since the political rights of Cubans were very limited, whether they opposed the regime or not. It was a dictatorship, and one that relied heavily on the support of the armed forces. Since Batista was in a position to fire anyone in disagreement with him, and did so, the regime cannot be called "disunited." Moreover, the coercion resources of the regime were considerable in terms of manpower and arms, though they were unimpressive in terms of training and efficiency. Ultimately, however, it was the lack of willingness on the part of the armed forces to fight the rebels that was the Achilles heel of the regime. For while Batista himself remained willing to the end to use whatever force seemed necessary to stay in power, his armed forces did not. They revealed a complex combination of extreme brutality (particularly the police) and at the same time an unwillingness to risk their lives to support the regime, particularly the army. The degree of unwillingness ranged from reluctance to fight and readiness to surrender, to outright conspiracy against the regime and defection to the rebels. Hence, the Cuban regime should be seen as highly oppressive on three of the four dimensions (political structure, regime unity, and coercion resources), but not on the part of the fourth (regime and armed force willingness to coerce).

If my analysis is correct, why have so many analysts (see Draper, 1962, p. 14) of the Cuban case agreed that it substantiates Batista's Chief of Staff's assertion (quoted earlier) that "...there is no army, once the people get up in arms, that can suppress it."? According to my analysis, the case could more legitimately be seen as supporting the very different view that a rebellion cannot succeed unless the regime's armed forces are disloyal to it. Yet, as I have previously mentioned, Andreski (1967, p. 247), for one, maintains that the Cuban case disproves exactly this generalization; although prior to the Cuban rebellion, he believed it to be one of the most widely accepted generalizations in this area. How is it that the same data can be interpreted in such entirely different ways?

In their book, *The Politics of Violence: Revolution in the Modern World,* Leiden and Schmitt (1968) assert that:

> No army is immune to the forces that spawn revolution.... All soldiers, after all, are related to the general population by a multiplicity of contracts; they are not generically different from other people; and they have stakes that are affected, along with those of others, by revolution or its failure [p. 26].

These authors allow that the armed forces may behave in different ways in a revolutionary situation, and I agree with them—the members of the armed forces are indeed affected by personal, social, and economic factors. But many scholars of revolution see the Cuban case as showing that "the people" beat the army, rather than that part of the army joined "the people." They go a step further than Leiden and Schmitt and assume, often only implicitly, that the behavior of the armed forces is a "dependent variable," a mere reflection, or symptom, of more basic societal conflicts. This is a convenient assumption to make (and widely held); for it then becomes possible to accept simultaneously that for a rebellion to succeed, the help of at least a section of the regime's armed forces is required, *and* that a successful rebellion will occur if certain "preconditions" (not related directly to the armed forces) exist.

But how reasonable are these assumptions? To assume that armed-force disloyalty automatically occurs when "the time is ripe" is indeed optimistic. And this assumption has led students of rebellion to neglect analyzing why the armed forces behave in a particular way in a particular situation. If they are not disloyal, the time must not be ripe. The reasoning often becomes circular. So, in the case of Cuba, the lack of motivation of Batista's armed forces is often seen as proof that an army can hardly be "effective against the wellsprings of social change."[4] This view may be true, but it deserves to be tested since it is by no means self-evident.

It is generally accepted that the Cuban regime was highly oppressive and that the armed forces grew increasingly unwilling to fight for the regime. The usual interpretation of these facts is that oppression cannot last: an alternative explanation is that oppression can last as long as the regime is able to maintain the loyalty of the armed forces. One way of evaluating which of these interpretations is correct is to consider the case of South Africa. It also has a very oppressive regime. If analysis reveals it to be as oppressive or more oppressive than the Cuban regime, then doubt is cast on the validity of the view that oppression leads to rebellion that ultimately is successful. For while there has certainly been considerable unrest in South Africa, there has been no successful rebellion. Nor does the unrest that has occurred qualify as an unsuccessful rebellion.

The description and analysis of the South African case focuses on the early 1960s, though data on preconditions cover the 1950s as well. The reasons for examining this period, rather than the situation in 1973, are, first, that unrest reached a peak at that time. Second, the nonoccurrence of a successful rebellion then or subsequently cannot be evaded so easily by saying that it is imminent, since it has had 10–12 years in which to happen. However, a successful rebellion in South Africa *could* be "just around the corner." As I have noted earlier, one of the aims of this study is to develop the basis for making a sound prediction as to whether a rebellion can succeed in South Africa, should one occur.

Since many readers may not be familiar with the South African situation, some important background information is given before examining the oppressive nature of its regime. (It is important to remember that the data to follow applies to South Africa in the early 1960s, unless otherwise specified.)

SOUTH AFRICA

When a white South African is asked how many people there are in the country, the answer is quite likely to be 3 million. This is approximately the number of *whites*–out of a total of approximately 16 million people. Such an answer is just one of many indications that South Africa is a pigmen-

---

[4]Leiden and Schmitt (1968, p. 26) hereby reveal that they, too, see the armed forces as merely a dependent variable.

tocracy. At the bottom of the ladder is the largest group—11 million Africans (the term, "Africans," is the preferred term for black South Africans). A ½ million "Indians" (immigrants from India) are on the next-lowest rung, together with over 1½ million "Coloureds."[5] The 3 million whites, who call themselves Europeans, are at the top. Van den Berghe (1965, p. 53) refers to these four groups as color-castes, since they are hierarchically ranked in relation to each other, "almost entirely endogamous, and mobility between groups is, with a few exceptions, impossible." This seems an appropriate label, though as van den Berghe (Ibid., p. 54) himself points out, there is such an enormous gap in terms of power and privilege between the whites and the other three groups, that for many purposes it is reasonable to regard South Africa as a two-color-caste situation, there being roughly one white to every four nonwhites (or one nonblack to every four blacks).[6]

For simplicity, however, most of the following analysis focuses on the situation of the Africans, and the relations between them and the whites, since they constitute just over two-thirds of the total population (Coloureds, just under 10%; Indians, about 3%), and there could hardly be a mass rebellion without this group being the major one involved.

Policy of Apartheid

Since the Afrikaners gained power in 1948, South Africa's racial policy has come to be known both within and outside its borders by the word, "apartheid." White South Africans translate this word to mean "separate

[5]South African "Coloureds" tend to be lighter skinned than Africans. Their forebears were Africans (such as the Khoikhoi), Asians (some of whom were brought to South Africa as slaves, others were political refugees), and whites.

Because social pressure has failed to prevent sexual unions and even marriages between whites and Africans or Asians, laws have been enacted for this purpose. Yet even criminal penalties have failed to curb the growth of the Coloured population through miscegenation. Unlike the Africans, the Coloureds do not have a distinct culture, but share that of white South Africans.

For some purposes the "Asians" (Chinese and Malayan) are regarded as Coloured, but sometimes they are considered of higher status; and the few Japanese in South Africa are regarded as "honorary whites" in recognition of the economic relations South Africa enjoys with Japan.

The Coloureds suffer less legal discrimination than the Indians, but the latter are slightly better off in terms of income and education.

[6]Since the distinctions made between black Africans, Indians, Coloureds, and Europeans are so important in South Africa, it is a bit deceptive to use the nondifferentiating word "black" when referring to all the non-European groups. On the other hand, the word "nonwhite," or "non-European," is disliked by many radicals in South Africa since it classifies people on the basis of a quality they do not have. Hence, I shall use the word black when referring to all peoples who are not regarded as white.

development," rather than a more appropriate phrase, like "white domination." The phrase, separate development, is supposed to conjure up an innocuous vision of each race preserving its own unique culture by living in its own area and ruling itself. Such an image is belied by the fact that the Africans' area consists of 264 separate pieces of land, known as the "Reserves," which *together* constitute less than 13% of the land.[7] The government did propose to consolidate these scattered areas into eight "Bantustans," each of which was supposed to become a "homeland" for the members of particular tribal groups, and each of which was supposed to become self-governing. However, in the early 1960s only one area, the Transkei, was thus organized.[8]

Yet, self-governing is hardly an appropriate description of the Transkei. Only 45 of the 109 members of the Legislative Assembly are elected by Transkeian citizens, the remaining 64 are chiefs appointed by the white government; and the Prime Minister is picked for his support of apartheid (van den Berghe, 1965, p. 147). Furthermore, the white government also has the power to veto all legislation passed in the Transkeian Assembly. And most important, the white Parliament maintaines all control over "foreign affairs, defense, internal security, immigration, customs, transport, post and telegraphs, and currency [*Ibid.*]." So much for self-government!

Oppressiveness of the South African Regime

Political Structure

The Rights of the Law-Abiding. The political history of South Africa shows a definite and strong trend toward a greater and greater monopolization of power in the hands of the white minority (van den Berghe, 1965, p. 73). Africans are completely disenfranchised; they have no representation in the government and no vote in the elections (except in the "homelands"). As van den Berghe puts it, the Africans are "ruled entirely as subject peoples under laws passed by the white Parliament [p. 75]." There used to be two legal African political organizations, the African National Congress (ANC), which was formed in 1912, and the Pan African Congress (PAC), which broke off from the ANC in 1959, but both were banned in 1960. Prior to this time, they functioned entirely outside of the Parliamentary system.

In general, Africans are denied even the most basic rights in the so-called "white areas," despite the fact that nearly two-thirds of the African population

[7]According to the Tomlinson Commission Report (1959), there were 254 separate pieces of land in 1955. In 1968, the regime announced that there were 276 (Rogers, 1972, p. 14).

[8]By October 1972, four "homelands" had been given "self-government," Bophuthatswana, Ciskei, Lebowa, and Transkei.

live in white areas. For example, Africans do not have the legal right to live in these areas, let alone to own land there. Because permission for an African to live in 87% of South Africa can be revoked by a minor official at any time, if for some reason their services are no longer needed by whites, Africans are liable to be deported to an African area (this is called "endorsed out"). What this means is that Africans are forced to leave their homes and often their families to return to their "homeland," even if they have never been there, have no relatives there, and have no job or survival prospects there.

The so-called "pass system" has been devised in order to better control the Africans. The word, "pass," refers to the reference book that all African adults are required to carry at all times. It contains information on their current employment situation, their employment history, tax receipts, permits, and other documents. At any time of the day or night, an African may be asked to show his pass to the police; if he does not have it on his person, he is subject to arrest and imprisonment, with the likelihood of job loss and hence deportation. If he has the pass on his person, but it is not "in order"—for example, he may have been laid off his job without reporting this to the labor bureau within 72 hours, or he may have reported to the labor bureau, but exceeded the 2 weeks permitted to find another job—then he is also subject to deportation. Close to a half-million Africans (464,726) were "endorsed out" of 23 "major towns" between 1956 and 1963, according to Horrell (1964, p. 189) and the number of deportations during the next 8 years has probably been considerably greater.

Hence, thousands upon thousands of African families are not permitted to reside together, because family ties are ignored in the interests of pursuing the policy of apartheid. In addition, thousands more are split up because the husband has to seek work in the city, for the "homeland" cannot sustain him and his family even at a subsistence level. And even if both husband and wife have permission to stay in the city, they often may not live together. As Sandor (1963) observes:

> An African wife may live with her husband in a town if he has established his "qualifications." But to do so she must be able to prove that she ordinarily and lawfully resides with him. Since African men are increasingly only being allowed to seek work in town provided they take accommodation in the so-called "bachelor" quarters, it is often impossible for their wives to establish "ordinary" residence with them. Nor may a wife be with her husband for the period he is establishing his "qualifications." She may visit him for periods of up to seventy-two hours without permission, though if she is picked up in town it is up to her to prove she has not been there for longer than seventy-two hours. Special extensions of the seventy-two hours regulation may be granted for women who wish to conceive [p. 15].

In addition, most domestic servants live in the homes of their white employers; thus, they are separated from their spouses and children, as well as from friends. Aside from the treatment of slaves, it is rare indeed that family relations, even of oppressed peoples, are treated as so entirely secondary to the economic and political interests of the oppressors. The consequence is that an enormous number of Africans are isolated from their families and any other primary group.

It is the pass system that seems to be regarded by Africans as the most detested aspect of apartheid, tyrannizing their daily lives and making the concept of a police state very real. According to van den Berghe (1965, p. 193), there are 300,000–400,000 arrests and convictions for breach of the pass laws each year.[9] The system effectively keeps "the masses under the continuous control of the police [p. 133]." It also restricts African migration to the cities and prevents reservoirs of unemployed Africans from forming in the urban areas. Van den Berghe sums up the situation well:

> In short, an adult African may not reside anywhere without permission, may not move outside his allotted place of residence without approval of the authorities, is subject to a curfew at night, may not live in any "white" area without being gainfully employed, may not own land in free hold (aside from some insignificant exceptions), and may be expelled from his residence and deported to any place, when the administration deems his presence to be 'undesirable' or 'redundant.' In a number of cases, persons have literally no right to live *anywhere* in their own country, and are susceptible to be arrested for illicit residence no matter where they are [*Ibid.*].

Such are the rights of the law-abiding Africans. What then of individuals who actively oppose the system that treats them so cruelly?

The Rights of the Opponents of Apartheid. Pierre van den Berghe (1965), one of the leading American sociologists writing on South Africa, summarizes the legislation passed in the 1950s designed to suppress all opposition, as follows:

> . . .a number of laws give the government wide powers of perquisition, confiscation of property, banning of organizations, exile, extradition, arrest, and detention without trial. The most important of them are the Suppression of Communism Act of 1950. . .the Criminal Law Amendment Act of 1952, the Public Safety Act of 1953, the Riotous Assemblies Act of 1956 and the Unlawful Organizations Act of 1960 (which resulted in the banning of the ANC and PAC). These acts, which followed waves of non-white protest, forbid practically any form of opposition by peaceful means or otherwise, and enable the government to repress the non-white liberatory movements [pp. 130–131].

---

[9]Arrest and prosecution for pass-law offenses have increased enormously. The highest figures on record (and such figures usually exclude prosecutions under municipal by-laws) are 937,098 (a daily average of 2,567) for the year ending June 30, 1968 (Horrell, 1969, p. 151).

More than to indicate the quantity of repressive legislation that was passed, this quotation is included to convey the consistent and rapid movement toward the greater and greater repression of the opponents of apartheid by the government. To convey something about the quality of the legislation, some of the provisions of these laws are described below.

In 1950, the Suppression of Communism Act was passed, ostensibly to outlaw the Communist Party and suppress communists. The main purpose, however, has been to suppress all effective and potentially effective opposition, most of which has not been communist. The definition of communism is so broad that it can apply to even the most anticommunist opposition. By this Act, Bunting (1964) states, communism includes any doctrine or scheme "which aims at bringing about any political, industrial, social, or economic change within the Union by the promotion of disturbance or disorder, by unlawful acts or omissions or by the threat of such acts or omissions ... [p. 165]." Also included is any doctrine or scheme "which aims at the encouragement of feelings of hostility between the European and non-European races of the Union the consequences of which are calculated to further the achievement of any object referred to" in the preceding sentence (Ibid.).

While communism, by this definition, can cover most forms of opposition, the government does not want to waste time prosecuting "communists" in the courts. Therefore, the Act permits the government to bypass the courts, by equipping it with "a formidable battery of administrative weapons for striking down its political opponents [Ibid., p. 166]." For example, the Governor General has the power to outlaw any organization engaged in activities that further the achievements of communism—defined in the extraordinarily broad terms quoted previously. In addition, people can be banned, and the banning provisions are, indeed, among the most potent and frequently used in the statute. While the terms vary widely, there are features common to every banning order served on a person in South Africa (persons abroad can be, and are also banned). The main ones are:

1. The banned person may not be in a gathering—defined as three or more persons—even in his or her home.
2. He or she is restricted to a certain area.
3. He or she may never be quoted by anyone, neither verbally, in writing, nor in any other way.
4. He or she must report in person to the police at regular intervals, such as every 12 or 24 hours.
5. He or she may not communicate in any way with another banned person.

Two other laws were passed in the early 1960s that carry the repressive trend several steps further. The first was the General Law Amendment Act (known as the "Sabotage Act"), which was passed in 1962. Conviction under this law results in a minimum sentence of 5 years and a maximum penalty of death; the burden of proof of innocence is placed on the accused. Once again, one of the outstanding features is the broad definition of what constitutes sabotage. It is "sabotage"

> [for] anyone to commit any wrongful or willful act whereby he obstructs, injures, tampers with, or destroys: (a) the health or safety of the public; the maintenance of law and order; (b) the supply of water, light, power, fuel, or foodstuffs, sanitary, medical, or fire extinguishing services; postal, telephone, telegraph, or radio services, or the free movement of traffic; (c) any property; or if, in contravention of any law, he possesses any explosives, fire arm or weapon, or *enters or is upon any land or building* [in Bunting, 1964, p. 183; italics in original].

Trespass, then, can result in at least 5 years in prison, unless the accused can *prove* that:

> ...his offense was not committed with intent: (a) to cause or promote general dislocation, disturbance, or disorder; (b) to cripple any industry or the production and distribution of commodities; (c) to seriously injure or endanger the safety of any person or to cause substantial financial loss to any person or to the State; (d) to further the achievement of any political aim, including the bringing about of any social or economic change in the Republic; (e) to cause and encourage feelings of hostility between different sections of the population; (f) to cause forcible resistance to the government *or to embarrass the administration of the affairs of State.* [*Ibid.*, pp. 183–184; italics added].

A report of the International Commission of Jurists on this law states that it "reduced the liberty of the citizen to a degree not surpassed in the most extreme dictatorships of the Left or Right."

The following year, 1963, saw another General Law Amendment Act (known as the "No-Trial Act") passed. From this time on:

> ...any commissioned police officer may without warrant arrest or cause to be arrested any person whom he suspects upon reasonable grounds of having committed or having intended to commit any offense under the Suppression of Communism Act, or the Unlawful Organizations Act (outlawing the ANC and PAC), or the offense of sabotage, and cause him to be detained for interrogation in any place for up to ninety days .... No person save a magistrate shall have access to such person and no court shall have jurisdiction to order his release [*Ibid.*, p. 190].

These are the laws passed prior to 1963, with the cooperation and support of the so-called Opposition United Party. More repressive laws were to follow. The South African political structure can thus be regarded as extremely oppressive. Let us turn to the second dimension of oppressiveness to be considered, the unity within the government regarding the willingness to oppress.

Regime Unity

In South Africa the regime is representative of the whole white ruling caste, so that in considering regime unity, we are also learning about unity within the entire white caste. Just as there are many different tribes in the African caste, there are two tribes in the white caste: the Dutch Afrikaners (57%) and the English South Africans (43%). At the end of the last century and at the beginning of the twentieth, the Afrikaners and the English South Africans were literally at war with each other, but since then, their mutual hostility has been expressed in less blatant ways. The English South Africans have always been more urbanized and wealthier than the Afrikaners, and substantially overrepresented in the professions and business. Since 1948, however, the/ have lost the political power to the Afrikaners. Aside from their relative positions in the social structure, these two tribes have different languages and religions, and they practice voluntary segregation as evidenced by low intermarriage rates, and separate living areas, schools, and universities. (The law plays a part in this segregation—in so far as children are required to be educated in their mother tongue.)

Despite their mutual dislike and sometimes hatred, there can be no doubt that when it comes to keeping the Africans "in their place," there is considerable unity and harmony between Afrikaners and English South Africans. Again and again, the United Party—the political party of the English South Africans, and the main opposition party since 1948—has been, as van den Berghe points out (1965), "willing to give sweeping powers to the government in order to keep control over Africans. . .[p. 86]." I think van den Berghe is quite right when he concludes that:

> . . . the English prefer to acquiesce and even to collaborate behind the scenes with the govenment they despise. "White Unity" and "swart gevaar" (literally, Black danger) are but two aspects of the same reality. As racial tension between Whites and Africans mounted, and as non-White political consciousness increased, the Afrikaner–English conflict receded in importance [p. 107].

Simmel's observation that a common enemy unites its foes aptly describes what has happened with white South Africans: as the threat of the "enemy" has grown, so has white unity.

But *considerable* unity is not the same as *complete* unity. There have always been some whites who have opposed the system, a few, even to the extent of favoring and working for a revolution. More, however, have been in favor of reforms. Most of the white dissidents belong to the English subculture, but there have also been some heated disagreements within the Afrikaner group regarding Government policies toward Africans [see Adams (1971, pp. 169–182)]. Much attention is often given to these conflicts in the domestic and foreign press. Unfortunately, this does not alter the fact that by far the more important trend is toward greater unity within the white caste.

So, regime and caste unity with regard to policies toward the regime's political opponents, and the blacks in general, should be regarded as high in South Africa, despite the underlying rivalry and hostility between Afrikaners and English South Africans, and some of the differences within each group. What, then, are the coercion resources available to the whites?

Coercion Resources

The main role of the army and police in South Africa is to defend white supremacy against the blacks. To this end, the whites do everything they can to maintain a monopoly of coercive force. Hence, no blacks are permitted to serve in the army, and black police may not bear firearms (they may carry only such weapons as sticks, clubs, and occasionally spears). Nor are black civilians permitted to own or use firearms: "The sale, and even the loss through theft, of weapons and ammunition to Africans are severely punishable offenses [van den Berghe, 1965, p. 77]." In addition, Horrell (1964) states that there are severe penalties against blacks for taking military training both within and outside South Africa, or even "to have taken any steps to that end [p. 38]." This low access to the means of coercion is in striking contrast to that available to anyone with a white skin.

In 1960, there were 9,019 white men in the Permanent Force; this number increased to 15,288 in 1963 [van den Berghe (1965, p. 136); Legum and Legum (1964, p. 207)]. Backing up the Permanent Force are the Commandos (part-time rural militia), and the Citizen Force. White males over 19 years of age are given training for 9 months, followed by 3 months a year for the following 3 years. This recruitment policy produces approximately 10,000 men a year for the Citizen Force. In 1963, this force consisted of 70,000 potentially mobilizable men (Legum and Legum, 1964, p. 210). Able-bodied white South African males who are in neither the Permanent nor the Citizen Forces are required to serve in the Commandos for 4 years (*Ibid.*, p. 207). From this source alone, 80,000 men could have been mobilized in 1963 (*Ibid.;* van den Berghe, 1965, p. 136). In this same year, there were 29,343 men in the police force; 12,200 were white [Legum and Legum (1965, p. 207); van den Berghe (1965) places the total figure at 28,385 members of the police]. About 15,000 citizens (including Coloureds and Indians, but not Africans) form a voluntary police reserve whose purpose is to assist the white police in emergencies. There are also women's shooting clubs where thousands of women are trained to handle guns, and white civilian protection organizations were formed in a number of towns in 1963; these are coordinated with the police reserve, increasing its strength considerably.

It is clear that every attempt is made to recruit all white males into the struggle to maintain white supremacy. And, indicative of the whites' fear of blacks, nearly every white home houses several guns or other weapons—in anticipation of trouble. In addition, the military budget nearly trebled 1961–1964 (van den Berghe, 1965, p. 137). In 1964, expenditures on defense amounted to 26.8% of the government's total expenditures (Horrell, 1964, p. 34).

Development of the arms industry in South Africa has been described by van den Berghe (1965, p. 137) as "meteoric," and there is agreement that this escalation is attributable to the fear of an international arms embargo, and mobilization of the other African states against South Africa. Hence, in 1962, the figure spent on weapon production had increased tenfold over 1961; by 1963, it had increased fortyfold (Ibid.). South Africa was then, Legum and Legum (1964) report, "virtually self-reliant for its munitions [p. 208]." In addition, the possibility of chemical bacteriological warfare was discussed, and research into nuclear power, poison gas, and rockets was underway (Ibid., p. 211).

The substantial nature of white South Africa's resources for coercion in the early 1960s may be highlighted by the Legums' conclusion that: "If the military forces of all the African states were to combine, they would not be able to offer a frontal challenge to the Republic for reasons of logistics [Ibid., p. 204]." There cannot be many societies where the regime has such a monopoly of the means of coercion. What, then, about the willingness to use these means?

Regime and Armed Force Willingness to Coerce

Prime Minister Verwoerd summed up the common sentiment of white South Africa perfectly when he said in 1962: "For a nation with its back to the wall, there is nothing to do but fight or vanish [Legum and Legum, 1964, p. 17]." Adam (1971a, p. 11) argues that this fear whites have of blacks is realistic in South Africa insofar as the whites' status and power is based on the underprivileged position of the black majority; in other words, a majority government would necessarily mean the loss of this privileged position. But even if these fears were not realistic, the important point is that Verwoerd's attitude is shared by most white South Africans. Hence, their willingness to use all available resources to preserve their "existence," to say nothing of their wealth and privileges, is about as high as it could be.

Since the whites in the armed forces also are affected by these considerations, their enthusiastic loyalty to the regime can be relied upon, no matter

how much upheaval and turmoil there is. Adam (1971a) puts it this way:
"In the case of larger military conflict it can be expected that the whites
of South Africa will fight with the same determination as the Israelis demonstrate against the Arabs [p. 124]."

In summary then, the South African regime and ruling caste may be
regarded as highly oppressive insofar as: (1) they are united in their determination to preserve their own privileged position by keeping the blacks down;
(2) they enjoy a virtual monopoly of the coercive resources; (3) they are
passionately willing to use these coercive resources to suppress the blacks;
and (4) the entire political structure grants few human rights to even the
most law-abiding Africans, and fewer still to those suspected of being active
opponents of the regime. In short, if the thesis that oppression sows the
seeds of its own destruction, is correct, then a rebellion should have occurred
in South Africa.

How have the blacks responded to this oppression? This is the subject
of the section to follow.

African Reaction to Oppression in South Africa

In the *Oxford History of South Africa,* Kuper (1971, p. 459) describes
the period 1948–1964 in South Africa as a "counter-revolution" by whites.
"This does not imply," writes Kuper, "that Africans attempted a revolution,
though it was threatened, or that the counter-revolution was a reaction
to the threatened revolution: on the contrary, it was planned in advance
[*Ibid.*]." Kuper uses the term counter-revolution to refer to the build up
of the structure and machinery of oppression just described.

In 1952, a mass campaign of civil disobedience was organized by representatives of Africans, Indians, and Coloureds to repeal some of the discriminat-
ory legislation that was passed by the whites. There were 8,557 highly
organized passive resisters (Kuper, 1971, p. 462). Resistance reached a peak
in October 1952, after which the campaign rapidly declined following
outbreaks of violence and the repressive reaction of the government (*Ibid.*).
None of the explicit aims of the Defiance Campaign, as it was called, were
achieved; indeed, if anything, ground was lost with the passing of two
additional repressive laws, that would make another similar campaign
much more difficult to organize (*Ibid.*). [For a more detailed account see
Kuper (1960); this is one of the 12,651 publications, films, and records
banned in South Africa since 1956 (Horrell, 1971).]

From 1957 to 1962, there were a number of peasant uprisings in Zululand,
Sekhukhuneland, the Hurutshe Reserve and east Pondoland [Kuper (1971,
p. 464); see also Mbeki (1964).] Some took the form of protest demonstra-

tions, which erupted into "destructive riots" after the police intervened in violent fashion. The most significant of these uprisings, described by van den Berghe (1965) as a "large-scale peasant revolt [p. 162]," occurred in eastern Pondoland in 1960: 6,000 Pondos refused to pay taxes and boycotted white-run stores (Bunting, 1964, pp. 176–177). Organization and discipline were maintained through committees and people's courts (Kuper, 1971, p. 465). This, as with all the other peasant uprisings, was suppressed "with much brutality." In Pondoland, in particular "the government used military force, Sten guns, and armoured cars against the peasants and carried out mass arrests under emergency regulations proclaimed for the Transkei [Ibid.]."

In the cities, too, "the year 1960 saw the most widespread wave of pro-test to date" (van den Berghe, 1965, p. 162). Such occurrences suggest that 1960 was the year in which the regime was most threatened by the ac-tions of the oppressed. For it can be argued that the "threat" comes from the show of numbers, rather than the tactics used—the tactics were always nonviolent; almost all violence that occurred was on the part of the regime. In this respect, the upheaval in 1960 had more the quality of a massacre than an unsuccessful, violent rebellion. Nevertheless, the regime was severly shaken.

In 1960, the Pan African Congress (PAC) organized a national, non-violent antipass campaign (Horrell, 1959–1960, p. 55) which Robert Sobukwe, the PAC leader, stated was the first step toward "freedom and independence" for the Africans; the target date was 1963. Africans were called upon "to leave their passes at home and surrender themselves for arrest at the nearest police station [Ibid.]." Thousands upon thousands of Africans participated in these and associated activities on 21 March 1960. The now notorious Sharpeville massacre was the result in one town, where 5,000–20,000 unarmed Africans had gathered by the police station in response to the PAC campaign. The official figures cite 69 Africans dead and 178 wounded, most having been shot in the back (Ibid., p. 58). There were also a number of casualties in Langa, Cape Town.

In response to the massacre, ex-Chief Luthuli of the African National Congress (ANC) called for a day of mourning on March 28, and about 57,000 Africans stayed away from work (Ibid., p. 62). Moreover both before and after March 28, thousands of Africans stayed away from work to march peacefully in protest (Ibid.).

On 24 March 1960, legislation was introduced to ban the ANC and PAC. And on March 30, the government declared a state of emergency. According to a press report quoting "official sources," 365 Africans were wounded and 83 killed in the upheaval that occurred March 21–April 9 (Ibid., p. 68). But official sources usually grossly underestimate African casualties. Regime forces suffered only three fatalities (all African police-men), according to the Minister of Justice *(Ibid.)*.

Following the declaration of the state of emergency, some 2,000 leading opponents of apartheid were detained without trial for up to 5 months. In addition, Bunting (1964) states, "almost 20,000 Africans were *arrested* . . . [and subsequently] . . . sent to prisons or work camps after conviction at secret trials held in the jails [p. 175]."

According to van den Berghe (1965), 1960 saw the end of the large-scale, peaceful (on the part of the Africans) protest actions, and the beginning of "a new phase of the liberatory struggle [p. 162]." Acts of sabotage became quite commonplace; van den Berghe mentions 45 reported sabotage attempts in a 2½-month period. By 1962, there were three underground organizations that condoned violent tactics. One was an offshoot of the banned ANC (*Umkonto we Sizwe*, translated "Spear of the Nation"), another was allegedly connected with the banned PAC (*Poqo*, translated "We Stand Alone"), and a third was the African Resistance Movement, most of whose members were white, ex-Liberal Party[10] members. However, aside from small-scale sabotage, few rebellious acts have survived the planning stage before exposure, followed by severe punishment of participants. During 1963, 3,355 people were arrested, detained, or banned under security laws, 1,186 of them without being charged (van den Berghe, 1965, p. 135). There had been dramatic trials, exciting dreams, and inspiring speeches, but no actions offered any serious threat to the government. By 1964, Kuper (1971a) concludes, "there was little evidence of independent African political action [p. 470]." From this analysis of the South African situa-tion, it seems clear that the confident assertion—oppression brings about its own demise—has to be questioned.

CUBA AND SOUTH AFRICA COMPARED

It is not easy to compare regime oppression in these two countries, par-ticularly since in Cuba it is possible to use data on the regime's reaction to substantial threat, whereas in South Africa, the regime has never really been severely threatened. Yet it still seems possible to say that the South African regime is, in several ways, substantially more oppressive than was the Cuban regime. First, the civil rights of the majority of its citizens are

---

[10]The Liberal Party stood for universal suffrage and peaceful tactics. It was a multiracial party but was dominated by whites. It disbanded in the 1960's, when a law was passed outlawing multiracial political parties.

practically nonexistent: in Cuba even the most oppressed citizens had free-dom of movement; Cubans could live where they wished, and with their families; they could walk around without being subject to arrest for failure to carry a "pass." Second, if we examine the oppressiveness of the laws applicable to the opponents of the regime, in South Africa such laws are far more severe. Imprisonment for 5–20 years for carrying out an insurrection in Cuba, and 3–10 years for "any act aimed at bringing about an armed uprising," is mild indeed compared to the laws in South Africa where it is possible to get from 5 years to death for stopping traffic or for trespass if the accused cannot prove his or her intent was not to embarrass the administration of the affairs of state (Bunting, 1964, pp. 183–184).

In practice, however, Batista and his agents were not restrained by the law and certainly behaved brutally. Furthermore, a dictatorship is inherently an oppressive political structure. But in South Africa the system is more oppressive than it was in Cuba, insofar as Africans are treated as non-people without even the right to live with their families, as but one example.

On the dimension of regime unity, there is little difference between South Africa and Cuba: in each case the rulers were united in their desire to suppress opposition. In the case of South Africa, the unity includes a desire to continue the subjugation of the subordinate castes.

Both countries also possessed great resources for coercion, and in both, the regimes showed great willingness to use these resources to the limit to preserve their power. In Cuba, it was the unwillingness of the armed forces to coerce the rebels that was the one factor undermining the monolithic nature of its oppressiveness. This is the factor that has not been put to the test in South Africa.

It might be argued by an advocate of the view that "oppression cannot last," that the reason there has been no rebellion in South Africa is not because South Africa is not sufficiently oppressive, but because the various other conditions—often regarded as "causes" of rebellion—are either miss-ing or weak. Could the absence of forces pushing for rebellion explain the absence of a rebellion in South Africa? In order to consider this possibility, it would help to know what the causes of rebellion are! Unfortunately, there is no consensus on this question. Nevertheless, in Chapter Three I attempt to evaluate whether the absence of a rebellion in South Africa can be explained by the absence of causes, or preconditions.

3

South Africa's Missing Rebellion: A Search for Explanations

The most obvious explanation for South Africa's missing rebellion is that South Africa is so unique a situation that the usual laws of rebellion do not apply. After all, this country has a caste system where the upper ruling caste is in a very small minority, yet maintains a virtual monopoly of positions of power, prestige, and wealth. It could be argued that these circumstances place South Africa in a different category from other societies, and make comparison with, for example, the Cuban situation unfruitful.

Clearly the South African situation is unique. But how may its unique characteristics make it harder for a successful rebellion to occur? In Chapter Two we saw how common is the notion that oppression provokes rebellion. Since the structure of South African society makes it uniquely oppressive, South Africa should be even more predisposed to rebellion if this view were correct. And indeed wide acceptance of this assumption is a major reason for so many predictions of rebellion or revolution in South Africa. For example, Adam (1971a), in his recent extensive analysis of the literature on South Africa, writes:

The total suppression of non-white opposition organizations after a series of "treason trials"[1] excluded the possibility of a legal change of power. Since then, it is argued, all the prerequisites for revolutionary change are present. The opposing blocks of African and Afrikaner Nationalism have become increasingly polarized, and both display readiness to use force. An end of communication between the antagonists parallels a refusal to compromise and negotiate; a lack of consensus about the rules of the game accompany the mutual denial of legitimate right to power; gradual reform, instead of revolution, is thus ruled out by the South African political system according to these analyses. *Hence, almost all social science studies on South Africa published during the sixties have predicted violence, bloodbath, unrest, and upheaval* for this polarized situation [p. 13; italics added].

A statement of the Central Committee of the South African Communist Party (Pomeroy, 1968) expresses essentially the same point of view as that of the social scientists, though the language is more dramatic. Indeed, this view has become almost a platitude of both liberals and radicals within and outside South Africa:

Where every protest and every demand is met merely by bloody suppression by the state, it becomes clear to one section of the people after another that the state is the obstacle to any sort of advance, and that no sort of happy or tolerable future is possible without the removal of this tyrannical state and its replacement by one which embodies the will of the majority of the people [p. 272].

This view is reminiscent of Draper's (1962) analysis of why the rebellion in Cuba was able to succeed. A second statement from the same source follows. It may sound like rhetoric, but it is widely believed by scholars and nonscholars alike; see, for example, the quotations from Gurr in the Introduction of this volume. "A minority, however heavily armed, cannot prevail over the great majority of the people when the majority is organized, determined and clear in its purpose. Every new act of tyranny and oppression by the government calls forth acts of revolutionary protest and resistance by the masses [Pomeroy, 1968, pp. 270–271]."

Most contemporary thinking on the topic apparently sees the uniqueness of South Africa as creating a particularly revolutionary situation. Why then, has there been no rebellion? Leaving aside for the time the issue of whether oppression creates a revolutionary situation, is the absence of rebellion due to the absence of the usual preconditions or "causes" of such upheavals?

[1] In 1956, 156 South Africans were arrested on charges of treason; 91 were brought to trial Although all were acquitted in 1961, van den Berghe (1965) states that the trial succeeded "in rendering many key persons almost as politically impotent as if they had been convicted [p. 84]."

Tilly (1964a) brings some order to the theories of causation by categorizing them under four headings[2]:

1. *The misery thesis:* economic hardship is considered to be the major cause of rebellion.
2. *The uprooting thesis:* the forces that uproot people are seen as the cause of rebellion.
3. *The organization thesis:* factors that permit or encourage the organization of potential rebels is stressed as the key cause of rebellion.
4. *The elitist thesis:* some kind of change in the position and organization of the elite is regarded as the all-important factor in rebellion.

While these theses are not mutually exclusive, there is a tendency for scholars in this area to treat them as if they were. All four theses are considered later, including some variations of the misery thesis, as well as others that do not fit into Tilly's categorization.

Data on the occupational structure and the distributions of income, land, education, and health in South Africa will be presented now, since these facts are necessary in evaluating whether or not the various notions of preconditions apply. (Data on employment are of course highly relevant, but Rogers (1971) states that "there are no published figures for African unemployment [p. 14].") Once again, I focus on the early 1960s and the years before, rather than on the current situation.

EVALUATING THE PRESENCE OF "PRECONDITIONS" FOR REBELLION

Income Distribution and Health

While South Africa is by far the most economically developed country in Africa, it is "at once an underdeveloped colonial area and an industrial power (van den Berghe, 1965, p. 96)" with enormous disparities of income and living conditions between whites and Africans. The living standard of white South Africans is the fourth highest in the world (Rogers, 1971, p. 3): that of blacks, one of the lowest. According to Legum and Legum, (1965, p. 269), in the early 1960s about 60% of black South Africans were living below the breadline (that is, the minimum living standard according to the South African goverment).

---

[2]It is I who am characterizing these as theories of causation. Tilly (1964a) himself described them as four general ideas about the relation between popular participation in the French Revolutionary movements and major changes in French society.

Focusing on urban areas, Sandor (1963) quotes the Council for Social and Industrial Research as maintaining that "half the African families in the main urban centres live below the poverty datum line [p. 19]." Other figures are higher; for example, in Capetown, 80% of the African families are estimated to live in poverty *(Ibid.)*. Rogers (1971) makes some correction for the fact that the breadline "is not a 'human' standard of living [p. 1]" by estimating an "Effective Minimum Level," which is "half as much again as the Poverty Datum Line [p. 13]"; she then suggests that perhaps 85–95% of all African urban families live below the revised minimum level *(Ibid.)*. This assessment applies to both the 1960s and the 1970s.

Two notable South African economists—Horowitz (1967, p. 422) and Houghton (1964, p. 59)—agree that accurate estimates of the distribution of income between whites and Africans are not possible. It is not surprising then that there is disagreement on this issue. According to van den Berghe (1965, p. 303), the whites received over two-thirds of the national income in 1960. On a per-capita basis, this estimate means whites enjoyed nine times the income of Africans (see also Bunting, 1964, pp. 269–70). However, according to van den Berghe (p. 184), in 1954, they enjoyed 12 times the income of Africans, so that the gap slighly diminished. Until 1954, the whites were practically the sole beneficiaries of economic prosperity. In the preceding 15 years, the purchasing power of Africans had actually decreased by 6.5%, in comparison with an increase for the whites of 46% *(Ibid.)*. But "since the late 1950s, rises in non-white wages are slowly reversing that trend, so that non-whites may now look forward to being slightly better off vis-a-vis Europeans than they were after the great Depresson some thirty years ago [van den Berghe, 1965, p. 185]."[3]

While other sources (for example, Rogers, 1971, p. 10) are in agreement with van den Berghe's picture of deterioration prior to 1954, some do

[3]Slightly confusing here is that Adam (1971a, p. 99) gives figures for 1962 according to which whites earn twelve and a half times the wages of Africans: this suggests a deterioration from van den Berghe's figures for 1960, where whites earned nine times as much as Africans. However, like van den Berghe, Adam stresses that the economic situation of the Africans did improve in the decade of the 1960s, although according to him, the gap between the earnings of the Africans and whites increased still more (pp. 97–99) .

Since we are interested in the question of "absolute misery," as well as "relative misery," it is interesting that even though Adam argues there were real wage increases for all groups in the 1960s, he states that the average household income for Africans in this period is still below the breadline in most of the areas for which data are given (p. 97). For example: "In 1967 some 68 percent of African families in Soweto, Johannesburg, had monthly incomes below the austere minimum requirements of R 53.32 ($74.65), even though, as the city council had discovered, average wages had risen by approximately 14 percent between 1962 and 1967 [p. 97]."

not accept his view that the situation for Africans has improved since then. Rogers, who does a far more thorough analysis of the economic situation than does van den Berghe, concludes that: "If the money increases are compared with the rising cost of living for Africans, . . . real income appears to have declined [Ibid.]." While this applies to 32% of Africans living in urban areas, the situation for Africans "in other areas appears to have been even worse [Ibid.]." For example, "in mining, African real wage rates have not risen since 1911, and have certainly fallen in real terms since 1935 [Ibid.]." For the 31% of Africans living on white farms in the rural areas, Rogers (1971) reports that "African real wages are often below the level of 60 years ago [p. 12]." And in the reserves, where the remaining 37% of Africans reside, "income per head has dropped" in real terms, by over 30% [Ibid.].[4]

Sandor's (1963) analysis is consistent with Rogers'. Commenting on the period of the 1950s, she asserts, for example, that "with a few exceptions, the real wages of Africans in the main urban centers, declined [p. 19]." (See Sandor, 1963, p. 20, as well.) Carstens (1973) specifically takes van den Berghe to task for his analysis of the economic situation, arguing that van den Berghe neglected to take account of the rise in the cost of living for Africans, their disproportionate tax burden, and the drain on the incomes of urban Africans due to the increasing subsubsistence situation in the reserves. He cites many government sources and South African economists sympathetic to the regime to support his conclusion that "the trend over the past twenty-five years would therefore seem to be downward in real terms or, at best, static [Ibid.]."

The sources, then, present a conflicting picture. One view is that there has been a slight improvement in the economic situation of Africans, relative to whites; another is that there has been a steady deterioration; and a third is that the Africans' economic situation has been essentially static.

Both the "absolute misery" of the Africans' economic circumstances, as well as the extremely large disparity between the daily experiences of blacks and whites, is powerfully brought home by the Legums' (1965) observation that "despite the fact that South Africa is incomparably the richest country in Africa, it has the highest record incidence of infant mortality due to malnutrition [p. 269]." According to Sandor (1963), "African children die at 25 times the rate of white children between the ages of one and four [p. 20]." Sandor asserts that "in parts of South Africa, the in-

[4]See also Wilson's data in Information Service Manual on Southern Africa (1968, p. 54E); and Horrell (1970, p. 113). Rogers' (1971) analysis also disagrees with Adam's picture of economic improvement in the 1960s. According to her, "African real income per head seems . . . to have declined about 1.7 percent a year in the twelve years ending in 1970 [p. 13]."

cidence of diseases of malnutrition is said to be the highest recorded in the world [p. 20]," and that "57% of Africans die before they reach 5 years; the equivalent figure for whites is 5% [*Ibid.*]." First, Steele, and Gurney (1972), quoting a UNESCO report, assert that by 1960 "sixty to seventy per cent of African children suffered from malnutrition [p. 51]."

Land Distribution

As I have already noted, Africans have the right to own land only in scattered areas designated as "Bantu areas," or "Reserves," comprising less than 13% of the total land mass. These areas are underdeveloped and often ruined by overpopulation, failing to sustain the 37% of the African population that endeavors to live there. If the government policy of apartheid were fully implemented, then all Africans would have to live where not even one-third can now do so. Hence, 68% of the population (the Africans) have 13% of the land, while just less than 20% of the population (the whites) own or control 87% of it (the roughly 10% of Coloureds and 3% Indians are segregated within the white areas).

Occupational Structure

From the figures on income distribution cited above, it will come as no surprise to learn that the Africans are relegated to the lowest-paid, least-skilled jobs. And there are laws to maintain the "occupational color-bar" or "job reservation"—the phrases used in South Africa to describe the protection of white workers from black competition. These laws, as van den Berghe (1965) notes, require that whites have "a virtual monopoly of skilled manual jobs, as well as higher clerical, managerial, civil service, and professional posts, at rates of pay from *five* to *fifteen* times those of unskilled non-white jobs [p. 56]." Even though job reservation is economically advantageous for the white caste as a whole, laws are instituted because where this policy is uneconomical for the individual employer, he may set racial considerations aside in hiring workers. In 1956, only 1% of whites were classified as unskilled manual workers compared with 80% of the Africans (*Ibid.*, p. 307). And everything necessary is done to ensure that "a non-White is never in a position of authority over a White person [p. 75]."

However, as in the United States, such gross job discrimination does not preclude an African elite. Since it is preferred that whites avoid all relationships—even professional—with Africans, a class of African professional and business persons is permitted in order to serve Africans. Except for this small elite, "it is virtually impossible for a non-White to be anything but a domestic servant, a subsistence farmer or farm worker, or an unskilled or, at best, semi-skilled labourer [*Ibid.,* p. 196]."

Moreover, the right to strike for better wages and working conditions is denied Africans. While it was strikes rather than African trade unions that were outlawed in 1953, the unions were not formally recognized and were therefore "unable to use the machinery for collective bargaining [Bunting, 1964, p. 266]" provided by the same act. When a dispute breaks out, police and other officials are immediately sent for, and if the Africans do not go back to work, they may be arrested on the spot and subjected to police harassment or brutality (*Ibid.,* pp. 267–268).

Education

Van den Berghe (1965) reports that in 1953 "the government spent 16 times as much for White as for African school children [p. 47]." And since the Bantu Education Act was passed that year, education for Africans has actually deteriorated. For example, the expenditure per African pupil in state and state-aided schools declined by about 30% between 1953 and 1960–1961 (Horrell, 1962, p. 178). The Act was designed to indoctrinate and train African youngsters for lives as hewers of wood and drawers of water. English was designated their third language thereby effectively cutting off most Africans from the more liberal ideas of the rest of the world. Also, according to van den Berghe (1965), "manual labour is stressed (in school) to prepare the child for his subservient role in South African society and Whites may use African school children for farm labour [p. 130]." Such a law fits well with the statement of Verwoerd before he became Prime Minister, that: "Good race relations cannot exist when the education is given under the supervision of people who . . . believe in a policy of equality [*Ibid.*]."

Until a few years ago 50% of African children did not attend school at all (*Ibid.,* p. 46). "In 1958 only 3.2% of all African school children were in secondary schools, compared with 22.7% of White children [*Ibid.,* p. 47]." And then only "about one African child out of four thousand finishes his secondary schooling [*Ibid.*]." At the university level the disparity between the opportunities of the white and the African is even more extreme; in 1957 about 1 white in 100 was a student compared with 1 African in 6,000 (*Ibid.*).

ARE THE "CAUSES" OF REBELLION ABSENT?

Having presented some of the basic facts needed for an evaluation of whether or not the preconditions for rebellion exist in South Africa, we will start by considering the "misery theories." The *absolute misery* theory, often regarded as one of the elements of the Marxist view, holds that people will rebel when they have "nothing to lose but their chains." However, the data presented make it clear that a majority of Africans in South Africa are in a "miserable" economic situation—in an absolute sense.[5] But there is no rebellion.

Another quite different but also popular theory, usually attributed to de Tocqueville, is that a rising standard of living is a precondition for rebellion (see Davies, 1962, p. 5). As I have already noted, scholars are not agreed on whether there has been a rise in the standard of living for Africans, a decline, or little change in the 1950s and in the 1960s. If the view that there has been an improvement is correct, then apparently a rise in the standard of living is not a sufficient condition for rebellion.[6]

There are an enormous number of relative-deprivation theories; the most systematically developed is that of Ted Gurr (1970b). He maintains that people rebel when there is a discrepancy between what they feel are legitimate expectations and what they in fact have (*Ibid.*, p. 25). One of the problems in applying Gurr's theory is that the deprivation may be relative in so many different ways. For example, it may be relative to "an individual's own past condition, an abstract ideal, the standards articulated by a leader, as well as a reference group [*Ibid.*]." Although there is not a consensus regarding whether there has been a deterioration in the economic conditions in which Africans live, the data presented make it clear that there has been considerable deterioration in terms of political rights and educational opportunities during the 1950s (and the 1960s). Hence, it seems reasonable to consider that in 1960, Africans were deprived in an overall sense relative to the past. Africans have also been deprived in terms of the standards articulated by their major leaders. It is not known whether Africans perceive whites as a reference group; but certainly all the disparities in income, education, health, power, political and civil

---

[5]It also seems to me that most people *do* prefer their accustomed "chains" to imprisonment, torture, or death.

[6]The obvious truth of this fact should not be allowed to conceal the point that theorists—because they ignore unsuccessful cases (or noncases like South Africa)—often do treat such factors as if they were sufficient.

rights described earlier constitute a striking case of African deprivation relative to whites which no one living in South Africa can fail to notice. South Africa, then, seems to be a case where both absolute and relative misery (or deprivation) occurs. Yet these conditions have not resulted in rebellion.

The case of South Africa dramatizes the uselessness of theories of causation that focus exclusively on the situation or the state of mind of rebels or potential rebels. Such theories assume that variables descriptive of the rebels determine whether rebellions occur or not, and often determine their outcome as well. While many of these theories acknowledge that the regime *can* affect the state of mind of the people, the idea of the regime as a serious or even insurmountable obstacle to the occurrence or success of a rebellion is usually denied, even though statements to the contrary are sometimes made. For example, when Davies (1962) published his first formulation of the J-curve theory of revolution, he made several statements about how it was possible for a regime to be so coercive that the people would be docile; and he referred to Nazi concentration camps to illustrate the point. However, more recently he (1969) has argued that: "If the frustration is sufficiently widespread, intense, and focused on government, the violence will become a revolution that displaces irrevocably the ruling government and changes markedly the power structure of the society [p. 690]." Davies does go on to modify this extreme statement by acknowledging that the violence may also "be contained within the system, which it modifies but does not replace [*Ibid.*]." Nevertheless, it is clear that basically Davies attributes no weight to the type of structural context within which the states of mind of the people function; apparently whether the people are violently opposed to a modern totalitarian dictatorship, or a weak, inefficient, disunited regime, is not seen as sufficiently important to consider. To Davies, social structure is a variable of no import. The South African case, however, makes Davies' position look rather naive.

Another theory that focuses on the situation of the rebels, but is a structural rather than a psychological theory, is what Tilly has called the "uprooting" thesis. Kornhauser (1959), for example, argues that mass movements (including revolutionary movements) are made up of people who have become isolated form primary group ties. Hence, when events occur that "uproot" masses of people—such as industrialization, economic crises, or natural disasters—there is an army of potential recruits for a mass revolutionary movement. It is the uprooted who make rebellions.

In South Africa, it is largely government policy that is responsible for uprooting thousands upon thousands of Africans. In Chapter Two it was seen that the African family does not have the right to maintain itself as a residential unit and often cannot do so for economic as well as political reasons. It was also pointed out that from 1956 to 1963, 464,726 Africans were deported from 23 major towns (Horrell, 1964, p. 189). In addition, a considerable percentage of African miners and other city workers are migratory laborers whose homes are in the reserves. Therefore, the number of uprooted Africans is very high. Clearly the uprooting thesis is not supported by these data.

This brings us to a test of another popular theory of revolution on the South African data. In the 1960s, Chalmers Johnson (1964) developed an equation for revolution: multiple dysfunctions plus elite intransigence plus an accelerator equals revolution (p. 12). An accelerator, Johnson (1966) explained, is "the event which triggers revolution in a society that is disequilibrated and that has a discredited base of authority [p. 98]." Examples of such an accelerator are the rise of a prophet or messiah in a dysfunctional society, or the defeat of the regime in a foreign war (1964, p. 12), or the spread of a belief that the armed forces can be overcome (1966, p. 104). "Dysfunction," according to Johnson (1964), "is the condition that demands the response of social change—and of revolution [p. 5]." This definition is quite circular. However, the general idea emerges that serious social problems like poverty, unemployment, and economic depression are regarded as dysfunctions, and together they constitute multiple dysfunctions. An intransigent elite is "one that opposes change [*Ibid.*, p. 10]." South Africa certainly suffers from multiple dysfunctions and has an intransigent elite; therefore, according to Johnson's equation, a revolution has not occurred because for years no accelerator has appeared. This conclusion is very unilluminating. In Johnson's model, the rules of correspondence that might enable one to connect the abstract concepts with events in the real world are lacking entirely, and thus the model is not really usable. Still, many scholars subscribe to at least part of the theory; that is, they believe that terrible, stressful conditions (multiple dysfunctions) cause rebellion. But, again, this theory is not borne out in South Africa. For few would argue that the conditions there are not extremely stressful for the blacks.

Marx's theory of revolution is complex, and a complete evaluation of it will not be made here. But some of his views are particularly relevant in the case of South Africa. For Marx, a precondition of a revolution against capitalism is a growing polarization of the haves and the have-nots—the capitalists and the workers. In addition, the workers are supposed to form a growing and increasingly miserable majority, in terms of wages, unemployment, and powerlessness. These conditions seem to be met in

South Africa.[7] Yet there is little working class solidarity. As Simons and Simons (1969) point out: "civic status is determined at birth and for life by colour rather than class, by geneology rather than function . . . [p.618]." Such an analysis suggests that Marx seriously underestimated the significance of racism. For without the element of racism to explain it, the combination of an advanced industrialism and an "absolute, degenerate colonial order [*Ibid.*, p. 610]" is anomalous. As Adam (1971a) writes:

> The more the machinery of law and police interferes with the chances of the masses, the more it would seem to reinforce the revolutionary potential, not only in terms of the subjective preconditions of a revolution but also by the increased objective gap between advancing levels of production and retarded modes of production. [p. 5]."

Yet no rebellion or revolution has occurred in South Africa.

Perhaps one element of Marx's theory may be helpful in understanding why there has been no rebellion in South Africa. For Marx, the factory is of central importance in the development of the revolutionary consciousness of the workers. Unlike the conditions of work for isolated peasants, the factory brings workers together, enabling them to see their oppression in their common problems. Out of this consciousness, organized trade unions develop through which the workers fight for their interests. In South Africa, this process has been disrupted. The development of African trade unions has been severely controlled, and any militant action energetically suppressed. This has also been the fate of all organizations formed to pursue the Africans' political interests, for example, African political parties. Under these conditions, the great potential power of Africans to withhold their labor, thereby crippling the economy, is extremely difficult and perhaps impossible to realize. If an effective organization were to occur, it would have to do so spontaneously. However, this possibility is unlikely: the workers can easily be replaced because they are unskilled, and there is a great deal of unemployment among Africans; hence, there is a buyers' market for labor. Furthermore, workers have no income to fall back on, and survival itself is a struggle. Finally, given the oppressive nature of the South African

----

[7]As Adam (1971a) puts it:

> From the perspective of most authors on South Africa, two apparently diametrically opposed race or class castes face each other in visible polarization: white and non-white, ruler and ruled, privileged and underprivileged, exploiter and exploited, a numerical minority against a four-times stronger majority which has the support of an almost unanimous world opinion and is backed by the historical tendencies of a declining colonial era [p. 9]."

regime, if solidarity were not complete, all who stuck out their necks would certainly get them severed.[8]

Whether or not it is appropriate to categorize Marx as subscribing to the organization thesis (Tilly, 1964a, does so), this thesis is one of the few that seems to survive the South African test. Marx did not consider that organization might be continuously prevented by regime action, but he did give organization a central place. An answer then to the original question as to why no rebellion has occurred in South Africa might be that the oppressiveness of the regime has made it impossible for the subordinate caste to organize.

Perhaps this begins to sound like another version of the elitist thesis. Here the view is that a rebellion or revolution can succeed only if the regime or elite is disintegrating or disunited, or loses confidence in itself, or stops believing that it has the right to keep the power. Previously data were presented showing that the regime in South Africa is united and resolute: the whites do seem to believe that they have the right to do what they are doing (though some theorists assume that "at some level" the whites must know it is "wrong" to oppress the blacks). The whites also appear confident that they can maintain a position of power, though a contradictory fear of Africans is also apparent. Hence, it is clear that the South African elite is not disintegrating, and if a disintegrating elite is a necessary condition for rebellion, then it is apparent why a rebellion has not occurred in South Africa.

Summary

Van den Berghe (1965) considers: "That South Africa has survived so long in such an acute state of disequilibrium is indeed highly problematic for sociological theory [p. 213]." In my analysis, too, the case of South Africa seems to challenge the validity and usefulness of most theories of causation of rebellion and revolution. Most of the theories focus on conditions that affect the rebels and do not consider the conditions that affect the regime and its agents, or the wider structural context of rebellion. That is why they are useless in understanding the South African situation where

---

[8]It may be noted that South Africa has a daily average prison population about six times the figure for France, and five times that of Britain (Horrell, 1971, p. 72). In addition, South Africa accounted for nearly half (47%) the world's legal executions during the early 1960s; as most of the rest of the world's use of the death penalty is decreasing, South Africa's is increasing (Sachs 1970, p. 3).

it is probably not that the push for rebellion is weak, but that the obstacles are so enormous. The elitist thesis is essentially one that focuses on obstacles, and that is presumably why it is one of the few that is consistent with the lack of a substantial rebellion in South Africa. Since the South African regime makes it virtually impossible for Africans to organize themselves into a revolutionary force, the organization thesis comes to be inseparable from the elitist thesis in this particular situation.[9]

Since so many of these theories of causation apply so poorly to South Africa, they are apparently in need of serious and critical review. To this end a useful step would be to accept Eckstein's (1965) distinction between preconditions for internal war and obstacles to it. He conceives of preconditions as the positive forces that make for internal war, and obstacles as the negative forces that work against it (p. 159). The probability of an internal war occurring, then, depends on the relative strengths of these positive and negative forces. Thus, it is perfectly possible that in a particular case the preconditions might be present, but the obstacles might be too considerable for rebellion to occur. Currently, many theorists do not acknowledge this possibility, since the role of obstacles in rebellion is not generally recognized. Another useful step would be to consider the probability that there are preconditions that relate to regimes, as well as rebels.

The theory presented in Chapter Two—oppressiveness ultimately provokes the forces that will destroy it—may not fit the South African case, but it is at least consistent with the fact that an oppressive regime was overthrown in Cuba. Yet on closer examination, it turned out that in the Cuban case, too, there was one "weakness" in the oppressiveness complex— the unwillingness of the armed forces to keep fighting for the regime. As I have already noted, many opinions have been expressed regarding whether this is a prerequisite for successful rebellion. But the answer has never been arrived at through a systematic comparative study.

I have argued that it seems extremely unlikely that the armed forces in South Africa will be disloyal to the regime. Therefore, an answer to the

---

[9]It should not be thought that all other theories of causation are found wanting when put to the test of the South African situation. For example, a popular theory formulated by Davies (1969) holds that:

> . . .revolution is most likely to take place when a prolonged period of rising expectations and rising gratifications is followed by a short period of sharp reversal during which the gap between expectations and gratifications quickly widens and becomes intolerable [p. 690]."

This theory is not discredited by the absence of a rebellion in South Africa, since there has been no prolonged period of economic improvement followed by a sharp reversal.

general question, whether armed-force disloyalty is a necessary condition for successful rebellion, also bears on the specific question of a successful rebellion in South Africa. In order to answer this question, I undertook a systematic study of the behavior of the armed forces in 14 rebellions; 7 are successful and 7 are unsuccessful rebellions.

4

Rebellion and Revolution: Conceputual Clarifications

In the first chapters of this volume I was interested in what makes rebellions succeed or fail; and more specifically, I considered the relation between the oppressiveness of the regime and its agents, and the outcome of rebellion. I later narrowed the focus of my concern still further to the relation between the loyalty of the armed forces to the regime and the outcome of rebellion. The comparative study described in the following chapters allows a test of the hypothesis that as long as the regime retains the loyalty of the armed forces, no rebellion can succeed. But I want to go beyond a yes-or-no answer to this question, and clarify the relation between the degree of armed-force disloyalty and the outcome of rebellion. This requires an examination of unsuccessful as well as successful cases.

In beginning such an analysis it is necessary to define the kind of event to be studied, that is, rebellion; to consider its relation to revolution; and to describe the general theoretical context within which these concepts are viewed.

DEFINITION OF REBELLION AND RATIONALE

Rebellion is defined as *a form of violent power struggle in which the overthrow of the regime is threatened by means that include violence.* Many people would regard this as a reasonable definition of *revolution*. Later, I explain why I use the term "rebellion" rather than "revolution," and how I conceive of the relation between these terms.

The use of the word "revolution" is, of course, extremely varied. For Barrington Moore, only four have ever occurred[1]; whereas for Pitirim Sorokin (1962), there have been over a thousand. Disagreement on how the concept should be used often leads to very heated argument, presumably because the phenomenon of violent political upheaval and radical social change are difficult to view neutrally.[2] And while it might be clear to most people that Sorokin and Moore are not studying the same phenomenon, this is often less clear among those whose definitions of revolution are less divergent. To complicate matters further, students in this area often fail to stick to one use of the word themselves.

Confusion over definitions is common enough in the social sciences. More serious is what seems to me to be the unnecessary confusion and muddled thinking that has occurred as a result of the failure to distinguish between the type of upheaval itself, its causes, and its consequences. Tilly and Rule (1965) pointed this out very explicitly in *Measuring Political Upheaval*:

> In attempting to measure political upheaval, one must distinguish three clusters of phenomena. First, there are those characteristics of the social units undergoing upheaval which enter into the explanation of the upheaval. Second, there are the characteristics of the upheaval itself. Third, there are its consequences, real or supposed.
> These distinctions are more subtle than they seem—more subtle, because it is so easy to slip into definitions, measurements, and classifications strongly influenced by the precipitating conditions or the consequences of the events under analysis. . . . The most intensely political approaches to internal upheaval, for example, treat the transfer of power as the event to be explained and thus (a) relegate "unsuccessful" attempts to second-class citizenship, and (b) include within the phenomenon events which narrower statements of the problem would treat as its consequences. . . [p. 2–3].

Tilly and Rule provide a very plausible explanation for the common equation of revolution with *successful* revolution, and the extraordinary lack of attention to unsuccessful attempts to effect revolutions. A corollary of this is, perhaps, the lack of interest in the factors relevant to the success or failure of rebellions. Failure to distinguish between the causes, form, and consequences of the upheaval is also probably responsible for the common

---

[1]This is ascertained from his question of me in 1966 when I told him of my interest in revolution. It was, "which of the four have you studied?"

[2]Initially, when I told people I was studying revolution, I experienced many irate reactions when it was learned that this or that "famous" case did not fulfill my definitional criteria, for example, the Spanish "Civil War," the "revolution" in Egypt in 1952, the Algerian "revolution," etc. It was as if I were belittling the importance of these cases.

assumption that if there is no rebellion or revolutionary attempt, then the "causes" are either absent or weakly developed.

It is interesting that in 1915 Michels made precisely the distinction between the nature of the upheaval and its consequences that Tilly and Rule advise and that is stressed here. In Michels' (1915) own words:

> The expression "revolutionary" is frequently applied simply to the struggle for liberty conducted by inferior classes of the population against superior (sic), if this struggle assumes a violent form, whereas logically. . .revolution implies nothing but a fundamental transformation, and the use of the term cannot be restricted to describe the acts of any particular class, nor should it be associated with any definite external form of violence. . .[p. 3].

In the first part of this quotation we have a more picturesque way of describing what I call *mass rebellion,* and in the second part, what I refer to as *revolution.*

In keeping with Michels, and Tilly and Rule, rebellion is defined *as a form* of power struggle, independent of its causes and consequences. The long-term consequences of rebellion may be successful or unsuccessful revolution. *Successful revolution* is defined as *substantial (or fundamental) social change resulting from rebellion.* This definition thus excludes the possibility that revolution can occur without being preceded by a rebellion.[3]

Depending on whether one prefers working with dichotomies or trichotomies, one may speak of *partially successful revolutions* when some social change results from rebellion, and *unsuccessful revolutions* when the social changes that follow are minimal, superficial, or nonexistent. More complex definitions could include specifications regarding the direction of change and the time period within which change should occur. In the diagrammatic presentation of the conceptual distinctions to be made in this study (see Figure 4.1), a simple dichotomy is used: *successful revolution* is *substantial social change following a rebellion; unsuccessful revolution* is *nonsubstantial social change following a rebellion.* A simple dichotomization of the short-term outcome of mass rebellion is also used. *Rebellions in which the regime is overthrown, that is, the rebels or their chosen representatives subsequently take over the positions of power,* are regarded as *successful,* and *rebellions in which the overthrow is not achieved, that is, the rebels or their chosen representatives do not take over the positions of power,* are regarded as *unsuccessful.*

An additional argument in favor of a distinction between rebellion and

---

[3]Here, my definition deviates from Michels since, to be faithful to his viewpoint I would have to be willing to regard the so-called "Industrial Revolution" as a revolution. I would only be willing to do this if the industrialization came as a consequence of a rebellion.

revolution is that it makes the task of arriving at usable, reasonably operational definitions more manageable, and hence facilitates testing hypotheses. For example, most definitions require that the ancien regime be overthrown *and* that fundamental social change be attempted *and* that fundamental change be effected. Naturally it is easier to define one criterion in an operational way than a composite of three criteria. Also, regime overthrow is easier to define operationally than either of the other two criteria. To invent usable measures for determining the degree of social change that has occurred, or its fundamental nature, and then to find the data that would be needed to apply these measures to a number of cases, would be extremely difficult. Perhaps this difficulty explains Eckstein's (1965) conclusion noted earlier that: "Despite the protracted normative argument between pro-revolutionaries and anti-revolutionaries. . .almost nothing careful and systematic has been written about the long-run social effects of internal wars. . .[p. 136]."

For definitions that require fundamental social change as the goal of the rebels, the task of defining "revolutionary goals" in an operational way is even more difficult. Obtaining reliable data on goals is inordinately hard, particularly for unsuccessful rebellions. Indeed, it is not really clear what should be regarded as reliable data in these cases. For a movement to be explicit about its aim to overthrow a regime and "reconstitute" a society is to invite suppression. Therefore, for strategic reasons, many movements claim reform as their goal. In addition, there are well-studied movements that appear to remain reformist until the very end. For example, the Hungarian students did not gather in the streets on October 23, 1956 with the intension of trying to overthrow the regime. [See the accounts in, for example, Kecskemet, (1961), Váli (1961), and Zinner (1962).] A movement can become rebellious or "revolutionary" while it is happening. To require explicit rebellious or "revolutionary" goals would be to bias the study toward a particular type of rebellion, that is, the type that has an organized underground movement and/or a guerrilla force, versus the "spontaneous" kind—like the Hungarian case. And then there are rebellions in which both these aspects are present, for example, the Russian case of 1917. Can we be sure that the people who demonstrated in the streets on 8 March 1917 were aiming to overthrow the Romanov autocracy? Here we must bear in mind that *wanting* and *planning* are by no means the same thing: the Africans in Rhodesia no doubt want the overthrow of the current Smith regime, but that is not the same as organizing around this as a definite goal.

Finally, there are often as many different goals in a movement as there are factions. In particular, a combination of persons with reformist and "revolutionary" goals is exceedingly common. This makes it difficult to categorize a movement's goals in any meaningful way.

It is not surprising, then, that in a well-received contemporary case study of a "counter-revolution," Tilly (1964b) avoids any analysis of the rebels' ideology and focuses instead on who they were and what they did. Nor is it surprising that no one before has made a systematic comparison of successful and unsuccessful revolutions—for if the definition of revolution requires that a regime be overthrown by people with "revolutionary goals," and that fundamental social changes consequently occur, what is an unsuccessful revolution? One that fails by any one, or two, or all three of these criteria?

These are just some of the problems that are encountered in attempts to operationalize some of the most widely accepted definitions of revolution. Most students of revolution have not tried to solve them. Yet, by separating these elements, an unmanageable task can become manageable.

TYPOLOGY OF REBELLION

In addition to the distinction between rebellion and revolution, three different types of rebellion are also distinguished for reasons that will become clear shortly: *mass rebellions,* which occur within autonomous political systems, and in which the participants are largely from the masses; *military rebellions,* which occur within autonomous political systems, but in which the overthrow is threatened by military forces; and *anticolonial rebellions,* which are intersocietal power struggles in which the overthrow of colonial systems are threatened by violent means.[4]

This study will focus on *mass rebellions* for a number of reasons. First, they bear most directly (at least more so than military rebellions) on the question of whether or not oppression can last. Mass rebellions are, after all, one of the few unambiguous indications that a large number of the members of a society are dissatisfied, want change, and are mobilized against the government to try to effect change. Second, I am interested in the outcome of rebellions. There are good grounds for believing that the differences among mass, military, and anticolonial rebellions are

---

[4]While violence is one of my defining criteria of rebellion, if one were interested in, say, studying the effectiveness of violence as a tactic, the definition could easily be adapted. For example, nonviolent rebellion could be defined as a form of power struggle in which the overthrow of the regime is threatened by nonviolent means; violent rebellions, by violent means. The frequency and conditions in which such nonviolent rebellions lead to substantial social changes (or are associated with such changes) could then be compared, and the same for violent rebellions. Mass, military, and anticolonial rebellions could be looked at together or separately for such a comparison.

very relevant to success and failure, since, among other things, the kinds of power dislocations involved in successful instances of these three kinds of rebellion are so different. For example: in anticolonial rebellions, withdrawal by the colonial power is a possible outcome, in striking contrast to mass rebellions, where those overthrown have nowhere to withdraw. They lose their power, whereas for a defeated colonial regime, power is merely limited. Presumably, this difference between the stakes involved for colonial and noncolonial powers who face rebellions has an important effect on the motivation of the regime and its agents to suppress the rebels. Chorley (1943) points out other differences between these kinds of rebellions that have implications for the likelihood of the rebels achieving success (her term, "social revolt," is roughly equivalent to mass rebellion, and "nationalist revolt" to anticolonial rebellion):

> In social revolts it is unlikely that the revolutionaries will have the benefit of a homogeneous population behind them. Nor is it likely that they will have the benefit of any compact geographical region to use as an undisturbed base for training their levies and assembling their supplies.
> The social revolt presents, therefore, on the whole a more difficult problem than the nationalist revolt [p. 246].[5]

The distinction between mass and military rebellions is even more salient, given that this study focuses on the relation between the loyalty of the armed forces to the regime and the outcome of the rebellion. In military rebellions at least a portion of the armed forces, must, by definition, be disloyal.

The conceptual distinctions made thus far are diagramed in Figure 4.1.

[5]Earlier, Chorley (1943) goes into more detail regarding the greater ease with which nationalist revolts can be effected:

> It will generally be found that a nationalist revolt is better placed technically than an internal revolt. Where a subject province or country rises against its rulers, it can be safely premised that on the whole the active rebels will have a sympathetic and homogeneous population behind them. Moreover, the rebellion will be grounded on a clearly cut geographical as well as on a clearly cut political unit. This gives a great advantage in guerrilla warfare where the fighters must rely on a sympathetic population. But in an internal social revolt the dividing line between revolutionaries and counter-revolutionaries will probably be clear-cut neither geographically nor politically. Geographically, active insurrection will be based on focal points dotted over a country and,owing to difficulty of communication, linked together precariously or not at all. Time and again plans for concerted rebellion at various separate centres have come to grief. And even in cases where rebellion is based on a widespread peasant jacquerie the difficulty of bringing the towns into line with the rural areas may prove insuperable. Politically, internal insurrection suffers almost invariably from the absence of a homogeneous population behind the revolutionaries. The dividing line comes between various classes of the population and is therefore bound to entail confusion and uncertainty [pp. 19–20]."

A number of important research questions arise out of this conceptual scheme—questions that cannot be asked or investigated if the more common definitions of revolution are accepted. These questions include: in what circumstances do rebellions result in successful revolution? How common is it for unsuccessful rebellions to lead to successful revolutions?[6] When do some of the frequently hypothesized preconditions of rebellion lead to successful revolutions, and when do they not?

RATIONALE FOR DEFINITION OF MASS REBELLION

I hope I have now provided an adequate rationale for distinguishing between the concepts rebellion and revolution, and for the exclusion of both social change and rebel goals as defining characteristics of rebellion. However, as yet I have not provided a rationale for what has been *included* in the definition of mass rebellion. In following the rationale here it is important to realize that the definition had to be as operational as possible, since with it I had to develop a universe of successful and unsuccessful mass rebellions from historical sources. (If the reader is uninterested in such a detailed rationale and uninterested in the problematic task of delineating a theoretical subject,[7] he or she is advised to skip the rest of this chapter.)

Since every element in the definitions is discussed in this section, a repetition of them seems advisable:

1. *Mass rebellion* is a form of violent power struggle, occurring within an autonomous political system, in which the overthrow of the regime is threatened by means that include violence, and in which the participants are largely from the masses.
2. *A successful mass rebellion* is one in which the regime is overthrown; that is, the rebels or their chosen representatives subsequently take over the positions of power.
3. *An unsuccessful mass rebellion* is one in which the overthrow of the regime is not achieved; that is, the rebels or their chosen representatives do not subsequently take over the positions of power.

Some mass rebellions do not have outcomes that fall neatly into one of these two categories. Some end in secession, for example, Biafra and Bangladesh. In others, the group in power is displaced, but not by the

---

[6]Eckstein (1965) interprets an article by Levy as suggesting "that internal wars always succeed in changing societies, regardless of who wins them, even if the changes do not accord with anyone's intentions . . . [p. 27]."

[7]Eckstein (1965) defines a theoretical subject as "a set of phenomena about which one can develop informative, testable generalizations that hold for all instances of the subject, and some of which apply to those instances alone [p. 8]." He argues that the first task that must be undertaken in order to advance the subject of "internal war" beyond the pretheoretical stage is to delineate a theoretical subject.

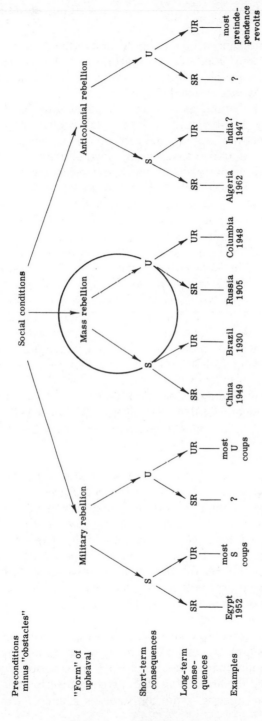

Figure 4.1 Conceptual framework for the study of rebellion. I am following Eckstein's (1965, p. 153) conception of preconditions as "forces that propel societies" toward violent rebellion, and obstacles as forces that "inhibit, or obstruct" this occurrence. My study is located within the circle in the figure. The examples given in the figure should be regarded as suggestions only. (S = successful; U = unsuccessful; SR = successful revolution; UR = unsuccessful revolution.)

63

rebels or their representatives; this happens quite often in Latin America, where a right-wing coup is effected in reaction to a developing mass rebellion. In order to simplify the assessment of outcome, rebellions with such outcomes were excluded from my study.

There are also many instances of violent political struggles that do not culminate in a really decisive confrontation. Such is often the case when rebellious movements are institutionalized with a continuing organizational base, such as a trade union or a "revolutionary" party. It can happen that there are many relatively minor confrontations over a period of years without any decisive defeat. This was the situation, for example, in Spain prior to the "Civil War," though some confrontations were major. Criteria for what constitutes a decisive confrontation were developed to meet such eventualities (see Appendix I).

There are several reasons for including *violence* as a defining characteristic, both for the means used by the rebels, and the power struggle as a whole. First, the phrase *violent power struggle* is intended to indicate that attention is limited to serious conflicts over the distribution of power within a society. Other kinds of conflicts, for example, nonpolitical ones, are ignored. The phrase also suggests that the event may be of considerable duration, which makes it preferable to "violent political upheaval." There are many kinds of violent power struggle that are in fact excluded, such as those in which the regime is not directly involved, for example, the struggle between the Front de Liberation Nationale (FLN) and the Mouvement Nationaliste Algeria (MNA) in Algeria, the Bolsheviks and the Mensheviks in Russia, the Kuomintang and the Communists in China prior to 1927.

Second, as Tilly and Rule (1965) point out, the appearance of violence "almost guarantees the seriousness of the collective action [p. 6]." In the case of rebel violence it is an indication that the "rules are suspended" and that the conflict "is serious enough for people to take risks and violate taboos [*Ibid.*]." These authors give a third important reason for including violence as a defining criterion: "Collective violence rarely escapes the attention of reporters and agents of social control, while other forms of coercion often slip by undetected. And neither direct observers nor readers of accounts of completed events have much difficulty deciding whether or not violence occurred [p. 7]."

However, if there is no regime violence *in response* to rebel violence, then we are not dealing with the kind of power struggle that is investigated here. As Johnson (1966) argues: "Abdication by an elite may usher in changes of revolutionary magnitude, but it is not an instance of revolution if all actors, including the abdicating elite, agree to the changes [p. 97]." Clearly, an abdicating regime is not the same as a violently overthrown regime.[8] However, if the regime abdicates only after having tried to defend itself through the customary violent means, then the case does qualify; for example, Batista finally abdicated at the end of 1958, but only after a violent struggle.

Requiring that the rebellion occur within an *autonomous political system* means that we are not concerned with anticolonial rebellions, nor with rebellions in which a second society (or several) intervene in any substantial way, either on the side of the rebels or the regime. And as Tilly and Rule (1965), who also limit their attention to political upheaval occurring within autonomous political systems, point out, "...partisan resistance to military occupation and enduring civil wars within fragile political unions are marginal cases in this respect [pp. 4–5]." But exactly what criteria can be used to decide, for example, whether the American "Civil War," the Spanish "Civil War," or the Chinese "Revolution" are mass rebellions or civil wars?

"Civil war" seems a more appropriate term to use than mass rebellion when there is a violent conflict between two semiautonomous political systems, each with its own regime, and in which each side enjoys considerable means of coercion in fairly distinct geographical areas. Also, in contrast to mass rebellions, separation or secession is a possible outcome of civil war. Examples are: the American "Civil War," the Pakistan–Indian conflict of 1948, and the more recent conflicts between the federal government of Nigeria and Biafra, and the struggle of Bangaladesh to separate from Pakistan. Unfortunately, the distinction between a civil war and a mass rebellion is not always as simple as this discussion might suggest. Sometimes there are intrasocietal conflicts between two "regimes," each enjoying a relative monopoly of the means of coercion in their respective areas; for example, the Communists in the north of China versus the Kuomintang in the south and west. Yet separatism was not the issue at all in China. What should be done with these marginal cases?

Since separation is such a very different outcome from regime overthrow, the factors predictive of successful separation are unlikely to be the same as those predictive of successful overthrow, except maybe at a very general level. Violent separatist conflicts, like the Nigerian one, have more in common with anticolonial rebellions than with mass rebellions,

---

[8]The rises to power of Mussolini and Hitler constitute borderline cases here, since there were certainly violent confrontations between their supporters and the Italian and German regimes. Yet Hitler was elected to office, which hardly constitutes a violent overthrow, and the Italian government finally abdicated to Mussolini after the nonviolent March on Rome. For this reason, both cases were excluded from the universe of cases collected.

and some of the arguments put forward earlier in this chapter for differentiating between mass rebellions and anticolonial rebellions are also relevant here.[9]

There is another sound reason for disqualifying violent intrasocietal struggles in which separatism or secession or autonomy is the issue or outcome. My definition of successful rebellion disallows inclusion of separatist outcomes, since the overthrow of the regime must be threatened in rebellion. Hence, the United States "Civil War" does not qualify since it was separatist, but the Chinese "revolution" does qualify since separatism was not involved. (The Spanish "Civil War" was excluded on other grounds, specifically because the rebellion was initiated and led by the military, and because there was considerable international intervention.)

The question now arises as to what to do with cases in which there is no real regime at all. Leach (1964) argues that rebellions are not really possible when there is no central regime to overthrow—not an uncommon situation even in twentieth century societies. For example, after the successful overthrow of the Manchu dynasty in China in 1912, and until the Kuomintang ascendancy in 1927–1928, there really was no central regime against which to rebel. The major struggle was between two movements neither of which represented the official regime. Given the central place occupied by the "overthrow" criterion in my definition, cases that occur in these kinds of social contexts are excluded.

In summary, as a result of including in my definition of mass rebellion the requirement that the upheaval occur within an *autonomous political system*, violent power struggles that occur in the following social contexts do not qualify for inclusion in the universe:

1. Societies that are not structurally independent of a foreign power at the time of the conclusion of the struggle, either because they have not yet achieved independence, or because they were recently conquered or occupied by another nation. However, nations may be engaged in international conflict or wars.

2. Societies without a real central government.

[9]Unfortunately, separatism as a differentiating criterion has the great disadvantage of requiring information on rebel aims. Earlier the argument was presented that an effort should be made to avoid requiring such information. However, in the case of this distinction it seems unavoidable. But it seems that obtaining information on separatist aims might be somewhat easier than obtaining information on the aims of nonseparatist rebellions. First, for the matter to result in civil war, it must be evident that one side wishes to prevent the other side from breaking away. If both sides agree to separation, then there is no civil war—only when one side opposes separation is there a violent confrontation. So the aims are more apparent than is often the case for mass rebellions. Second, separatist aims and territorial separation of the two sides, each with its own "regime," usually occur together. Data on the latter, then, can alert one to look more carefully for data relevant to separatist aims.

3. Societies in which there is substantial external intervention, in that people from another country (or other countries) or an international body like the United Nations, assist by fighting on behalf of the rebels or the regime. Other kinds of intervention do not require the case be disqualified. The reasons for disqualifying cases in which a second power contributes a significant amount of manpower is that it is easier to get data on manpower than many of the other types of intervention (see Appendix I for a discussion of what exactly constitutes "a significant amount" of manpower). Also, if the participants in a rebellion have to be "local," a mass rebellion cannot be "manufactured" by another power. Hence, it indicates local discontent, which, as already noted, is the kind of situation most relevant to the question of whether coercion can work or not.

In addition, the following types of violent power struggle must be excluded:

4. Civil wars, where the struggle is over "self-determination," "autonomy," or "secession," not the overthrow of the regime.
5. Wars, which involve more than one autonomous political system.

My definition of mass rebellion requires that the *participants be largely from the masses*. The word, "mass," is meant to include peasants, workers, students, and the middle class. While my definition can easily be adapted to differentiate between middle class, peasant, or proletarian mass rebellions, this distinction is not made in this study. Lasswell and Kaplan (1950) define "the elite" as "those with most power in a group," and "the mass" as those with "least power [p. 201]." They also use the concept of a "mid-elite," who are "those with less power" than the elite. If their mid-elite and mass categories are collapsed, we have the meaning of mass in my definition. Requiring that participants be largely from the masses serves, then, to exclude power struggles that occur between individuals or groups within the elite, and power struggles that are initiated or led by the armed forces. The latter qualify as military rebellions. Despite the fact that some military rebellions do receive active mass support, it is often very difficult to know whether this is real, cynical (that is, the desire to be on the side of the winner, whoever that may be), or only proclaimed. But cases in which the armed forces *participate* with the rebels will obviously not be excluded, since it is the hypothesis that no rebellion can succeed without such participation that is to be tested.

To qualify as a rebellion, *the overthrow of the regime must be threatened*. Where this is the case, we can be sure we are dealing with an important struggle for power. (This does not imply, of course, that all those upheavals where overthrow is not threatened, or where it is threatened by the armed forces, are unimportant.) There have been, after all, thousands

of messianic and millennarian movements that are violent and have "revolutionary goals" but that provide no real challenge to the regime.
Such failures would not provide an interesting comparison group for successful rebellions.

But determining whether the overthrow of the regime has been threatened
by an unsuccessful rebellion is no easy task. It might seem that to stipulate
that the movement must at least be *attempting* to overthrow the regime
would simplify it (that is, replace the word "threatened" with "attempted"), but I have earlier pointed out the enormous pitfalls involved
in determining the aims of a movement. Assuming that the larger the
scale of the rebellion, the more threatening it is, the criteria decided
upon for evaluating whether overthrow is threatened or not are:

1. the amount of violence;
2. the number of rebels;
3. the social–geographical area involved;
4. the duration of the rebellion.

All these criteria have the virtue of being quantifiable. It is assumed that the
more violence, the greater the number of rebels, the larger the social-
geographical area involved, and the longer the duration of the rebellion,
the greater is the threat of overthrow to the regime. These critereia are
very similar to those Sorokin (1962) used for measuring the magnitude of
"revolutions" in his classic study done in the 1930s. Indeed, for the
social-geographical area criterion, Sorokin's seven categories have been
collapsed into three to fit my cruder index (*Ibid.*, p. 394).[10]

The actual index developed for evaluating the scale (degree of threat)
of the rebellion is presented in Table 4.1. The scoring system is crude,
and the cut-off points for each category inevitably arbitrary. The scoring
system's virtues are its explicitness and the fact that it makes possible
a systematic evaluation of how large-scale a rebellion is, rather than an
impressionistic, implicit evaluation. In addition, it can allow for missing
data: where precise data are not available, qualitative data are used to
make estimates. However, when there is no good basis for estimation,
the criterion is not used in calculating the scale score. Since the mean
score is used, this missing datum does not distort the score. The scale score
has to be at least 1.1 to qualify for inclusion in the study.

Since evaluation of the amount of violence requires knowledge of the
number of deaths, and since sometimes the only information available is

[10]For another of his criteria, Sorokin combined the amount of violence and social change into
a single dimension. Given the importance of separating the form of the upheaval from its consequences, this combination seems unfortunate. It makes it impossible to examine the relation
between violence and social change.

the number of dead and wounded, or the number of "casualties" which includes wounded and dead, Bodart's formula is used; this formula was developed to deal with just such incomplete data. Richardson (1960) used this formula in his study of "deadly quarrels", his rationale seems sound (see also Bodart, 1916):

> From "a comparative investigation of several hundred battles of modern and recent times" . . . Bodard concluded that for every 450 men put out action, 100 on the average were killed on the spot, and of the remaining 350 about 47 later died of their wounds. So if our only information is that the number of soldiers killed or wounded was $k + w$ it is permissable to deduce the number of those who died by $d + (k + w)/3$ [p. 10].

TABLE 4.1

Index for Evaluating the Scale of Mass Rebellion

---

a. *Amount of violence*
    0 = minimal (<150 deaths)
    1 = some (151–500 deaths)
    2 = considerable (501 + deaths)
b. *Number of active rebels*
    0 = few (500)
    1 = some (501–1000)
    2 = considerable (1000 +)
c. *Social–geographical area involved*
    0 = a disturbance of a local character in a rural county or similar limited area; a similar disturbance in several rural counties, or in a small town; a disturbance in a larger town; a disturbance in several towns of medium size, or in one important city, or in a small province
    1 = a disturbance in a larger province, or in a part of capital city; a disturbance in several large provinces, or in the whole capital city
    2 = a disturbance in the capital city and spread over several provinces; a disturbance where almost the whole country is involved; a disturbance in the entire country
d. *Duration of the event*
    0 = < 1 week
    1 = 1 week–6 months
    2 = 6 months +

NOTE: If the only information available cites figures of dead and wounded or "casualties" (which presumably includes wounded, as well well as dead), the number of dead are calculated by Bodart's formula (Richardson, 1960, p. 10):

$$\text{Dead} = \frac{(k + w)}{3}, \quad \text{where } k = \text{killed}, \ w = \text{wounded.}$$

5

Method: The Whys and Wherefores
of an Empirical Study

Chapter Four was devoted to precisely defining the phenomenon of mass rebellion. This was necessary to enable first, the creation of a universe of successful and unsuccessful rebellions, and second, the drawing of a random sample therefrom. In this chapter, a careful description of how these tasks were carried out is presented.

The study was limited to twentieth-century rebellions; and, since my interest in understanding the phenomenon of rebellion is so bound up with my concern with the fate of South Africa, it seemed reasonable to focus on cases of rebellion that occurred in the past 70 years. Moreover, by focusing on the present century, fewer cases were likely to be disqualified because they were "premodern," that is, where the rebels are without a real central authority against which to rebel.

A universe of mass rebellions was created by going through the historical sections in the *Encyclopaedia Britannica* of all nations that were members of the United Nations in 1968. United Nations membership was used since the definition of mass rebellion requires that countries have achieved independent status. When considerations other than political independence entered into United Nations membership, it was not adhered to; for example, Communist China and East Germany were added, and Byelorussia and Ukraine were excluded.[1] This provided me with a list of 122 countries.

In looking through the histories of these countries—as recorded in the *Encyclopaedia Britannica (EB)*—any evidence that suggested the occurrence of a violent political upheaval for which at least an approximate date could be inferred, was recorded, unless there was information that indicated it did not meet my definitional criteria of mass rebellion. For example, if the event was described as a "bloodless" upheaval, or as involving the intervention of a substantial number of troops from another country, or if the conflict was initiated by the army, it was not recorded.[2] This procedure resulted in a list of approximately 160 possible cases. Further information was obtained for all of these events from the *New International Yearbook (NIYB)*.

Both *EB* and *NIYB* suffer from a serious bias. The amount of space allotted to each country is highly correlated with degree of economic development and past historic "importance." Information on Third World countries is often very limited.[3] In order to compensate for this bias in *EB*, the practice of having a lower "recording threshold" for countries given relatively little space was followed. Vaguer phrases such as "considerable unrest," a "general strike," a "coup," "serious riots," and "rural unrest," were followed up, as were vaguer dates. For example, if a sentence

[1] There are countries that no longer exist, having been swallowed up by others in the course of the century's conflicts; for example, Latvia. If the history of these territories has not been included in that of the nations that incorporated them, then to that extent the claim cannot be made that the histories of all countries that have existed in the twentieth century have been searched for instances of rebellion.

[2] While sometimes there is a great deal of information in *EB* on a particular rebellion, at other times there is no more than a phrase or two, such as "violent conflict," "bloody revolt," or "revolutionary unrest." For this reason, cases with very little information were often more likely to be recorded than cases where there was sufficient information for it to be clear that one or two of the definitial criteria were not met. Hence, the number of upheavals that were recorded cannot be regarded as meaningful data for, say, an evaluation of the stability or instability of different decades or regions, or for the plotting of instability curves over time in the manner of Sorokin (1962).

[3] An additional bias of *NIYB* resulted from its United States origin. Particularly in the sections on Latin America, a disproportionate amount of space is given to any incident affecting United States–Latin American relations. I doubt, however, whether this latter bias led to the exclusion of any cases of rebellion.

I chose *NIYB* after examining a number of different yearbooks because it seemed the best in terms of the amount of space given each country, in the kind of information given, and in that it started as early as 1907, in contrast, say, to the *Encyclopaedia Britannica* yearbook. Since I could find no adequate substitute for *NIYB* for the years 1900–1906, my cases were limited to post-1906 rebellions.

like the one that follows were used to describe the situation in a country with a low-recording threshold—"between 1925 and 1932, there were several abortive revolutions"—further information for each of the 8 years would be sought in *NIYB*.

Many cases still remained in doubt after following up the approximately 160 cases in *NIYB*.[4] If there were more than two definitional criteria in doubt at this point, the case was disqualified. If there were two criteria or less in doubt, further information was sought in other yearbooks, for example, *Annual Register of World Events*, *Facts-on-File*, *Keesing's Archives*, and *Statesman's Yearbook*. The reason for introducing such criteria was that a disproportionate amount of time was being spent on case selection. For the interested reader, a step-by-step description of the way in which the universe was created and the cases selected is diagrammed in Appendix II.

After carrying out the second stage of the case-selection procedure, most of the original 160 potential cases were disqualified, leaving a meager universe of only 28 cases, approximately 18% of the potential universe. Two random samples were drawn from these 28 cases, one from the list of successful rebellions, the other from the list of unsuccessful rebellions. Both samples are listed in Table 5.1 in the order of selection, with the date at which the outcome was determined.

Even after the samples were drawn, if it became clear from a more intensive study of the historical materials that a case did not fulfill one or more of the defining criteria, it was still possible to disqualify it. Since only *EB* and *NIYB* data were used up to this point, it is surprising that only one case had to be disqualified: the Nazi rebellion in Austria in 1934.[5] Honduras, the eighth case of unsuccessful rebellion to be drawn, replaced the Austrian case in the random sample.

The next task was to go through as many historical and yearbook accounts on each of these cases as seemed necessary to obtain data required to further check the qualifiability of the case, and to obtain data on the loyalty or disloyalty of the armed forces. The data gathered, the degree of disloyalty had to be assessed in each of the 14 cases. A scale was developed for this purpose. The three constituents of the scale are as follows:

  1. *The degree of disloyalty (D)*, where the minimal degree of disloyalty that can be scored is when the armed forces are unwilling to fight for

---

[4] It is due to this rule of low-threshold recording that only an approximate figure can be given for the total number of cases recorded from *EB*.

[5] Most of the historical accounts provided evidence that Hitler and the German Nazis played an important role in the Nazi rebellion in Austria. Hence, Austria was disqualified on the grounds that it was not an autonomous political system.

TABLE 5.1

Universe and Random Samples of Mass Rebellion[a]

Successful rebellions		Unsuccessful rebellions	
1. Albania	1924	1. Columbia	1948
2. Mexico	1911	2. Spain	1934
3. Bolivia	1952	3. Cuba	1912
4. Afghanistan	1929	4. Burma	1954
5. China	1949	5. Austria	1934
6. Cuba	1958	6. Italy	1914
7. Brazil	1930	7. Honduras	1933
8. Bolivia	1930	8. Bolivia	1949
9. Russia	1917	9. Cameroon	1960
10. Portugal	1915	10. Ceylon	1958
11. Tanzania	1964	11. Philippines	1954
12. Cuba	1933	12. Ireland	1923
		13. Portugal	1927
		14. Spain	1930
		15. Bulgaria	1923
		16. Rumania	1907

[a]The rebellions are listed in the order in which they were drawn. The first seven cases in each sample constitute the random samples. The date indicates when the outcome of the rebellion was determined.

the regime, and the degree of maximum disloyalty that can be scored is when the armed forces fight on the side of the rebels.

2. *The timing of the disloyalty (T),* where the minimal disloyalty occurs when the armed forces defect near the end of the rebellion, and the maximum, when they defect at the start.
3. *The proportion of the armed forces who are disloyal at a particular time (P),* where the minimal disloyalty occurs when only 2–10% of the armed forces are disloyal, and the maximum when more than 95% are disloyal. "The armed forces" include the army, the navy, the airforce, and the police.

Often, precise figures are not available on the proportion of the armed forces who are disloyal at a particular time. Historians appear to prefer vague phrases like "a majority of the armed forces," or "some of the troops," or "a few soldiers." This is why instead of developing an equal-interval percentage scale, categories were developed that would

TABLE 5.2

Armed Force Disloyalty Scale

---

1. Degree of disloyalty *(D)*
    0 = willing, enthusiastic fighters
    1 = unwilling fighters, e.g., surrendered readily
    2 = neutral, e.g., stood by without resisting, ran away
    3 = actively helped rebels, e.g., gave arms, informed rebels of troop maneuvers
        and battle plans
    4 = fought on the side of the rebels

2. Time at which disloyal *(T)*
    0 = never (in the last 5% of the duration)
    1 = near the end (in the last 6–25% of the duration)
    2 = about halfway through (from 26–75% of the duration)
    3 = near the beginning (in the first 6–25% of the duration)
    4 = from the start (in the first 0–5% of the duration)

3. Proportion of armed forces disloyal at a particular time *(P)*
    0 = none (0–1%)
    ½ = few (2–10%)
    1 = some (11–25%)
    2 = considerable (26–50%)
    3 = majority (51–95%)
    4 = all (96–100%)

---

have a meaningful relation with imprecise phrases like those with which I had to work. Data on the degree and the timing of disloyalty were also often imprecise, so here, too, categories were devised with this unfortunate situation in mind.

The major task of data collection involved a search for the most precise data obtainable on the three elements of disloyalty required to arrive at a disloyalty assessment. When data were imprecise, an intelligent estimate was made. The way in which the formula for combining these three elements was developed is described below.

Preliminary formula:
(1)
$$D \times T \times P,$$

where D = degree of disloyalty; T = time at which disloyal; P = proportion of armed forces disloyal at a particular time.

Example: If about one-third of the armed forces start fighting on the side of the rebels about halfway through the rebellion, the disloyalty score would be:

$$4_D \times 2_T \times 2_P = 16.$$

However, such simple descriptions of the role of the armed forces are frequently inadequate: different parts of the armed forces may behave differently at different times. Therefore, the formula was changed so as to be able to deal with more complex conclusions.

Preliminary formula:

(2) $(D_1 \times T_1 \times P_1) + (D_2 \times T_2 \times P_2) + \cdots + (D_n + T_n + P_n).$

Example: The police force, constituting about 5% of all the armed forces, actively helped the rebels by giving them arms and letting them attack buildings freely, from the start of the rebellion. The army, however, remained loyal until about halfway through, when the majority of them became unwilling to fight, surrendering readily to the rebels. A few of them at this time went so far as to fight on the side of the rebels. This would be scored:

$$(3_D \times 4_T \times 0.5_P) + (1_D \times 2_T \times 4_P) + (4_D \times 2_T \times 0.5_P)$$
$$= 6 + 8 + 4$$
$$= 18.$$

But there was also a problem with this formula. Cases of long duration, or cases about which there was a great deal of data, are more likely to get more $D \times T \times P$ expressions and, hence, to score higher on disloyalty. Hence, it seemed important to standardize the number of expressions that could contribute to the final disloyalty score for each case. It was therefore decided that only the two expressions that contributed most to the disloyalty score would be used. So, in the last example used to demonstrate preliminary formula (2), the expression that added only four points to the final disloyalty score would be omitted, since it was the lowest. This is by no means an ideal solution since it is likely to result in some underestimation of disloyalty for cases where more than two expressions would otherwise be used. However, in this study, it turned out that the Chinese rebellion was the only one for which this was the case. Thus, the problem turns out to be minor.

Final disloyalty score formula:

(3) $(D_1 \times T_1 \times P_1) + (D_2 \times T_2 \times P_2)$,

where (1) and (2) are the two expressions that contribute most to the disloyalty score.

The reason for a multiplicative rather than an additive formula is simply that after experimenting with all the different possibilities, it seemed that the multiplicative formula better expressed the cumulative way in which disloyalty works.

6

Analysis, Conclusions,
and Implications

Since the results of the case analyses take very little space to report, and the journey through 14 case studies is, in contrast, lengthy, it seems advisable to present the results and discuss their implications prior to the case presentations. The danger that the results and conclusions would get buried in all the data seems too great to follow the more conventional order of presentation.

Verbal descriptions of the disloyalty-score expressions for all 14 cases are presented in a highly abbreviated form in Table 6.1, together with their quantitative expressions. (The formula and scale by which these quantitative expressions were obtained are on pages 76 and 74, respectively.) A simple examination of the disloyalty scores of the seven successful mass rebellions presented in this table makes it clear that *in no case of successful rebellion did the regime retain the loyalty of the armed forces*. While the extent of disloyalty varied considerably—from 10.5 in the case of Cuba, to 40 in the case of Albania—this does not alter the fact that some disloyalty occurred in *all* successful cases.

TABLE 6.1

Disloyalty Scores for Successful and Unsuccessful Rebellions

Successful rebellions	Early[a]	Middle	Late	Disloyalty score
1. Afghanistan 1929	$1_D \times 4_T \times 3_P = 12$ Majority unwilling from start	$3_D \times 2_T \times 1_P = 6$ Some helped rebels half way	—	18.0
2. Albania 1924	$4_D \times 4_T \times 2_P = 32$ Considerable number fought for rebels from start	$4_D \times 2_T \times 1_P = 8$ Some fought for rebels half way	—	40.0
3. Bolivia 1952	$4_D \times 4_T \times 1_P = 16$ Some fought for rebels from start	—	—	16.0
4. Brazil 1930	$4_D \times 4_T \times 1_P = 16$ Some fought for rebels from start	—	$4_D \times 1_T \times 2_P = 8$ Considerable number fought for rebels near end	24.0
5. China 1949	$4_D \times 3_T \times 0.5_P = 6^b$ Few fought for rebels near start	$4_D \times 2_T \times 1_P = 8$ Some fought for rebels half way	$4_D \times 1_T \times 3_P = 12$ Majority fought for rebels near end	20.0
6. Cuba 1958		$4_D \times 2_T \times 0.75_P = 6$ Between a few and some fought for rebels half way	$1.5_D \times 1_T \times 3_P = 4.5$ Majority unwilling/ neutral near end	10.5
7. Mexico 1911	$4_D \times 3_T \times 0.5_P = 6$ Few fought for rebels near start	$4_D \times 2_T \times 1_P = 8$ Some fought for rebels half way	—	14.0

As previously noted, Andreski (1967, p. 247) argues that the Cuban rebellion of 1958 showed that rebellions could be successful even without the cooperation of the armed forces. My analysis of the Cuban case does not permit this conclusion. Even though the disloyalty score for Cuba is quite low (10.5), particularly in comparison with the mean disloyalty score for successful rebellions (20.3), the fact remains that there was definitely more than token armed-force disloyalty there.

Scanning of the data presented in Table 6.1 makes at least two things clear:

TABLE 6.1 *(continued)*

Unsuccessful rebellions	Early[a]	Middle	Late	Disloyalty score
1. Austria 1934	—	—	—	0
2. Burma 1954	$4_D \times 3_T \times 3_P = 36$ Majority fought for rebels near start	—	—	36
3. Columbia 1948	$4_D \times 4_T \times 1_P = 16$ Some fought for rebels from start	—	—	16
4. Cuba 1912	—	—	—	0
5. Honduras 1933	$4_D \times 3_T \times 0.5_P = 6$ Few fought for rebels near start	$4_D \times 2_T \times 0.5_P = 4$ Few fought for rebels half way	—	10
6. Italy 1914	—	—	—	0
7. Spain 1934	—	—	—	0

[a]This category includes "from the start" and "near start," i.e., within the first 25% of the duration. These two time categories were collapsed because it turned out that in none of the cases were there disloyalty score expressions at both of them.

[b]This expression is excluded from the total score since only the two expressions that contribute most to the disloyalty score may be included.

1. Armed-force disloyalty is necessary for a successful outcome of rebellion, but it is not a sufficient condition. There are three unsuccessful cases where there was a substantial amount of disloyalty. One of them, Burma, had the second highest disloyalty score of all the cases in both samples. Or, put another way, Burma had a score nearly double the mean disloyalty score for the successful rebellions.

2. Several unsuccessful rebellions failed to win any disloyalty from the armed forces whatsoever.

The question left unanswered is whether there is a statistically significant relationship between the disloyalty of the armed forces and the outcome of rebellion, such that the greater the disloyalty, the more likely the outcome of the rebellion will be successful. The possibility of this relationship was tested in two different ways. The mean disloyalty scores for the successful and the unsuccessful cases were calculated (it was 20.3 for the successful rebellions, and 8.9 for the unsuccessful cases), and the t test was used to determine whether the difference between them was statistically significant or not. However, since the assumptions required by the t test—that the populations sampled are normally distributed and that the variances of the populations are homogeneous—seem questionable in the case of successful and unsuccessful rebellions, a chi-square test was also used to ascertain whether there was a significant association between armed-force disloyalty and the outcome of mass rebellion.

Using the t test, it was found that the difference between the mean disloyalty score for the successful rebellions was significantly different from the mean disloyalty score for the unsuccessful rebellions (at better than the .05 level). And using the chi-square test of association it was found that the association between armed-force disloyalty and the outcome of mass rebellion was significant at better than the 0.02 level.

What are some of the implications of these results?

IMPLICATIONS OF STUDY

In 1943 Chorley asserted that: "In a revolutionary situation the attitude of the army is. . .of supreme importance. It is the decisive factor on which will depend success or failure [p. 243]." My study does not reveal whether or not the attitude (I prefer the word, behavior) of the armed forces is *the* decisive factor. But it certainly provides solid evidence that it is *a* decisive factor. Chorley, Brinton, Lenin, Trotsky, Le Bon, Mosca, and Calvert have been proven correct in their view that successful rebellions require some defection on the part of the armed forces. And the view of Mao, Guevara, Debray, Mills, Hobsbawm, and Leiden and Schmitt, that "popular forces can win a war against the army [Guevara, 1968, p. 1]," when subject to no qualifier about the loyalty of the armed forces, has to be rejected. Only if it were reasonable to assume that armed-force disloyalty automatically occurs whenever a mass rebellion gets underway might this view be valid. But the unsuccessful cases of rebellion analyzed in this study make it clear that popular uprisings do not always find such support in the armed forces. And cases like South Africa, where the basis for armed-force loyalty is so obviously strong, make it clear how unwise it is to take armed-force disloyalty for granted.

In Chapter One, Pettee's belief that armies always join revolutions if all the "causes" of revolution are present was mentioned. For Pettee and the many others who hold this view (though most of them are less explicit about it), the behavior of the armed forces is seen as merely a dependent variable; it is not credited as capable of being an independent force. It seems to me that Trotsky's (1959) more complex view on this matter is much nearer the truth:

> There is no doubt that the fate of every revolution at a certain point is decided by a break in the disposition of the army. Against a numerous, disciplined, well-armed and ably led military force, unarmed or almost unarmed masses of the people cannot possibly gain a victory. But no deep national crisis can fail to affect the army to some extent. Thus along with the conditions of a truly popular revolution there develops a possibility—not, of course, a guarantee—of its victory. However, the going over of the army to the insurrection does not happen of itself, nor as a result of mere agitation [p. 116].

The question that cries out for research, then, is what factors explain "the going over of the army to the insurrection"? My study has shown only the significance of armed-force loyalty to the outcome of mass rebellion. It is for another study to uncover what factors determine whether the armed forces are likely to be loyal or disloyal. Some of the variables that might be examined in such a study are: the social-class composition of the armed forces on both the officer and conscript level; the proportion of officers to men; the closeness of contacts between the armed forces and the civilian population; whether the army is a long-service, professional army or a short-service, conscript army, or something in between; the recruitment criteria, for example, political versus military; the pay, status, and promotion opportunities, and how these compare with opportunities outside of the armed forces; the emphasis in the training on discipline, courage, efficiency, and obedience; the existence of an ideology shared with the regime; and how well or badly the troops are treated. Lip service given to the important role of the armed forces must be replaced by thorough examination of the effect of factors such as these on their loyalty to the regime.

The fact that armed-force disloyalty is necessary for a successful rebellion to occur suggests that when the regime and its armed forces remain willing to use their coercion resources to suppress the rebels, they can. This fact undermines one of the basic assumptions of the "integration" or value theory of society, that "every functioning social structure is based on a consensus of values among its members [Dahrendorf, 1959, p. 161]." As I have noted earlier, outside of sociology too, many people seem unable to accept the notion that a really oppressive regime may be quite stable and long lasting. This comforting belief is, unfortunately, quite undermined by the results of this study. Examining only one element of oppressiveness —the loyalty of the armed forces to the regime—I found that this element alone plays a decisive role in rebellion, since, if the armed forces remain loyal to the regime, a mass rebellion cannot succeed. This fact supports the unhappy conclusion that oppression *can* last—which does not mean it always will, but does mean that we have to give up the overly optimistic notion that "good" necessarily triumphs in the end.

And what are the implications of my study for South Africa? The fact that the armed forces in that country are almost exclusively white was pointed out in Chapter Two. It is unusual in this day and age, at least in noncolonial situations, to find armed forces exclusively recruited from the elite, and of a different racial and cultural group from the majority of the people. This is one major difference between Cuba and South Africa, and since the whites in the armed forces share with the whites in the rest of society an enormously strong interest in maintaining the status quo, the chance of their behaving as did Batista's forces in Cuba seems to be absolutely nil. Given the results of my study, this leads me to predict that as long as there is no external intervention on behalf of the blacks in South Africa, there can be no successful rebellion. My prediction is based not only on the assumption that the armed forces will not defect, but also on the assumption that, because South Africa is highly oppressive on all the other dimensions of oppressiveness analyzed (that is, regime unity, coercion resources, the willingness of the regime to use these resources to coerce, and the repressiveness of the entire political structure), a successful mass rebellion is even more improbable.

It should be clear by now that by making this prediction, I am directly contradicting the predictions made by most people regarding South Africa. Adam (1971a), one of the few whose prediction is the same as mine, in a recent analysis of the South African situation confirms my point:

> ...almost all critical analysts of South Africa have predicted that the Apartheid endeavor would inevitably fail. No country in the Third World, it is said, either in Latin America or among the feudal states of Asia, has been riper for a violent revolution, certain to take place in the forseeable future. The magnitude of this revolution has been viewed as likely to exceed all other colonial revolutions because of the severity of suppression, the technological development of the country, and the divergent interests at stake for the two uncompromising antagonists [p. 4].[1]

---

[1]For example, Leo Marquard (1969) concludes that "in attempting to retain political control, the European inhabitants adopt policies that create the very forces that must, in the long run, overthrow their rule [p. 269]."

But it is not only most analysts of the South African case who need to come to terms with a harsher reality; many other theorists and activists have to do so too.[2] Unfortunately the views of Franz Neumann (1957, pp. 266–267) seem to have a great deal of validity. He points out that in the twentieth century, those who hold political power have available to them physical coercion, all instruments of economic power (the means of production, consumer goods, wages, and prices), and all psychological means of coercion (that is, propaganda and education.) Neumann then asserts:

> It seems to be impossible to overthrow the holder of political power who is in unlimited possession of all these instruments and techniques. Indeed, there exists in modern history no example of a successful revolution against a halfway strong state. . . . Every strong state can deal with its opposition; totalitarian politics have no difficulty whatever with this. . . . In the modern period of conscious precedence of politics, revolution can be successful only within the ruling class and only with the help of the political machinery itself [p. 267].

In the study described in this volume it is important to note that all cases of successful rebellion occurred in countries that were neither highly industrialized nor highly developed enconomically. The same is true of the five successful cases that were not included in the random sample (Bolivia, 1930; Russia, 1917; Portugal, 1915; Tanzania, 1964; and Cuba, 1933). Indeed, with the exception of Austria, 1934, the countries in which unsuccessful rebellions occurred were also at an early stage of industrial development. As Tannenbaum (1960) observes:

> All of our social revolutions[3] have been in agricultural countries where the population was preponderantly rural. . . . It surely is no accident that in spite of the Marxist

---

[2]For example, Taber (1970) asserts: "Where the cause appears just, the situation is intolerable, and oppression past all appeal, the way to action is clear [p. 32]." Taber goes on to say how victory for the rebels can easily follow.

Aside from cases like South Africa and Rhodesia, one wonders how the ubiquity and antiquity of the oppression of women can be explained by those who subscribe to this viewpoint. Perhaps its very universality has made it hard for many people even to recognize it for what it is. But while the oppression of women has much in common with other forms of oppression, it is also unique, but not only by virtue of its universality. Because the separation of women is so profoundly imbedded in the institutions of society, and most women are tied in deep and complex ways to members of the very group that oppresses them, it could be argued that the oppression of women is unique in its potential for lasting, and that other groups are less vulnerable since their fragmentation can be overcome more easily.

[3]By "social revolution," Tannenbaum means successful mass rebellions followed by substantial social change.

doctrine of proletarian revolutions we have no single example of a serious effort
by an industrial populace to capture its government and distribute the property. . .
[pp. 45–46].[4]

This is one of the few hard facts we have about rebellion and revolution,
and it is an extremely important, though ignored, one.

It is noteworthy that it is students of less-developed nations who are
most apt to espouse some variant of the view that oppression cannot last. At
least this is consistent with the fact that there have been successful mass
rebellions in less economically developed societies. Nevertheless, their
optimism does not seem justified, insofar as they claim that an oppressed
people must ultimately be victorious, strong and resolute armed forces
notwithstanding. They are even less justified in arguing this view for highly
industrialized nations.

Much of the revolutionary rhetoric now flourishing in the United States
and other highly industrialized societies also naively assumes that the writings
of Mao, Guevara, Fanon, and DeBray can be directly applied to these
societies. They completely ignore the relevance of the structural context.
Taber's (1970) comment in *The War of the Flea* is typical: "Popular revolutionary forces *can* defeat regular armies. This is the fundamental lesson of
China [p. 47]." And this is supposed to apply to industrial nations as well.
"[M]odern industrial societies, with all their awesome destructive capability,
cannot suppress popular insurgencies, once firmly rooted [p. 11]." Indeed
Taber goes on to assert that such societies are particularly vulnerable to
guerrilla warfare: "The weakness peculiar to the modern, bouregois-
democratic, capitalistic state (but shared in some measure by all modern
states) make popular war possible . . . [p. 26]." I regard these views as
overly optimistic and unfounded rhetoric.

It is important to point out here that many students of rebellion and
revolution do not distinguish between anticolonial and mass rebellion, or
a war like that between the United States and North Vietnam. Therefore,
it is important to emphasize that the findings of this study, as well as my
comments and conclusions, are limited to mass rebellions. For many reasons,
some of which were discussed in Chapter Four, the conditions for success
are likely to be different for these different kinds of power struggles. And

---

[4]For a similar statement, see also Tannenbaum (1962, pp. 222–223). While Hungary in
1956 was an industrial nation, this rebellion had far more in common with an anticolonial
than a mass rebellion (de-Russification was a major goal). And it was Russia's intervention
to maintain her colonial control over Hungary that made its success so shortlived. In Chapter
Four some reasons were given for why the factors making for success and failure differ for mass
and anticolonial rebellions.

it might well be that armed-force disloyalty is not a prerequisite for success in anticolonial rebellions, or for success in wars against foreign powers.

IN SUMMARY

My hope is that this book will contribute toward a much-needed redirection in studies of rebellion and revolution. To that end, I bring together in this chapter the suggestions scattered throughout this volume on what I think is necessary to achieve this redirection and why this is needed.

Studies on rebellion have been plagued by the failure to distinguish among the causes, the form, and the consequences of the event. I have developed a particular typology of different kinds of rebellion and used a simple dichotomy of the short-term outcome of rebellion to facilitate an analysis of the particular questions that interested me. Presumably, with different questions, their usefulness will fall away. But the usefulness of distinguishing causes, form, and consequences should go far beyond this study. The failure to make these distinctions has left a number of really important questions unasked and unstudied; for example, in what circumstances do "preconditions" lead to rebellion and in what circumstances do they fail to result in rebellion? Or what determines whether a successful mass rebellion will lead to a successful revolution? In addition, the failure to make these distinctions has resulted in an almost complete failure to see unsuccessful cases of rebellion as deserving of study, since if causes, form, and consequences are seen as an inseparable whole, then unsuccessful cases are really *noncases*. As I have pointed out earlier, Brinton (1952) describes the "abortive revolution" as if it were a distinct type. Leiden and Schmitt (1968) devote only 2 out of 215 pages to the topic of "abortive revolutions" in their book *The Politics of Violence: Revolution in the Modern World.* They mention casually that ". . .of course, many revolts are simply suppressed [p. 60]." But that, apparently, is that. There is no attempt to consider what is similar and what is different about the rebellions that suffer this fate and rebellions that succeed.

The common failure to distinguish between the conditions leading to a rebellion and the conditions enabling the rebellion to succeed has meant that when rebellions do not succeed, the tendency is to attribute this to some weak or absent "precondition" or "cause." This is why we lack studies on the determinants of the outcome of rebellions. And it also helps to account for the extraordinary lack of consensus regarding causes, since an excessive burden is placed upon "preconditions" to explain all phases of the upheaval and all consequences as well.

Another reason for the serious misdirection of studies in this field is that so many studies seem to fall into either of two schools of thought. The first is guilty of a naive psychologism: the adherents of this school focus so heavily on the importance of the state of mind of the rebels or potential rebels, that they ignore the social structure within which these minds exist [for example, Davies (1962, 1969); LeBon (1960); and in some of his work, Gurr, (1970b)]. The second school is guilty of a naive structuralism. These analysts place all the emphasis on the social-structural conditions as if "structural conduciveness" and successful rebellion inevitably go together [for example, Wolf (1969a);Moore (1966); and sometimes Johnson (1964, 1966)]. If the rebellion does not succeed, the structuralists are likely to explain it as due to "defective" structural conditions (such as that the economy is still at a prerevolutionary phase or the degree of industrialization is insufficient). In explaining why a rebellion does not succeed, the psychologists (who often are not, in fact, psychologists by disciplinary affiliation), in contrast, are likely to examine the factors that might have resulted in the rebels losing hope, or lowering their expectations, or changing their beliefs about the legitimacy of their demands. Studies of rebellion must go beyond either of these extremes.

Interestingly enough, the two schools join forces when it comes to attributing little importance to regime or military variables in either the incidence or outcome of rebellion. It does not seem *logical* for the psychologists to ignore the state of mind of the regime and their agents—but they do. Similarly, it does not seem logical that the structuralists should ignore these institutions that, after all, constitute a significant part of the social structure—but they do. Both schools of thought are equally optimistic insofar as they assume that when people need and demand change, they ultimately get change (psychological school); or when the social structure requires change, it will happen (structural school). I question whether such optimism is justified.

It should be added that neither of these schools is self-acknowledged. Yet perhaps this analysis will help some of these undeclared adherents to recognize their allegiance , together with its limitations. This could then open the way to more balanced views that recognize that not only can the regime and the armed forces play determining roles in rebellion, but that the notion of "preconditions" should be applied to regimes too. Students of rebellion must grow accustomed to looking for regime preconditions with as much concern as is now given to rebel preconditions—indeed, I would say, more concern. I agree with Eckstein (1965) that some "hindrances may be absolute in character, in that wherever they exist internal war fails to materialize . . . [p. 153]." Armed forces loyal to the regime appear to be one such absolute hindrance or obstacle to successful mass rebellions.[5] High regime oppressiveness might be another, assuming there is no intervention in support of the oppressed by other societies.

People are apt to see theoretical and practical implications as poles apart, as if theoretical means nonpractical. But this view is not justifiable. As Franz Neumann (1957) said: "Far-reaching real consequences can flow from apparently merely theoretical differences such as those about the relation of economics and politics [p. 257]." This also applies to the importance of regime and armed force variables relative to rebel variables. What then are the practical implications of my findings?

The practical implications may seem to be very counter-revolutionary. But ultimately, the truth is neither revolutionary or counter-revolutionary, and both revolutionaries and counter-revolutionaries have to come to terms with it. For if it is true, as I believe my study shows, that no mass rebellion can succeed without the defection of some of the regime's armed forces, then it helps revolutionaries not one jot to act in ignorance of this. Only the romantic who believes that the impossible can become possible with faith, energy, and dedication, can really argue against this position. (And the fact that some successful revolutionaries have been romantics does not mean that they were successful *because* they were romantics.)

In a situation where people are rebelling, the behavior of the armed forces has been shown to be a decisive factor in the outcome of the rebellion. For revolutionaries to come to terms with this means that they must devote a great deal of thought to how to encourage defections from the police and army. It is probably unwise, for example, to treat the armed forces as the enemy. Revolutionaries should try to make it more likely that the armed force personnel can identify with them. This might be facilitated by fraternizing as much as possible with them, infiltrating the armed forces, playing down the differences between themselves and members of the armed forces instead of maximizing these differences, for example, in dress, public behavior, and language. Hence, an ideology that could see the armed force personnel as victims rather than exploiters would probably increase the likelihood of defections. These tactics and beliefs are quite the opposite

[5]The fact that in the sample of unsuccessful mass rebellions studied, there were some rebellions in which there was no armed force disloyalty, opens to question Eckstein's (1965) view that "internal wars seem rarely to occur even if other conditions favor them, if a regime's instruments of violence remain loyal [p. 157]." It is their winning that seems to be impossible in this situation.

of what rebels are often inclined to do. Calling people "pigs," for example, is hardly likely to attract their sympathy to the cause.

It is interesting to note in this context that what I am recommending is exactly what Castro practiced. Chapelle (1962), who visited the guerrillas in the Sierra Maestra and observed some of their engagements with Batista's forces, had this to say:

> Before I left the United States, the Castro underground in New York briefed me on the tactics this way: "We return prisoners without even intimidating them. We do not exchange them, you understand; not one of ours has ever been returned to the field. But we just disarm our enemies when we capture them and send them back through the Cuban Red Cross."
>
> I was cynical about this claim and once in Cuba, I remarked to a rebel officer that I would be much surprised to see unintimidated, unwounded prisoners being returned, not exchanged, in the middle of a shooting war. This remark was a mistake.
>
> That same evening, I watched the surrender of hundreds of *Batistianos* from a small town garrison. They were gathered within a hollow square of rebel Tommy gunners and harangued by Raul Castro. ̇
>
> "We hope that you will stay with us and fight against the master who so ill-used you. If you decide to refuse this invitation—and I am not going to repeat it—you will be delivered to the custody of the Cuban Red Cross tomorrow. Once you are under Batista's orders again, we hope that you will not take up arms against us. But, if you do, remember this.
>
> "We took you this time. We can take you again. And when we do, we will not frighten or torture or kill you, any more than we are doing to you at this moment. If you are captured a second time or even a third by us, we will again return you exactly as we are doing now [p. 237].

Mao's policy, too, was to encourage defection from the Nationalist forces. He completely accepted these defectors without punishment for past behavior; however, he did not release Nationalist troops who did not "repent."

More generally, acknowledging the importance of regime variables also has policy implications for potential rebels. There may not be much they can do about the regime's resources for coercion, but they may be able to act in certain ways to create disunity. Regimes have long practiced a divide-and-conquer policy toward oppressed peoples; rebels might themselves try this policy.

A last word must be said on South Africa, since it was my interest in its future that inspired this work.

The usual argument against intervention in South Africa has been that apartheid is a "domestic" issue. Underlying this policy has been the assumption so often mentioned—such oppression cannot last, and justice will ultimately be victorious. Even the African nations that have pressed for armed intervention for some years seem to share this assumption; they are simply impatient for its realization and insulted by the continuation of white domination and exploitation of blacks in South Africa.

This study suggests, on the contrary, that for radical change to occur in South Africa, external intervention on the side of the blacks *is* necessary. The nations of the world must choose whether to allow such a regime to continue its oppression for the forseeable future, or not. They have to face that this is a choice and realize that nonintervention on the side of the blacks means they are directly or indirectly supporting the oppression of the black majority by the white minority in South Africa. I use the word "directly" because most Western countries (and, to a lesser extent, most nonaligned and even some Communist countries) have been intervening in South African affairs in support of the regime, for a long time, some on a massive scale, for example, by investing in the country and by carrying on normal diplomatic and trade relations (see First, 1972). This has enabled the regime to equip its coercive arsenal with the very best hardware and software, and to develop the capacity to produce its own unaided, if the need should arise. But military hardware and software are changing at an unprecedented rate, so that if the rest of the world were to disengage itself from South Africa, it would not take many years for the effects to be felt in this critical area. Moreover, disengagement would seem to be a logical first step toward the more intense kind of intervention that will probably be required, in coordination with internal efforts, to make South Africa a more just society.

7

Successful Rebellions and the Behavior of the Armed Forces

In this chapter, a brief account will be given of each successful rebellion included in the sample. The accounts will give some flesh to my definition of rebellion and a sense of the variability in the types of upheaval that fall within my inquiry. They will also provide a context for the information on the role of the armed forces. (If the reader is familiar with the case, however, the summary case description can easily be skipped.)

Instead of presenting my own summary description based on all the sources used, I decided to present historians' accounts of the rebellions. Thus, I am rescued from the temptation of including in the summaries information that fits best with my definition of rebellion, and focuses most pointedly on my interests, when in reality the data are inconsistent and often ignore my interests. (Even if I were able to resist such a temptation, the reader's trust on this score will not be put to the test.) The criteria used for selecting one case description rather than another were the length of the account, the quality of the historical work, and readability. In some instances I have permitted myself to do a little cutting, but I have never added to the accounts of the events described.

An analysis of the scale of each rebellion can be found in Appendix III. It may be remembered that the scale of the rebellion is used as a measure of whether the overthrow of the regime was threatened or not. A description and analysis of the behavior of the armed forces follows each case description, and each section includes a score indicative of the degree of disloyalty of the armed forces. (See pages 74–76 for a description of the method of calculating the disloyalty score.) The cases appear in alphabetical order.[1]

1. AFGHANISTAN—THE SUCCESSFUL REBELLION OF 1929

The rebellion in Afghanistan is unusual on many counts. First, it occurred in a premodern, tribal society. In theory, the king could call on the support of loyal tribesmen when he needed help in addition to his regular armed forces. Fletcher (1965) reports that on this occasion when the king called on tribesmen for help, he ended up arming his opponents; Habibullah Khan, who was to take his throne, was actually "given rifles and a general's commission in the Afghan army [p. 217]" after the rebellion had already started.

Second, it was a "reactionary" rebellion. Tribes normally hostile toward each other united against the king in opposition to his program of modernization and Westernization.

Third, since most of the fighting took place on a tribal level, in a sense there were really a number of rebellions going on simultaneously. Habilullah Khan, an illiterate brigand, assumed power, though he was looked down upon by the other tribes. Hence, it is only partially true that the "rebel leaders" took over power; Habibullah Khan can not be regarded as the leader of, say, the Shinwaris, who started the rebellion. Yet this fact does not seem to justify disqualifying the case, since he did represent the common rebel goal of overthrowing the king and putting a stop to the regime's reforms. This was why the other tribesmen would not follow the king's instructions to fight Habibullah Khan.

---

[1]The following abbreviations will be used in Chapters Seven and Eight, as well as in Appendix III:

AR: Annual Register	NIYB: New International Yearbook
EB: Encyclopedia Britannica	NYT: New York Times
F-on-F: Facts-on-File	NYTI: New York Times Index
HAR: Hispanic American Report	SY: Stateman's Yearbook
KA: Keesing's Archives	

It can be assumed (unless otherwise stated) that the year of the publication mentioned is the same as the year of the event, with the exception of EB, where only the 1967 edition was consulted.

Case Description[2]

By the end of September dissatisfaction and unrest was increasing throughout the country. The army, by means of which alone the king could hope to coerce his reluctant people into accepting so drastic a change in their accepted habits and customs, was miserably paid and inadequately housed. Its discipline and efficiency were deplorably neglected and its loyalty to the King's person, more than doubtful. The King's unpopularity was increasing and few persons outside the Court circle were disposed to support either him or his reforms. Trouble broke out in the Koh-i-Daman area north of Kabul under the leadership of a well-known brigand, Habibullah Khan, alias Bachha-i-Saqao or son of the water-carrier, but subsided shortly afterwards when the outlaw gangs dispersed to the hills.

Meanwhile the King continued to advocate his proposals for reform. In the month of October he delivered to a representative gathering of Afghans in Kabul a series of lectures covering in detail the various measures he proposed to adopt. He boldly pronounced himself to be a revolutionary, and asked his countrymen to follow him in a programme which, if carried into effect, would have entirely altered every aspect of Afghan social and official life. His audience listened and acclaimed his proposals, except for one dissentient voice whose owner was promptly relieved of his appointment. Even the action of the Queen in dramatically tearing off her veil was greeted with applause.

It was the last acclamation the King was to receive. Although the approach of winter was unfavourable to rebellion and there was no outstanding figure in the country to lead a revolt against constituted authority, resentment against the King was so widespread that an outbreak might be expected from any quarter. On 14 November the Shinwaris of the Eastern Province broke out and by the end of the month had invaded Jalalabad and destroyed the King's palace and the British Consulate. Disaffection then spread to the Mohmands and to the other tribes of the Eastern Province, which was soon completely out of Government control. The Khost area was the next to go. Zadrans and Jajis turned against the Government and seized outposts on the Peiwar Kotal and elsewhere. Meanwhile in Kabul the King appeared unwilling to take the only action which held out any hope of restoring the position. It appears that both Soviet and Turkish Ambassadors urged him to fight to the bitter end, and after defeating the rebels to impose his new reforms. The British representative saw that such a course would be fatal. The regular troops even if willing were in no state to face the tribesmen. The air force was not of sufficient size to affect the situation, and bombing of Afghans by Russian pilots would only stiffen resistance and throw additional odium on the King.[3] On 24 November Sir Francis Humphrys had an audience of the King at which he spoke strongly of the danger now besetting the regime. He told His Majesty frankly that he had alienated all classes of the population. Priests, agriculturists, merchants, and soldiers were all seething with discontent at the new reforms and at

[2]The description is taken from Fraser-Tytler (1967, pp. 213–216).

[3]It seems that the Russian pilots were used by Amanullah in his fight against the rebels. Since they appear not to have played a substantial role, and since the side they were on, lost, the case was not disqualified on the grounds of intervention.

increased taxation. The King should direct every effort towards conciliating the Shinwari leaders and localizing the rising. If the Mohmands joined the rebellion the capital would be in great danger.

This warning appears to have had some effect. The Foreign Minister, Ghulam Sadiq, was sent down to Jalalabad to parley with the rebels and to arrange a settlement. He returned early in December with the rebel terms, which included complete cancellation of the reforms, abolition of the ''hasht nafari'' system of conscription, the recall of Afghan girls sent to Europe for education, and an amnesty for all concerned in the rebellion. While these terms were under discussion further fighting broke out, and tribal reinforcements sent from Kabul were defeated and dispersed. It would appear that up to the middle of December the King did not take the rebellion seriously. The Eastern Province is a long way from Kabul and the rebel advance had not got within seventy-five miles of the capital. In Khost no rebel move in the direction of Kabul had taken place. The rest of the country appeared quiet though uneasy. But Afghan forces had been dissipated, the seizure of Jalalabad by the rebels had shaken the Central Government, and in the capital there was no genuine loyalty towards the King.

It was in such circumstances that Habibullah Khan, the Bachha-i-Saqao, made his dramatic entry on the scene. He was a Tajik of Kala Khan, a village situated in the Koh-i-Daman Valley, some twenty miles north of Kabul, from which it is separated by a low range of hills. He had had a varied career. Having deserted from the Afghan army after eighteen months' service and having spent a period in Peshawar as a tea-seller, he had received a sentence of eleven months' imprisonment in Parachinar in the Kurram Valley for house-breaking. He joined the rebels during the Khost rebellion of 1924, after which he became a highwayman. As leader of a gang of outlaws in the Koh-i-Daman Valley he had given considerable trouble to the Afghan authorities by raiding and robbing officials and wealthy travellers while showing much generosity to the poor. He was at large in the hill country north of Kabul at the beginning of the rebellion, and showed considerable astuteness by delaying his attack on the city until the Afghan Government was in difficulties over the Shinwari revolt and the defection of the army.

He seized the fort of Jabal-us-Siraj at the mouth of the Salang Valley on 10 December, when the garrison of 900 strong surrendered to him with their arms and equipment. On the 14th he advanced on Kabul down the north road past the British Legation, where the Minister closed the gates and warned him against an attack on the foreign Legations in and round Kabul. Between the Legation and the city the rebel forces captured the Koh-i-Lula forts with their stocks of arms and ammunition, and established themselves on the Asmai heights overlooking Kabul. For the next few days fierce fighting took place round the British Legation, which was completely cut off from the city and from communication with the outer world. Attempts were made by the royal troops to force an entry into the Legation precincts, which were throughout under heavy fire from the opposing forces, and British aeroplanes sent up to reconnoitre were also fired on. Sixty-two shells and thousands of bullets fell into the Legation grounds, all buildings were hit and the Military Attache's house was burnt to the ground. In the early morning of 23 December. . . the Legation ladies and children were conveyed under cover of darkness and by devious paths to the aerodrome, whence they were taken by air to Peshawar, further evacuations of European women and children being made on the following days. By 25 December the King's troops had got the upper hand and the rebels fell back on Jabal-us-Siraj, where they put out of action the hydro-electric station which supplied Kabul with electric light and power.

Reinforcements now began to reach Kabul, and on 3 January 1929 the Regent issued from the capital and joined battle with the rebels in the Koh-i-Daman Valley. He was heavily defeated and the rebels once more approached the outskirts of Kabul. On 5 January the king issued a proclamation cancelling all the more controversial of his recent reforms and granting concessions to the mullas [religious leaders]. The gesture came too late. Fighting continued till the 13th, when the Commander of the Royal Forces was surrounded and surrendered in a village a few miles north of Kabul, and by the evening of the 14th the Bachha-i-Saqao was in possession of all points of vantage. He had taken the aerodrome and was moving into the city.

On the 14th King Amanullah, in the hope of living to fight another day, thrust the crown into the unwilling hands of his elder brother, Inayatullah, and escaped out of the capital, making his way by road to Qandahar. Inayatullah lasted only three days. On the 17th the rebel troops were closing round the Arg (citadel) which contained the palace, the treasury, and the arsenal. A prolonged defence was out of the question and a massacre inevitable, when the chief priest of Kabul, the Hazrat Sahib of Shor Bazar, took the unprecedented step of asking the British Minister for help to save the royal party and the city from destruction. Sir Francis Humphrys took the responsibility, a very considerable one, of asking for aeroplanes to be sent from Peshawar on the guarantee of the Hazrat Sahib that they would not be fired on when they landed. This "cease-fire" order was faithfully observed and for the second time inside a week a King abdicated and fled from Kabul. The water-carrier's son was left in possession of the Durrani throne.

Discussion

Since Fraser-Tytler is by far the most careful source on the Afghanistan rebellion, it is unfortunate that he is not more specific on the matter of disloyalty. However, he does say that Habibullah Khan "showed considerable astuteness by delaying his attack on the city until the Afghan government was in difficulties over the Shinwari revolt and *the defection of the army* [*Ibid.*, p. 215; italics added]." Since it was the Shinwaris who started the rebellion, this suggests that there was disloyalty very early in the rebellion. Fraser-Tytler also gives the impression that the armed forces were far from eager fighters: "He [Habibullah] seized the fort of Jabal-us-Siraj at the mouth of the Salang Valley on 10 December, when the garrison of 900 strong surrendered to him with their arms and equipment [*Ibid.*]." Prior to this, Fraser-Tytler observes that the armed forces could not be trusted:

> The army, by means of which alone could the king hope to coerce his reluctant people into accepting so drastic a change in their accepted habits and customs, was miserably paid and housed. Its discipline and efficiency were deplorably neglected and its loyalty to the king's person more than doubtful [p. 213].

Fletcher (1965), too, has nothing relevant to say on disloyalty. It is the poorer sources—Shah, Sykes, and Wild—who have at least some information on the subject. Sykes (1940), when describing Habibullah Khan's attack on Kabul, writes that he "had been joined by many of the unpaid soldiers [p. 313]." This represents the maximal degree of disloyalty early in the rellion. However, Sykes gives no idea of the percentage of the armed forces who defected, beyond the word, "many." Later Sykes writes: "On January 14, realizing that his soldiers had deserted him [Ibid.]," the King abdicated in favor of his brother. The latter was then "bombarded by his own artillery men, who had joined Habibullah [Ibid.]."

Shah (1933) has little data relevant to the loyalty of the armed forces; he merely states that right at the beginning, when the Shinwaris began rebelling: "Many of Amanullah's officers were sent to quiet the disturbance, and all of them were imprisoned by the rebels [p. 151]." And later in his book, Shah mentions that the king placed "his hope in the army—the army which was already disgruntled, ill-paid, ill-clothed, and ill-fed [p. 157]," pointing out the King's foolishness in relying on such an army.

Wild (1933) makes a number of statements that suggest a great deal of defection on the part of the army. He is the only source to mention the police, of whom, near the end of his account, he says: "There were no police. They had reverted to civilian clothes and civilian occupations [p. 217]." With regard to the army, Wild makes the following remarks:

> Many of them deserted. Many of them sold their rifles and equipment to their enemies in return for food and money, both sadly lacking in all government ranks [p. 202].

> The next setback was the capture of Pesh Bolak Fort from the state troops, a feat which could only have been performed by the virtual surrender of the garrison. The daily depletion of the ranks could be noticed. The pride of Amanullah's (the King's) soldierly heart was humbled by desertions in mass [Ibid.].

Finally, Wild mentions the local people had noticed "the slight resistance of the government troops," and, when Kabul was being attacked he again writes "desertions were now common [p. 210]."

At least one phrase of the disloyalty score seems clear. That the majority

(51–95%) of the armed forces were unwilling fighters from the start (in the first 0–5% of the duration):

$$1_D \times 4_T \times 3_P = 12.$$

But it appears there was greater disloyalty than is expressed by this one phrase. In light of the vagueness and inconsistencies among sources, however, it was difficult to adequately express a second phrase of the disloyalty score. My decision was as follows: that some troops (11–25%) actively helped the rebels about halfway through (26–75% of the duration) the rebellion:

$$3_D \times 2_T \times 1_P = 6.$$

Hence, the *Disloyalty Score* for Afghanistan is 18.

2. ALBANIA — THE SUCCESSFUL REBELLION OF 1924

The Albanian rebellion is noteworthy in two ways. First, it was led and initiated by the elite, specifically, the opposition political parties and leaders of the armed forces. However, since rank-and-file members of the opposition parties formed the enormous majority of the rebel group (see the scale analysis in Appendix III), and since the civil and military leadership initiated the rebellion together, the case was not disqualified.

Second, Mousset (1930), Swire (1929), *NIYB,* and *AR* all point to the lack of regime resistance—barely sufficient to qualify by my criteria. It is consistent with this fact that there appear to have been few casualities; indeed, the case only just reaches the scale criterion. Hence, the Albanian rebellion narrowly escaped disqualification on several counts.

Case Description[4]

The Opposition were exasperated. They alleged that the incompetence of the Government was responsible for these murders.[5] Some alleged that the Government, under the influence of Ahmed Zogu [Prime Minister, December 1922–February 1924 *(EB)*] was implicated. To these charges Zogu replied, in a somewhat ill-advised speech, when it would have been wiser policy temporarily to efface himself *(Le Temps* 18.6.24). This completed the rift. The Democrats, with some of the Popular Party, forty-four deputies in all, withdrew from the Assembly, declaring that they would not again meet at Tirana, which was too close to Mati, Zogu's native district. As a result the Assembly was reduced to constitutional impotence,

[4]Swire (1929, pp. 429–434).
[5]"... on April 6, two American travellers were murdered by highwaymen... [*NIYB*]." About a month later, Rustem, a young Liberal member of the National Assembly, was killed.

being deprived of the quorum necessary for the purpose of passing legislation. The majority of the Opposition deputies, led by Monsignor Noli [a Bishop;
head of the Albanian Greek Orthodox Church] and Colonel Kassim Kiafzezi—commander of the troops in southern Albania—assembled at Valona, where a mass
meeting and demonstration took place, nominally to celebrate the funeral of
Avni Rustem [see note 5]. At the meeting it was declared that the Government
was but the instrument of Ahmed Zogu—which was to some extent correct—and
that no deputy of the Opposition was safe in Tirana; it was demanded that the
Assembly should meet elsewhere, and that Zogu, with certain of his supporters,
should leave the country.

Although the Government was still supported by a majority of the deputies,
and was therefore entitled to remain in office, it appreciated the seriousness of the
situation, and adopted a conciliatory attitude. There was some indication that
the greater number of those who had so impetuously registered their protest against
the Government regretted their ill-advised act, which was merely injurious to
the reputation of the country, and were willing to return to Tirana. In these circumstances, Elias Vrioni was dispatched to Valona to negotiate.

In the meantime, however, Gurakuchi [a nonmilitary figure—later to become
Minister of Finance], in northern Albania, had drawn up a manifesto which was
signed by the northern deputies of the Opposition and countersigned by Colonel
Redjeb Shala, commander of the troops in northern Albania, inviting Parliament to
meet at Skutari. Shala, a northern chieftan, was one of those who considered that
Skutari should replace Tirana as the capital, both because of its importance and for
commercial reasons. The Government at once and very properly dismissed Shala;
he ignored the Government, and declared martial law throughout his zone, while
Elez Yssuf, Bairam Tsuri—who had been condemned to death in consequence of his
escapade in January, 1923, and had sought refuge with Albanians across the border
—and others, called their followers to arms, and attacked the Government troops
around Krouma.

These events encouraged the southern section of the Opposition, who considered that matters had now gone too far for compromise, and Vrioni's mission
proved fruitless. Colonel Kiafzezi declared martial law throughout his zone, Shevket
Korcha, Commandant of the Gendarmerie, joined him, and the majority of
the troops under their command, together with irregular supporters, began to
concentrate at Valona and Berat. The Government thereupon proclaimed general
mobilization in Central Albania, which remained loyal. In the meantime the
northern insurgent forces drove from Skutari, after some desultory fighting, a
handful of gendarmerie which remained loyal to the Government, and advanced
upon Tirana . . . .

In view of the increasing gravity of the situation, Shevket Verlazi resigned
[from his position as Prime Minister] on the 1st of June, and he was appointed to
command the Government forces, many of whom were his own tenants. . . .
Elias Vrioni succeeded him as Prime Minister, while remaining Minister for Foreign
Affairs, and Abdurrahman Dibra took Verlazi's place as Minister of the Interior.
Otherwise the Cabinet remained unchanged. In the meantime, the United States
Minister, Mr. Grant-Smith, who alone of all the representatives of the Powers

had preserved a very reserved attitude towards Zogu, and therefore was in a better position than others to act, proposed that the League of Nations should be asked to arbitrate in the dispute. Here again, however, matters had gone too far, and neither side would accept the proposal without reservations unacceptable to the other.

Some sharp skirmishing took place around Alessio, which fell to Colonel Shala after a temporary success by the Government troops; Kiafzezi issued an ultimatum to the Government demanding unconditional surrender, and in the meantime ordered his troops to advance on Tirana and Elbasan. Vrioni, on the other hand, made one more bid for a compromise. Mufid Libohova was sent to treat with Kiafzezi, M. Fakhri with Shala. Neither of them returned. A Military Directorate was constituted at Valona, and in the meantime the advance continued in leisurely manner. Some skirmishing took place both before Elbasan and in Bregumatia, but there seems to have been, on both sides, except in isolated cases, a reluctance to shed much blood. Moreover, contemporary reports indicate that, at most, 12,000 Democrats and 4,000 Government supporters took part in the struggle—if, indeed, it may be described as such. There is no doubt that contemporary reports of fighting emanated chiefly from imaginative journalists, and that the vast majority of the population took no part on either side. . . .

The revolt of June, 1924, did, however, enjoy a large measure of popular support—in any case moral support—both in the south, where the failure of the Government to curtail the power of the Beys and introduce sweeping agrarian reforms, was a cause of discontent, and in the north, where jealousy of Ahmed Zogu, the claim of the Skutarenes that their town should be the capital, the desperate plight of the people, and the irredentist aspirations of the Kossovo Committee, all contributed to stir up hostility towards the Government. . . .The Cabinet, with the exception of Zogu, sought refuge in Italy. . . .

On the 9th of July the insurgent forces closed in upon Tirana, and Vrioni fled precipitately for the coast with Shevket Verlazi and a number of their colleagues. They sailed for Bari, where they met a hostile crowd of Albanians, who held them responsible for the state of their country, and some of the Beys were roughly handled before the police intervened. During the afternoon of the 10th Ahmed Zogu called a public meeting in Tirana and asked the people whether they preferred resistance or surrender; they decided in favor of the latter course, and accordingly white flags were hoisted upon the prominent buildings. In the evening Colonel Kiafzezi's troops occupied the capital. Ahmed Zogu retired with some five hundred adherents, and after some further skirmishing with Bairam Tsuri and Elez Yssuf, fled into Yugoslavia.

The country was now in the hands of the Democrats, and the Military Directorate, which had become the Supreme National Council, temporarily replaced the Government. Monsignor Noli was asked by the Council of Regency to form a Cabinet, which took office on the 17th. . . .

Discussion

It is very difficult in this case to decide when exactly the rebellion started, and hence to be sure that it was not the government's armed forces who took the initiative (in which case the rebellion would be disqualified from inclusion in the study). An argument could be made that the rebellion started when the Opposition, led by Bishop Noli and Colonel Kassim Kiafzezi, withdrew from the Assembly. Another possibility is when the manifesto was drawn up and signed by the northern deputies of the Opposition, and counter-signed by Colonel Redjeb Shala. Yet another is when Colonel Shala declared martial law, and Bairam Tsuri (an old guerrilla) and others called their followers to arms. However, the important factor is that on each of these occasions, according to Swire (1929), a combination of civilian and military personnel took part.

According to two of the other sources, however, the initiative was definitely civilian. Skendi (1957), for example, writes: "Bishop Noli and other exponents of Westernization" formed "a new group, the opposition party, which fomented disaffection in the army so that early in June, 1924 two columns of troops marched on Tirana [p. 14]." And *NIYB* reports that: "upon refusal of this demand [for a change], the Opposition left the assembly and openly revolted against the Government...." However, Mousset's (1930) account is closer to Swire's: "... une insurrection éclate dans le nord, à l'instigation d'un certain Redjeb Chalya, secondé par un vieux partisan ... Bairam Txour [pp. 53–54]." Since Swire seems the best source, we shall accept that the initiative was taken by the civilian and some of the military authorities as well, and hence, that there was maximal defection (fighting on the side of the rebels) from the start.

The next questions to settle are, what percentage of the armed forces defected at the start, and was there additional disloyalty later? According to Swire (1929, pp. 430–432) and Mousset (1930, p. 54), the rebellion broke out in the North, the South joining a little later (exactly how much later, is not clear). As Swire (1929) describes it there was very little resistance to the rebels in the North; there was some "desultory fighting" with "a handful of gendarmerie which remained loyal to the government [p. 431]." And the troops in Central Albania (populated by approximately one-third of the inhabitants of Albania) remained loyal to the government (*Ibid.,* pp. 430–31).

These data on disloyalty seem to be well summarized by the following two statements: a considerable proportion (26–50%) of the armed forces fought on the side of the rebels right from the start (in the first 5% of the duration):

$$4_D \times 4_T \times 2_P = 32.$$

And, some (11–25%) joined the rebels, fighting on their side, about half way through (from 26 to 75% of the duration):

$$4_D \times 2_T \times 1_P = 8.$$

Hence, the *Disloyalty Score* for Albania is 40.

3.   BOLIVIA — THE SUCCESSFUL REBELLION OF 1952

Of the twentieth-century rebellions that have occurred in Latin America, the Bolivian rebellion of 1952 is one of the best known—the Mexican and Cuban rebellions are the only two that are better known. This is probably because it is commonly thought that these three rebellions were the only ones in Latin America to be followed by successful revolutions, that is, substantial social change. Malloy (1970) describes the Bolivian rebellion as "Latin America's second 'great' revolution [p. 158]."

Case Description⁶

Early on the morning of April 9, La Paz was thrown into the confusion and bloodshed of a well-planned revolt⁷ aimed at overthrowing the military junta of General Hugo Ballivian. Eleven months after the military had taken control of the government to prevent the election of Victor Paz Estenssoro to the presidency, the Movimiento Nacionalista Revolucionario [the MNR, according to Malloy (1970, p. 164), was a "mass–based popular movement"] began its successful attempt to return its exiled leader to Bolivia and make him President. Paz Estenssoro, who had held the post of Minister of the Treasury in the Villarroel regime, left Bolivia in 1946, when a mob hanged President Villarroel from a lamppost on the main square of La Paz. In the presidential elections of May 1951, Paz Estenssoro received a plurality of popular ballots as the M. N. R. candidate in absentia, but fell short of the constitutionally required absolute majority. This left the final choice up to the Senate. Before any action was taken, President Mamerto Urriolagoitia resigned, leaving the military in control.

Hermán Siles Zuazo, who ran on the same ticket with Paz Estenssoro last May, headed the civilian faction of the revolt which broke out simultaneously in La Paz, Oruro, Cochabamba, Potosí, Trinidad, Sucre, and Santa Cruz. At first the military group loyal to General Ballivian seemed to be controlling the rebels, but by the second day of fighting it became apparent that the M. N. R. was to be victorious and General Ballivian took refuge in the Chilean Embassy. Heavy cannon fire destroyed many homes in the residential and workers' districts around the capital city, and more than 1,000 persons were killed. Reports on the number killed during the fighting ranged as high as 3,000. The third day, April 11, rebel forces stormed El Alto airbase, on the rim of the depression in which La Paz is located, and dealt a decisive defeat to the government troups. Siles Zuazo immediately proclaimed himself provisional President pending the arrival in the capital of Paz Estenssoro. A new cabinet was installed without delay. . . .

Dr. Paz Estenssoro, 44-year-old former economics professor, returned to

⁶*Hispanic American Report (HAR)*, Vol. 5, No. 4, May 1952, pp. 34–35.

⁷While *HAR* and *EB* are in agreement that the rebellion was well planned, Lieuwen (1961) describes it as a "spontaneous outburst of popular antagonism [p. 137]." However, this inconsistency does not bear on my analysis.

La Paz on April 15 and was sworn in as President of Bolivia the following day. His plane was met by hysterical crowds and the Bolivian people now expect him to solve the many pressing financial problems facing the nation.

Discussion

In this description of the Bolivian rebellion, there is no information on the role of the armed forces. In Alexander's (1958) opinion "the uprising was the result of a conspiracy between General Antonio Seleme, Chief of the Carabineros (the national military police) and the MNR [p. 44; see also p. 146]." (Malloy shares this opinion; see *Ibid.*, p. 156.) Together they formulated a plan for a coup, the idea being that Seleme would become President in "a united MNR-military cabinet [p. 156]." Simultaneously, negotiations were begun between the MNR and General Torres, chief of staff of the army, who had been in open conflict with General Ballivian, the head of the junta *(Ibid.)*. An alternative idea was that Torres would become President: but Torres backed out at the last minute *(Ibid.)*. "Fearful of exposure" writes Malloy, "the MNR decided to go ahead with Seleme and moved the date of the planned coup from April 15 to April 9 [*Ibid.*]." So, on April 9, the MNR "in conjunction with the national police under Seleme's command, initiated an insurrection [*Ibid.*, p. 157]. According to Malloy, however, "the bulk of the military remained loyal and moved to crush the rebellion [*Ibid.*]," so that "by the end of the first day, the insurrection appeared doomed and Seleme sought asylum [*Ibid.*]." (See Barton, 1968, p. 253.) Nevertheless, by the second day, armed workers began moving toward the capital. Together with the other rebels they managed to trap the capital troops "without hope of reinforcement [*Ibid.*]." The goverment therefore fell that very day.

It is quite clear from these data that the initiative for the rebellion was taken by both civilian and police forces. With regard to the army, Malloy's statement that the "bulk of the military remained loyal" is regrettably vague. Several other sources describe the army as remaining loyal to the military junta, or imply this; for example, Andreski (1967), Lieuwen (1961), and Alexander (1958), respectively, write as follows:

On 9 April 1952, there occurred in La Paz one of those rare occasions in which civilian rebels defeat an army in open battle . . . [p. 233].

The MNR began arming the workers, engineered the defection of the police, and in the revolution of April 1952 completely routed the army. The armed forces, *which had remained loyal to the oligarchy*, were now disbanded [pp. 71–80; italics added].

One of the first acts of the new regime was to retire antagonistic elements from the

army. Not only were 80 percent of the officers and non-commissioned officers
retired, but most enlisted men were sent back home. . . . The MNR had defeated it
[the army] in open battle and naturally did not trust its remnants to defend the
regime of the party which had routed it [p. 146]."

With regard to this last quotation from Alexander, one wonders why
only 80% of the officers were retired; if 20% helped the rebels, that would
be a very significant degree of defection. Other sources explicitly state
that a portion of the army was disloyal to the regime; for example, Patch
(1961) writes: "Civilian irregulars and a portion of the army quickly
defeated loyal army forces. . . [p. 127]." According to EB, the revolt
was "supported" by "certain army officers." And the Bulletin of
Hispanic Studies goes so far as to say that: "On April 9 part of the army
and the police force, led by General Antonio Seleme, seized control
of key points in the capital. Two regiments remaining loyal, a three-day
battle began. . . [pp. 102–103]."

How can these differences be reconciled? Often a good indicator of
the role of the military in a successful rebellion is the degree to which
the new regime contains military men. Osborne (1944) states that the
Cabinet that was formed consisted of "leading figures of the MNR movement together with three Labour Ministers . . . [p. 69]." Only one of
the members of the Cabinet was also in the military—General Froilán
Calleja, who was Minister of Interior Defense. But this fact, while lending
greater weight to the view that a portion of the army was not disloyal, by
no means successfully reconciles the inconsistency.

Before arriving at a disloyalty score, the degree of the defection has to
be assessed, as well as the proportion of the total armed forces (police and
army) who defected. The police, it seems, not only helped arm the civilian
rebels, according to Andreski (1967, p. 233), but fought on their side
from the start, under the direction of the Police Chief, General Antonio
Seleme (Alexander, 1958, p. 44 and Malloy, 1970, p. 157). Patch and
the Bulletin of Hispanic Studies both suggest that part of the army was
actively in rebellion from the start too, and that they also fought on the
rebels' side [see Patch (1961, p. 127) and Bulletin of Hispanic Studies
(pp. 102–103 and text for the quotations]. For those who participated,
then, disloyalty was maximal.

But what was the proportion of the armed forces (police and army) that
defected?

The SY (1952) reports that "the standing army numbers 8,000 to 10,000
men" (the figure of 9,000 will be used) but gives no figures on the police.
Lieuwen is no help here either.[8] Alexander's (1958) figure for the size of

[8]Even though Lieuwen's (1961) much-acclaimed book is titled Arms and Politics in Latin
America, "police" or "carabineros" are not even listed in the index.

the army is substantially discrepant with *SY;* he maintains that just prior to the 1952 rebellion there were 18,000 officers and men in the army. While unfortunately Alexander, too, provides no quantitative information on the size of the police force, he does give sufficient qualitative information about them to suggest that it was no meager force:

> In addition to the Army,...there was the Carabineros, a militarized national police force, patterned on that of Chile. Its principal job was maintenance of order in the countryside. There was a certain amount of rivalry between the Carabineros and the Army, although until the Nationalist Revolution of 1952 the Carabineros did not play an independent political role [*Ibid.*].

Once it is established that the police force was substantial—unlike, say the Honduran police force of 1933, which consisted of 250 men (League of Nations, 1933, p. 226)—the question becomes, how substantial? Assuming that there were a minimum of 1100 in the police force, this would mean that at least 11% of the armed forces were disloyal. Whether or not some of the army were disloyal and/or the police force somewhat larger than 1100 men, these numbers would have to have been quite substantial in order to raise the proportion of disloyalty from the "some" (11–25%) category to the "considerable" (26–50%) category. Yet had the numbers been so substantial, the sources would probably be less in conflict regarding the loyalty of the army. Hence, the estimate is that 11–25% of the armed forces fought on the rebels' side from the start of the rebellion (in the first 5% of the duration):

$$4_D \times 4_T \times 1_P = 16.$$

Hence, the *Disloyalty Score* for the Bolivian Rebellion is 16.

4.   BRAZIL — THE SUCCESSFUL REBELLION OF 1930

Brazil provides an unusual case because of the apparently small amount of violence, despite the fact that it was, without a doubt, an armed rebellion. The relative lack of violence was due to rebel strength.

There is a striking similarity between the Brazilian case and that of Bolivia and Honduras, as well as many other South American rebellions. Presidential elections are frequently a precipitant of rebellions, and the election losers the major civilian source of rebels. Such a situation is so common in South America that it raises the question of whether rebellion itself can become institutionalized. Interestingly, the Albanian rebellion of 1924 provides a comparable case.

Case Description[9]

President Washington Luiz thought he had secured sufficient support to insure the election of his presidential nominee, Júlio Prestes. The official election returns seemed to confirm his calculations. Prestes, whose ties to the incumbent President were reinforced by the fact that both were from the state of São Paulo, received 1,091,709 out of the 1,890,524 votes cast. But the opposition, which had campaigned under the label of the "Liberal Alliance" (Alianca Liberal), angrily rejected the official result. The political leaders of the states of Minas Gerais and Rio Grande do Sul, who dominated the opposition alliance, especially resented Washington Luiz's attempt to install another São Paulo politician in the presidency.

After past elections, especially those of 1910 and 1922, the losing candidates had claimed fraud in the counting of votes as well as claiming that force, threats or bribes had been used at the ballot box. And for a short time after the election of Júlio Prestes was officially announced in April, it appeared that the opposition might again restrict its protest to mere words. On May 30 Vargas issued a "manifesto" denouncing the "frauds and intimidations" practiced by the electoral officials "whose tricks and stratagems are stimulated and encouraged by the electoral legislation itself." But the defeated candidate tempered his attack with the assurance that he still believed the necessary modification "in our political habits and customs" could take place "within the existing order . . . ." Certain of the revolutionaries were, however, less willing to be satisfied with words, and finally organized a full-fledged conspiracy aimed at seizing power by armed rebellion. A few weeks after the election, young radicals such as Oswaldo Aranba and Lindolfo Collor made contact with disgruntled leaders of the Liberal Alliance in Minas Gerais and Paraíba. But the political patriachs of Rio Grande do Sul (Borges de Medeiros) and Minas Gerais (António Carlos) were at first cautious; since neither wished to initiate a revolt, each waited for the other.

The event which catalyzed the opposition into armed rebellion was the assassination of its former vice presidential candidate, João Pessoa of the northeastern state of Paraíba. On July 26 Pessoa fell before the bullets of the son of a bitter local political enemy of the former governor. His death was not atypical of the bloody clan politics in the northern coastal backwaters. At this tense moment in national politics, however, it had a traumatic effect because Washington Luiz had supported the political group to which the assassin was linked. The wavering conspirators among the opposition were swept along in the wave of indignation which the radicals promoted in order to create a revolutionary atmosphere. Borges de Medeiros now supported the revolution and aided greatly in recruiting military commanders into the conspiracy. A revolutionary general staff was organized, with Colonel Góes Monteiro as its chief. The date of the revolt was set for October 3.

The revolt began as scheduled, with Vargas exhorting the rebels in Rio Grande do Sul to lead the march on Rio de Janeiro. "Rio Grande, on your feet for Brazil! You cannot fail to meet your heroic destiny!" The "people" were rising "to re-acquire liberty, to restore the purity of the republican regime, to achieve national reconstruction," Vargas proclaimed.

[9]Skidmore (1967, pp. 4–7).

The conspiracy was supported by politicans of the Liberal Alliance and a group of revolutionary young military officers (tenentes). If this had been the limit of the rebels' strength, they would have constituted a serious but not necessarily a mortal threat to the incumbent government. With the military behind him, President Luiz could have imposed his new President on the country, as previous regimes had done against severe protests of the opposition in 1910 and 1922. But as the rebels marched on Rio de Janeiro from south (Rio Grande do Sul), north (Paraíba), and west (Minas Gerais), Washington Luiz found that he lacked the support of the military.

The incumbent President had been assured by his Minister of War, General Serzefredo dos Passos, that he could count on the armed forces to back him against the rebels. But many senior generals stationed in Rio de Janeiro were disturbed at the prospect of a civil war against what was now a formidable armed opposition in the states of Rio Grande do Sul, Santa Catarina, and Paraná. The leader of the dissident officers, Army Chief of Staff General Tasso Fragoso, later explained their apprehensions: "It seemed that an electric shock had passed through the political atmosphere." He held the President responsible "for the state of unrest and distrust in which we find ourselves. Unfortunately he set out on a rocky path and has already brought grave misfortunes upon the country." As for supporting Washington Luiz against the rebels, "No one wanted his son to put on a uniform and die fighting for a man frankly divorced from the common interest."

Some three weeks after the rebels began their march on Rio de Janeiro, Washington Luiz still did not yet appreciate how his authority had crumbled. By late October the revolt had reached such proportions that the generals in Rio decided to take matters into their own hands.

The dissident military, led by Generals Tasso Fragoso and Mena Barreto, moved on October 24 to seize power from the President and his military ministers. Tasso Fragoso explained that the commanders in Rio were forced to act because "agitation had erupted everywhere," presenting them with the threat of a "national revolution such as had never been seen."

The dissident generals issued a manifesto calling upon Washington Luiz to resign; they even forced an interview to make a personal appeal. Ever confident, Washington Luiz defied their ultimatum. Only after the personal intervention of Cardinal Leme of Rio de Janeiro was the President convinced that his position was lost and that he must leave office and abandon his plan to inaugurate Júlio Prestes in December.

The Junta ruled Rio de Janeiro in its own right for ten days before finally delivering power on November 4 to Getúlio Vargas, the acknowledged leader of the opposition movement. Any inclination on the part of the Junta to perpetuate themselves in power had been cut short by the growing pressure from the rebels, whose military forces were closing in on the capital city. In his speech accompanying the investiture of Vargas as "provisional President," General Fragoso noted that the military had decided to intervene out of a desire that "Brazilians cease spilling blood on behalf of a cause which was not endorsed by the national conscience . . . ."

The shift in political leadership resulting from Vargas' assumption of the presidency became known as the "Revolution of 1930." Subsequent events confirmed the accuracy of that description, at least in the political sphere. In the decade and a half after Vargas assumed power, nearly every feature of the political system and the administrative structure was subjected to the zeal for reform. Many of these changes remained juridical fictions. Enough were implemented by 1945, however, to have transformed irrevocably the world of government and politics which had produced the revolutionaries of 1930.

Discussion

Camacho (1952) describes the Brazilian rebellion of 1930 as ". . .a revolution in which the army largely supported Vargas. . . [p. 46]." And according to Lieuwen (1958), it "represented defeat for the traditional ruling groups, with the armed forces playing a decisive role although civilian politicians took the lead [p. 61]." Johnson (1964) also refers to the armed forces as "participating in the overthrow of the old regime [p. 206]."

More specifically, in detailed accounts of the rebellion there seems to be agreement with Skidmore's (1967) account quoted above that "a group of revolutionary young military officers [p. 5]" (tenentés) actually helped to plan the rebellion, that is, there was joint civilian–military initiative.

Young (1967) writes that after the rebellion had started,

> . . . the revolutionists began a propaganda campaign against loyal federal troops stationed in the state of Rio Grande do Sul. The theme was that brothers should not fight brothers. It was very effective for the majority of the federal troops were natives of Rio Grande do Sul [p. 59].

After the outbreak of the rebellion on 3 October 1930, Young states that: "By eleven o'clock that night, most of the federal troops of Pôrto Alegre had gone over to the rebels . . . . Most of the cities in Rio Grande do Sul went over to the revolutionists without fighting. . . [Ibid.]." Bello (1966) confirms this description. There follows a lengthy quotation from Bello, which is rich with data on armed force disloyalty (italics added):

> Although it had been repeatedly announced, the revolution caught the central and state government unprepared to defend themselves. There was no overall government plan, no coordination of objectives, only scattered, if intrepid, delaying actions that took the lives of many men loyal to the Union. *More and more military units went over to the rebels, or remained neutral,* which amounted to the same thing . . . . *The governments of the North fell with little or no struggle.* Thus, the rebel column that left Paraíba under the command of Captain Juarez Távora to assault Recife again had no trouble getting to Bahia; the first attack on Recife had been called off when expected reinforcements failed to join up. *The other northern states, except Pará, fell in the first skirmishes.*
>
> *The rebel troops of Rio Grande do Sul, consisting of army, police, and civilian battalions under the military command of Lt. Col. Góis Monteiro,* with Getúlio Vargas as supreme leader of the revolution, had little difficulty reaching the border between

Paraña and São Paulo; *the small core of resistance offered by the government of Santa Catarina* was isolated on its island capital. In Minas as in Rio Grande do Sul, the focal points of federal resistance were surprised and quickly overcome. The rebel columns, poorly trained and equipped, moved against the states of Rio de Janeiro and Espírito Santa; *the weak federal defenses crumbled everywhere, often by the treason of trusted military chiefs.* The region around Itararé, on the Paraña–São Paulo border, was expected to be the center of hostilities. The expected battle ("the greatest in Latin-American history, except that it didn't take place," was a famous quip of the period) would decide the success or failure of the revolution. According to the undoubtedly exaggerated statement of the revolutionists' high command, 30,000 men, who were perhaps quite unsure of victory, had moved up from the South. The governments of the Unión and São Paulo held the appreciable advantages of being closer to their supply centers and having better communications.

At this stage, *a group of high-ranking officers in the Rio garrison, who had already sent two unanswered ultimatums to the President, stepped into the fight, presumably by prior agreement with the rebel chiefs, and delivered the death blow* to the constitutional legality so bravely defended by Washington Luiz [pp. 272–273].

The account in *NIYB* is also quite consistent with Bello's, at least regarding the armed-force defection near the end of the rebellion.

[A] long-drawn-out civil war was in prospect. Then with unexpected suddenness, the struggle was terminated October 24, when a junta of army and naval officers headed by General Fragoso deserted the government and seized control of Rio de Janeiro.

[W]ith the outbreak of the revolution against the Federal government, the army and naval officers sensed that the populace was overwhelmingly in favor of a change of government and acted at the critical moment to end the civil war.

These data on the disloyalty of the armed forces were summarized by the following two expressions to arrive at a disloyalty score: some (11–25%) of the armed forces fought on the side of the rebels right from the start:

$$4_D \times 4_T \times 1_P = 16.$$

And by the end, a considerable additional proportion of the armed forces had joined the rebels, fighting (or willing to fight) on their side:

$$4_D \times 1_T \times 2_P = 8.$$

Hence, the *Disloyalty Score* for Brazil is 24.

5.   CHINA — THE SUCCESSFUL REBELLION OF 1949

Of all the rebellions analyzed in this study, the case of China is by far the most famous, probably because this rebellion was followed by so successful a revolution (that is, such substantial social change; (see Chapter Four for the rationale behind classifying the case of China as a mass rebellion, rather than a civil war.) For this and other reasons, the Chinese rebellion is often used as a lesson in possibilities by revolutionaries and romantics; the conclusion that is frequently drawn from this case is expressed by the quotation from Dr. Johnson that opens Fitzgerald's (1952) book, *Revolution in China*. " . . . [B]ut then, there is this consideration: that if the abuse be enormous, nature will rise up, and claiming her original rights, overturn a corrupted political system.[10]

China presents many problems for the analysis I have undertaken. First, when can the rebellion be said to have started? This is important, not so much for ascertaining the scale of the rebellion, but because the time at which disloyalty occurs in relation to the duration of the whole event is important for determining the disloyalty score. And there is the further "complication" of an 8-year war with Japan. How, then, to get around these difficulties.

One could perhaps regard the 1927–1937 period of conflict between the Kuomintang and the Communists as a distinct rebellious event whose outcome was indecisive due to the beginning of the Sino-Japanese war. In this case, it would be disqualified as having a marginal outcome. The next rebellious event, which did have a decisive outcome, might be thought of as starting as soon as the 8-year war with Japan ended in 1945. The period during the war of course does not qualify since China at that time cannot be described as an "autonomous political system."

However, since the continuity in leadership and ideology, for example, was very considerable for the periods 1927–1937 and 1945–1949, it seems artificial indeed to confine the analysis to the latter period, and to regard these events as discrete. Yet since there was officially, and to some extent in practice, a kind of moratorium on Communist–Kuomintang fighting during the Sino-Japanese War, (albeit a moratorium frequently flouted,) and because of the definitional criterion that no second, foreign power be substantially involved in the conflict, I decided to ignore this period, and to work with 1927–1937 and 1945–1949.

Case Description[11]

In June 1928 Kuomintang forces took Peking, completing the official unification of China and destroying the power of the northern warlords.

[10]It is this tendency to assume that a general conclusion can be drawn from a single case that makes comparative study so mandatory. And more particularly, I have already explained why I think *this* general conclusion especially requires being put to the comparative test. The Chinese case on its own simply *cannot* prove that serious oppression cannot last.

[11]*EB* and United States Department of State (1949). The first paragraph is from the State Department report; the second and following paragraphs are from *EB*.

In domestic politics the years 1928–37 were stormy, but, on the whole, progress toward a more stable regime was made. Throughout the period the most prominent figure in the central government was Chiang Kai-shek. So vigorous a man inevitably had his enemies, but he retained his control of the army and accordingly continued the dominant leader. . . .

The greatest domestic menace to Chiang Kai-shek and the Kuomintang was the Communist movement. After the purges of mid-1927 the Communist party turned to armed force to overthrow its rival. Only gradually was it able to create armed bands of peasants and deserting soldiers, seize control of inaccessible bits of territory and begin to create soviet districts. It appealed to tenant farmers, landless labourers and others upon whom the existing rural order bore most heavily. Terrorism was widespread, and persons of property were dealt with cruelly. In essence the movement depended on peasant revolt. By 1930 the Communist army had become a sizable force and Soviet regions covered large areas in Kiangsi, Fukien, Hunan and Hupeh.

The Nanking government launched five campaigns between Dec. 1930 and Oct. 1933 in an attempt to destroy the Communist army and capture the Soviet bases. Finally by Oct. 1934 the main Communist forces were driven out of their chief base in southern Kiangsi. They executed a long retreat, marching and fighting through most of the southern and western provinces of China, arriving in north Shensi one year later. In the meantime Japan had seized Manchuria and was seeking to detach north China. The Communists skillfully employed the rising patriotic sentiment to blunt the Nationalist attacks against themselves, urging an end of civil war and a united front of all parties and armies against Japan. This program appealed especially to the Manchurian troops of Chang Hsüeh-liang who were being used to fight the Communists in north Shensi. When Chiang Kai-shek, late in 1936, went to Sian to push the campaign, he was seized by Chang Hsüeh-liang, who demanded the end of the civil war against the Communists, a reorganization of the government with more toleration for the opposition and, above all, a united front against Japan.

Although Chiang Kai-shek was released without publicly acceding and Chang Hsüeh-liang was technically punished, in effect the dramatic incident was the precursor to the easing of the war against the Communists. . . .

Sino-Japanese War[12]

While the National Government was engaged in the problem of suppressing Communism, Japan embarked upon a series of encroachments on Chinese territory, beginning with occupation of Manchuria in 1931 and leading up to the Marco Polo Bridge incident on July 7, 1937.

The Japanese actions aroused large sectors of Chinese opinion . . . . [T]here was an upsurge of nationalism, particularly after 1935, when the loss of the northern provinces was threatened. The revival of patriotism included most of politically conscious China—elements ranging from warlords to students. Resistance against Japanese aggression became a popular slogan exploited not only by leftist intellectuals, such as those united in the National Salvation League, but also by dissident militarists. . . .

[12]The source is the State Department report, pp. 45–47.

The wartime entente between the Kuomintang and the Chinese Communist Party was never formalized by a written alliance, but rested upon a series of parallel documents issued by the two parties, by which the Kuomintang announced the change in Chinese Government policy from one of military suppression of communism to that of seeking a political settlement, and by which the Chinese Communist Party proclaimed the abandonment of forceful insurrection and sovietization in favor of cooperation with the Government against Japanese aggression. . . .

China after World War II[13]

Japan's defeat set off a struggle between the Nationalists and Communists for control of occupied China—from Manchuria in the north to Canton in the south. Nationalist troops, using transportation facilities of the U.S. army, air force and navy, were able to take over key cities and most railway lines in east and north China. But Communist troops, moving out from their guerrilla bases, occupied much of the hinterland in the north and in Manchuria. The stage was set for renewal of the civil war.

The united front had always been precarious. It had been tacitly understood by both the Nationalists and Communists that they would co-operate only until Japan had been defeated; until then, neither side could afford to compromise its title to nationalism by seeming to pursue internal aims at the cost of the national struggle. The growing wartime ineffectiveness and corruption of the Nationalists, who seemed, especially to the north Chinese, practically a government-in-exile in far-off Chungking, left the Communists on a rising tide in 1945. The U.S. government, while aiding the Nationalists materially, attempted, especially through the mission of Gen. George C. Marshall in 1946, to re-establish Chinese unity.

As Marshall stated in his farewell declaration of Jan. 7, 1947, he would have preferred to see the Chinese government in the hands of liberal statesmen of the political centre. However, sentiment in China had polarized, and such centre groupings as the Democratic league (founded 1941) were impotent. The league, commanding no military force, had initially been tolerated by the Nationalists, mainly to provide window dressing and a talking point for mediators in pressing the Communist party to give up its own army. When the league, as Marshall's sentiments indicated, seemed to become a possible non-Communist alternative to the Nationalists for U.S. support, Nationalist policy turned to suppression of the league and willing delivery of most of its remnants to the Communist side, thereby stripping the U.S. of its illusions for a compromise solution. The murder of Wen I-to—poet, professor and a leader of the league—in July 1946, hastened this development and the failure of the Marshall mission.

The civil war lasted from 1946 to 1949. During 1946 and early 1947 the Nationalists took most of the railways and recaptured important cities in the north. As Soviet troops withdrew from Manchuria, the Nationalists sent in their best armies to try to hold the vital railways and industrial centres. This proved to be strategically unsound. Communist forces, re-equipped with surrendered Japanese arms and, to an ominously growing extent, with U.S. arms captured from the Nationalists,

[13]*EB* is the source from this point until the end.

shifted from guerrilla warfare to large-scale offensive campaigns. In 1948 they destroyed the Nationalist armies in Manchuria and won impressive victories in north China. By the end of the year, Nationalist armies were disintegrating, and public support for them was evaporating. The Kuomintang was torn by factional strife. Debasement and manipulation of the currency brought galloping inflation and a wild flight of capital, causing a defeatist attitude among many Nationalists.

In 1949 the Communists captured the Nationalist capital, Nanking, and the two substitute mainland capitals, Canton and Chungking, in which the Nationalists successively took refuge. On Dec. 8, 1949, T'ai-pei, on the island of Formosa, to which Chiang Kai-shek and many of his followers had fled, was declared the Nationalist Capital.

In Sept. 1949 the Chinese People's Political Consultative conference met in Peiping to establish a new government. The conference included representatives of many parties, professions, organizations and ethnic minorities, but their selection was determined by the Communists. In Oct. 1949 the conference announced formation of the People's Republic of China, with its capital at Peiping, which was then again named Peking.

Discussion

There were defections from the Nationalist forces right from the start of the rebellion (that is, in the first 8½ months, which is within the first 5% of the total duration). But an assessment had to be made as to whether these defections constituted at least 2% of the Nationalist forces.[14] Some of the relevant data on the basis of which the decision was made, is presented below.

Chu Teh, Nationalist garrison commander of Nanchang, is credited by O'Ballance (1962) with being the "father of the Red Army." On 1 August 1927, 4 months after the beginning of the purge of the Communists by Chiang Kai-shek, he had led about 1000 soldiers from his garrison, and with the help of other armed forces (numbers are unclear), a successful uprising was effected in the city of Nanchang *(Ibid., pp. 38–39).*[15] When he heard of this uprising, Mao Tse-tung immediately organized a small communist force where he was in Hankow. While estimates of its strength vary, O'Ballance indicates that "it was probably about 1000 armed men, *some of whom were Nationalist troops from the Hankow garrison who had revolted* . . . [*Ibid.,* italics added]." However, quite

---

[14]Fred Taylor did some of the data collection and analysis of armed force disloyalty for China, and the assessment of disloyalty was made jointly.

[15]In fact, O'Ballance describes Chu Teh as having been "a secret Communist" for some time before this, making the question of whether he can be regarded as a defector somewhat ambiguous.

soon "the commander of his [Mao's] ex-Nationalist troops, with all the men, changed sides and returned to the Nationalist fold [*Ibid.*]."[16]

Isaacs (1961) describes the very early period as follows: "Scattered peasant detachments fled to the hills and resumed the role of partisan bands. They joined hands with *companies and regiments of Kuomintang soldiers who had mutined* and taken refuge in the mountains. . . [p. 324; italics added]." No numbers are given, unfortunately, but the general picture emerges from the sources that after the purge, the Communists consisted of fairly well-depleted, struggling bands.

By the summer of 1926, Chiang's army amounted to about 200,000, according to O'Ballance (1962, p. 30). This figure apparently applies to early 1927, as well. While this figure includes the Communists, it still seems unlikely (judging from O'Ballance's and Isaac's data) that the numbers involved in defections reached 2% of the armed forces (200,000)—the minimum criterion for contributing to the disloyalty score. Hence, these early defections were ignored in my analysis.

The period "near the beginning" (that is, within the first 6–25% of the duration) runs from about January 1928 to the end of 1930. By the summer of 1928, the Red Army was about 10,000 strong, Griffith writes (1967, p. 28). He adds that, "a fairly large proportion of recruits were deserters from the *min-t'van*—the landlord's private militia—or from provincial armies [p. 30]." And later, when discussing the "military advantages" enjoyed by the small Chu-Mao army in late 1928 and afterward, Griffith concludes:

> Finally, a psychological factor entered into the equation: the landlord militia and many White [i.e., Nationalist] provincial troops, poor peasants, too, were fundamentally sympathetic to the Communists and deserted to them before, during, and after battle. White commanders . . . hesitated to take the field with troops whose loyalty was at best questionable. Some Communist 'victories' were in fact victories in sham battles; some of the arms 'captured,' in fact bought [p. 33].

O'Ballance (1962) also mentions defections without saying what percentage of the armed forces were involved; for example, he states that: "In May 1928, Chu-Teh had about 10,000 followers all told at Chin Kan Shan, but only about a quarter were armed, mainly with a variety of rifles. Such arms as they had were those brought over by ex-Nationalists [p. 46]." While these statements are regrettably vague, it seems safe to say (particularly in view of my caution for the earliest period) that "a few" of the

---

[16]Early in the rebellion, defection by the defectors seems to have been quite a problem for the Red Army, and it was this fact that resulted in the great emphasis on the political reeducation of the soldiers. After this the problem was alleviated.

Nationalist armed forces defected, to the extent of fighting on the side of the Communists near the beginning of the rebellion.

From the end of 1930 to the beginning of the war with Japan in 1937 is the period that may be described as "about half way through."[17] The data relevant to assessing the amount of disloyalty during this period is presented below.

During the second campaign to "exterminate" the Communists in 1931, Griffith (1967) cites T. A. Bisson as writing that in the last two weeks of May: ". . . numerous units of the government troops, estimated at 20,000 men, had deserted and been incorporated into the Communist armies [p.325]." Twenty thousand is exactly 10% of the 200,000 Griffith reports the Nationalists had "mustered" for this campaign (Ibid., p. 39). However, Griffith's comment on Bisson's figure is that it is "probably somewhat exaggerated [p. 325]."

During the third extermination campaign, Griffith describes the first encounter with the Communists as "unpropitious," since "an isolated brigade went over to the enemy, lock stock and barrel [pp. 39–40]." Elsewhere Griffith writes that there were "generally" about 600 men to a brigade (p. 329).

Griffith also cites the Japanese government's estimate of the composition of the Communist army during the winter of 1931–1932 as 28% surrendered Nationalists (p. 329). Since Griffith quotes Nanking's estimate of Communist troops for May 1931 as approximately 117,000 (p. 39), and for June 1932 as about 100,000 (p. 42), then if the Japanese estimate is correct, there were about 28,000 surrendered Nationalists in the Red Army of 1931–1932. For the autumn of 1932 O'Ballance (1962) gives the following data on defections: "On this occasion the Nationalist 28th Route Army, under Ten Chin-tan, came over to the Red side almost en bloc. Ten brought with him about 20,000 armed soldiers . . . [p. 72]."

And after the Long March, in February 1936, the Communists entered Shansi, which was defended by Nationalist troops of "Model Governor" Yen Hsi-shan. Griffith (1967) describes the following result: "When they [the Communists] withdrew, hundreds of students returned with them to Shensi. Many of Yen's troops defected; some units went over intact. The Communists later claimed they enrolled 8,000 selected volunteers during their Shansi operations [p. 58]."

By late 1936, O'Ballance (1962) writes, there were 95,000 in the Communist army of which 10,000 were "Manchurian and Chinese Muslims who had been persuaded to come over to the Reds [p.113]." The Man-

---

[17]Strictly speaking, the first half of 1945 should be considered as belonging to this time period too, since the duration of the war is being ignored; but while mathematically more accurate, it does violence to the idea of the historical periods involved.

quite churians under Chiang must be considered Nationalists, and the Muslims were from a cavalry of what, O'Ballance says, were "semi-independent warlords," who were nevertheless allied with Chiang Kai-shek. Hence, this constitutes considerable defection.

All the above data for this period "about-halfway-through," suggests there were well over 60,000 defections from the Nationalists to fight on the side of the Communists. However, since Liu (1956) claims that the Nationalist forces in 1937 were "about 300,000 strong [p. 112]," it seems that we have to conclude that there were "some" (11–25%) rather than a "considerable" number (26–49%) of defections to the side of the rebels.

For the last period, 1946–1949, there is so much data to support the view that the majority of the Nationalist forces defected, that I shall restrict myself to an analysis of the best source, Gittings (1967), and simply make passing reference to the other sources.

According to Gittings: "In the first two years (1946–1948) two thirds of the PLA's [People's Liberation Army] manpower came from the peasantry, and only one third from captured KMT troops [*Ibid.*, p. 61]." Since elsewhere Gittings provides many sources for the figure, 2,800,000, for the Communist forces in June 1948 (p. 304), one-third of this number comes to just under 1,000,000 defectors. However, Gittings also reports that:

> According to the Communists' own statistics, the number of troops who surrendered or came over to the PLA was negligible in the first two years of the war (less than 50,000) but increased dramatically in the second two years beginning July 1948 (644,000) and over one million in 1948–1949 and 1949–1950 respectively [p. 69].

These data suggest that the previously mentioned figure of just under 1 million ex-KMT troops must refer to early defections as well as later ones. Elsewhere, Gittings goes into more detail:

> In June 1948 the PLA numbered 2,800,000; two years later it had increased to 5 million. Nearly 80 per cent of these were "young people," many of whom had defected from the Nationalist armies. Victory was hastened by the collapse of morale in these armies; this also meant that more KMT soldiers surrendered or let themselves be captured, while fewer got killed. According to PLA statistics, in the first two years of the war (1946–1948) about 50 per cent of KMT losses were casualties (1,450,000 out of 3,090,000). In the third year (1948–1949) losses were almost the same as for the previous two combined, but casualties amounted to less than 20 per cent of the total (571,610 out of 3,050,000). In the four years July 1946—June1950, the PLA claimed that it had captured a total of 4,586,750 ex-KMT soldiers, and that a further 1,773,490 surrendered and crossed sides of their own free will. Whatever the precise accuracy of these statistics, their dimensions roughly indicate the size of the problem [*Ibid.*, p. 19].

Although defections that occurred after January 1949 cannot be counted, since they occurred in the "near end" time period, it still seems reasonable to conclude that the majority of the Nationalist forces fought on the side of the rebels during the preceding period.

In summary: A few (2–10%) troops fought on the side of the rebels from early on in the rebellion (in the first 6–25% of the duration):

$$4_D \times 3_T \times 0.5_P = 6.$$

Some (11–25%) troops fought on the side of the rebels about halfway through (26–75% of the duration):

$$4_D \times 2_T \times 1_P = 8.$$

The majority of Nationalist troops (51–95%) fought on the side of the rebels near the end (in the last 6–25% of the duration):

$$4_D \times 1_T \times 3_P = 12.$$

Since the disloyalty score is made up of the two expressions that contribute most to the score: the *Disloyalty Score* for the Chinese Rebellion is 20.

6. CUBA — THE SUCCESSFUL REBELLION OF 1959

Cuba is one of the most interesting cases in this study, not merely because it is so well-known a rebellion, nor because it is so relevant to the whole debate as to whether oppression can last or not, but because of all the successful rebellions drawn in the sample, there was the least amount of armed-force disloyalty in Cuba.

Case Description[18]

On July 26, 1953, Fidel Castro learned something about the wrong way to destroy a military dictatorship. That was the date when he led two hundred anti-Batista underground rebels in the famous assault on Fort Moncada barracks just outside Santiago. He had hoped to take the fortress by surprise, then appeal to the Cuban people to revolt against the dictatorship. Instead, most of the rebels were cut down by machine-gun fire; Fidel and his brother Raúl escaped into the nearby Sierra Maestra, but they were captured shortly by an army patrol and sentenced to long prison terms on the Isle of Pines.

Following his mid-1955 pardon by the then confident and well-entrenched Batista, Fidel Castro went into exile to gather support for an invasion force. In Miami and

[18]Lieuwen (1958, pp. 263–265).

New York his appeals to Cuban exiles reportedly netted fifty thousand dollars, which he later used to purchase arms and a yacht. A residence in Mexico City became his headquarters, around which gathered eighty-one followers, most of them Cubans associated with the "26th-of-July" movement. One important exception was Dr. Ernesto "Ché" Guevara, a Communist-oriented, Argentine-born physician, who had been banished by Juan Perón and who later lent his revolutionary zeal and talents to the government of Jacobo Arbenz in Guatemala.

Early in 1956, Castro and his little band of followers began intensive training in guerrilla fighting at a ranch just outside Mexico City. The master hired to teach harassment tactics, hit-and-run maneuvers, sabotage operations, bomb making, and jungle survival, as well as use of firearms, was Colonel Aberto Bayo, a veteran guerrilla fighter of the Spanish Civil War. On November 20, 1956, the eighty-two-man invasion force sailed for eastern Cuba aboard the "Granma," a sixty-foot yacht of doubtful seaworthiness. Less than a week after landing, seventy had been either cut down by Batista's troops or captured and imprisoned. Only twelve (including Fidel, Raúl, and Guevara) managed to reach their destination—the Sierra Maestra. And yet these twelve became the nucleus of an amateur, civilian revolutionary army which in just two years time developed sufficient military capacity to overcome the allegedly invincible Batista army.

Castro's army was recruited primarily from the peasantry. The long-exploited *guajiros* gained new hope from Fidel's promise of land, and many became adept students of guerrilla warfare. To the Sierra Maestra also came a number of urban, middle-class refugees from the Batista tyranny. A rebel underground began to supply arms and conduct sabotage. Financial aid came from tyrannized middle-group elements, who looked to Fidel, long associated with the democratic Ortodoxo party, as their leader in the fight for restoration of civil rights and political freedoms. Cuban exiles in Miami sent vital material help by parachute. Additional arms and ammunition were secured by frequent ambush of Batista's army patrols.

Unequal to the guerrillas in isolated mountain skirmishes, Batista's army began mass assaults, but with equally frustrating results. It was not long before the regulars began to lose stomach for the dangerous business of pursuing the guerrillas. Finally, in May of 1958, Batista launched an all-out onslaught with 13,000 troops against Fidel's guerrillas, then estimated to number less than five hundred. But despite the twenty-five to one odds, the offensive failed. By August, the increasingly confident rebels had opened a second front in the Escambray Mountains in the center of the island. Meanwhile, Batista's armed forces began to become worried and restless. Batista had to crush a navy rebellion in Cienfuegos during 1957, and in late 1958 air force pilots refused to follow his orders to bomb rebel-held towns. Meanwhile, mounting opposition from urban middle-class elements steadily sapped the strength of the regime. The final rebel drive occurred in late December as the guerrillas, now eight thousand strong [this figure is much higher than figures given in other sources; see Appendix III for the discussion of scale] and overwhelmingly supported by the civilian populace, descended from their mountain fastnesses and attacked the cities of Santiago in the east and Santa Clara in the center. When tha latter fell, Batista's generals forced his resignation. On New Year's Day 1959, Major Fidel Castro, age thirty-two became the new ruler of Cuba.

Discussion

26 July 1953 is usually seen as the date on which the Cuban rebellion started, and 1 January 1959 as the date it ended. However, this obscures the fact that from July 1953 to December 1956 there really was no active rebellion (first, Castro was in jail in Cuba, then he was in Mexico planning and training for the rebellion), so that armed-force defection in favor of the rebels was not really possible during this period. Even after Castro and his fellow guerrillas "invaded" Cuba in November 1956, only about 12 of them escaped death, and this small band stayed in the Sierra Maestra mountains till quite near the end. While the rebels managed to increase their numbers, they were not really actively engaged in attempting to overthrow Batista's regime most of the time. For the purposes of assessing disloyalty, then, it is misleading to regard the rebellion as of 5½ years' duration. Instead, duration will be figured from the date the rebel band invaded Cuba, 1 December 1956 to January 1959—25 months.

The reader should be reminded, however, that even before Castro's invasion in 1956, a group of young army officers, under the direction of Colonel Ramón Barquin, had attempted a coup that was unsuccessful. And another group of right-wing officers had tried to stimulate disorder so as to create an excuse to execute a coup. These incidents (see Chapter Two) clearly indicate unwillingness of a few of the armed forces to support Batista. But the disloyalty scale was not developed to assess disloyalty independent of any civilian rebellious action, so these incidents were not calculated into the disloyalty score.

Thomas (1971) describes the top rank of the military as "disgruntled" from the start, and the army as being "dominated by a net of intrigue and distrust [p. 798]." As early as March 1957, Fagg (1965) writes, "Batista concentrated forces in Oriente province, but they could not penetrate the rebel territory in the Sierra Maestra and many soldiers sold their weapons to Castro or defected [p.96]." But few other sources either confirm or refute this particular episode. The event that *is* mentioned by most of the sources (and which was also mentioned in Chapter Two) occurred on 6 September 1957: just 10 months after the invasion, a section of the navy, in collaboration with Castro's 26 July movement, tried to overthrow the regime (Thomas, 1971, p. 961; Lieuwen, 1958, p. 100). For some months prior to this, the 26 July Movement had enjoyed a following among the younger officers of the navy (Thomas, 1971, p. 961). The plan was for uprisings to occur in a few different places, but the day before these were supposed to happen, there was an attempt to postpone them. The news did not reach the rebels in Cienfuegos, who managed to take over the naval and police stations there. However, the victory lasted only a morning.

But, according to Thomas, it was still "the largest action in the civil war so far [p. 964]." He estimated that about 400 rebels participated and about 300 were killed. Some of the participants, Macgaffey and Barnett (1965) report, "fled to the Escambray where they became the nucleus of the Second Front of the Escambray [a guerrilla group] [p. 290]." (See Goldenberg, 1965, p.157.)

The other event that is emphasized in many of the sources is the campaign of 24 May 1958, which has been described by Thomas (1971) as the "only major offensive of the war [p.996]." But even prior to this, Lieuwen (1958) maintains that: "It was not long before *the regulars began to lose stomach for the dangerous business of pursuing the guerrillas* [p. 265; italics added]." In addition, the still-imprisoned Colonel Barquin, whom Thomas describes as Castro's most "formidable rival," had a group of officers calling themselves the 4 April Movement and another rebel group working for his release by means of a coup on the Isle of Pines (1971, p. 994). At this point in the many-faceted rebellion, this show of disloyalty to the regime *does* contribute to the disloyalty score.

Brennan's (1959, pp. 229–231) description of Batista's all-out campaign of May 1958 against the rebels in the Sierra Maestra suggests that some of Batista's soldiers were unwilling to fight, some were neutral, some actively helped rebels, and others joined the rebels' side. According to Thomas (1971), however, for at least 25 days Batista's officers "drove their men on with energy and some zeal [p. 996]." However, by the time that only 4 square miles of territory remained in Castro's control, even Thomas relates that "the morale of the army was drooping. Many of the men, untrained for this sort of territory, were exhausted [p. 997]." And in the next few days Castro, still with fewer than 300 men, "decimated" one of the 1000-men battalions of Batista's soldiers. *(Ibid.)* According to Thomas:

> The consequences of this setback were extraordinary. Batista's High Command, now a demoralized gaggle of corrupt, cruel and lazy officers without combat experience, began to fear total extinction from an enemy of whose numbers and whereabouts they knew nothing accurate [*Ibid.*].

The army tried to withdraw, and "some deserted (for instance, thirty out of eighty on 24 July at El Cerro) [p. 998]." One of the battalions collapsed, "partly due to lack of food and drink," but partly also "because Castro entered into contact with Major Quevedo, whom he had known at the university and who afterwards joined the rebels [*Ibid.*]." According to Brennan (1959), the Major "wrote letters to fellow army officers urging them to cease fighting and consider going over to the Rebel cause. Many of them, in the months of 1958 that followed, did so [pp. 232–233]."

And Otero Echeverria (1959) claims that many of Batista's soldiers, when giving themselves up to the rebels, embraced them and said, "Long live Castro [p. 198]," and that many also remained in the Sierra to fight on the side of the rebels.

Unfortunately, none of the sources gives any precise figures or even estimates of the amount of armed-force disloyalty. Both the revolt at Cienfuegos and the Sierra Maestra fiasco occurred within the range of what constitutes "about halfway through," according to the disloyalty scale. Bearing in mind the events of disloyalty that have been described, a summary statement that probably errs in the direction of underestimation is as follows: between a "few" (2–10%) and "some" (11–25%) of the regime's armed forces fought on the side of the rebels about halfway through the rebellion:

$$4_D \times 2_T \times 0.75_P = 6.$$

Regarding the growing unwillingness of the majority of the armed forces to fight up to, and including, a couple of months before the end of the rebellion, we are inundated with qualitative evidence. Some of this material is presented below, with the passages indicating disloyalty italicized for emphasis. It should be pointed out that some of the disloyalty occurs so near the end that is should not contribute to the disloyalty score (according to the scale, disloyalty from about November 23 onward cannot contribute toward the score), but since the sources do not separate their data according to my coding categories for "time at which the armed forces are disloyal," it is simpler to leave it all together. This will also give the content more coherence:

LIEUWEN (1958):   *The regular army,* in the face of mass antagonism toward the regime and repeated guerrilla success, *began losing its will to fight. Airforce pilots began to desert rather than follow out orders to bomb defenseless cities.* Faced with this distasteful prospect of having to conduct wholesale slaughter in an attempt to quell the swelling popular opposition, *the army general went to Batista and forced his resignation* [p. 100].

THOMAS (1971):   At Guisa Castro faced 5,000 men of Batista's with 200 *guerrilleros,* of whom 100 were new to the combat. Batista's commanders were beginning to despair: "Our Army, tired and decimated by two years of fighting without relief, had completely lost its combat power. *Desertions to the enemy increased daily.* We lacked reserves and *a great part of the officers confined in the barracks maybe* [*were*] . . . *in contact with the enemy* [p. 1016]." [Surprisingly, Thomas does not give the source of this quotation.]

MACGAFFEY AND BARNETT (1965):   *The failure of Batista's army to fight during the last months of 1958* was the final and indisputable blow [p. 289].

FAGG (1965):   Batista made one last desperate effort to destroy the revolutionists. *His army swarmed into the affected area, only to surrender or melt away* [p. 98].

GOLDENBERG (1965):　Castro's problem there [in the Sierra Maestra] was more how to survive than how to protect himself against Batista's soldiers, *most of whom were not anxious to fight* even if they could find him in this impassable region [p. 55].

When Castro began his offensive [in August, 1958] and *most of the troops retreated without a fight* and appeared to be completely demoralized, the rebel army naturally began to grow . . . [p. 162].

In the Batista camp everything during the last December weeks was in a state of collapse. *Various generals were openly engaged in conspiracy. One of them, Cantillo, even flew to Fidel Castro for discussions. The leader of the army, Tabernilla, tried to persuade the American Ambassador to mediate.* In the middle of November, after the elections at which Rivero Aguero was, as expected, 'elected' President the situation seemed hopeless. *The bomber pilots . . . used their bombs only occasionally (on the civilian population) but usually dropped them where they would do no damage. Junior and senior officers gave themselves up or fled. Cantillo and others were planning the establishment of a military junta on December 26.* At the end of December, before the plan could be put into operation, the 'battle of Santa Clara' took place in the Central Province, ending in a total fiasco for the government troops and causing little bloodshed. [According to *HAR,* this battle left 3000 casualties— quite a discrepancy.] *An armoured train hastily sent to the spot–its commander fled before there was any fighting*—was put out of action and taken over by the rebels. Then Castro went from the mountains to Santiago, *after the commander of the Moncada garrison had gone over* to him [pp. 162–163].

Much more material could be presented to support these data. [See Andreski (1967, p. 248); Brennan (1959, p. 14); Draper (1962, p. 14); Huberman and Sweezy (1960, p. 64); Matthews (1964, p. 102); Otero Echeverria (1959, p. 219); Phillips (1960, p. 389); and Suárez (1967, p. 29).] It seems, therefore, that a reasonable summary statement of armed-force disloyalty near the end of the rebellion (that is, in the last 6–25% of its duration), is that the majority of regime troops (51–95%)ʼ were neutral or unwilling to fight for the regime any longer:

$$1.5_D \times 1_T \times 3_P = 4.5.$$

Hence, the *Disloyalty Score* for the Cuban Rebellion is 10.5.

7.　MEXICO—THE SUCCESSFUL REBELLION OF 1911

The overthrow of Díaz in 1911 is normally seen as but the first phase of the long-drawn-out Mexican Revolution. In this study, however, I focus on this first phase, since 1911 is when the first regime overthrow was accomplished.

Case Description[19]

The actual Madero Revolution of 1910 was scarcely the mass uprising of a downtrodden people. Nor was it the instrument of rapacious foreign capitalism. The few and feeble attempts that the Madero family made to obtain loans in the United States to carry on a revolt against Díaz were flatly turned down, on the basis that the whole scheme outlined in the Plan of San Luis Potosí seemed a poor business risk. The Madero Revolution was essentially a colossal bluff that succeeded. Many of the details about its critical episodes are still controversial; no thorough-going investigation has yet appeared. But the available published materials point unmistakably to the conclusion that less than 20,000 men, and less than 1.5 million dollars (raised in Mexico) killed an era. Even by Mexican standards it was a small affair, but its repercussions were great.

Tiny bands of devoted Maderistas rallied to the Plan of San Luis Potosí which denounced the election of Díaz as fraudulent. Premature outbreaks occurred on November 18, 1910 and sporadic local fighting sizzled thereafter at widely separated points in the Republic. The strength of the Madero forces, if such they could be called, lay in the Northwest. Venustiano Carranza, Pancho Villa, Pascual Orozco—all destined soon for wider recognition—here recruited ranchers, smugglers, drifters, and patriots to the Madero cause. Unable to operate effectively in his home state of Morelos, a peasant leader, Emiliano Zapata, and his more dreaded brother, terrorized Guerrero, while lesser chieftains in Sinaloa, Puebla, Zacatecas, and the isolated peninsula of Yucatán moved in narrower circles behind Díaz' main lines.

Gustavo Madero, main organizer for his brother, kept careful account of the effectives at the movement's disposal; his estimates reveal how small and regionalized was the affair, even at its apogee in May 1911. More than three-quarters (76.8 percent) of the total fighting strength of the Madero revolution was concentrated in the western and northern states of Mexico. All told, the number of guerrillas was less than 17.5 thousand.

But the Maderos had difficulty keeping even this small force supplied with arms and ammunition, almost the sole source of which lay in the United States. With no funds coming from the United States commercial circles, the Maderos were forced to raise all the loans they could on their own properties, to the point where they were reduced to having their laundry done on credit in Texas. Small sums came from captured villages. Bannerman and Company, suppliers of arms to revolutionists throughout the Latin-American world, were unsentimental enough to want cash on the barrelhead. Lack of cash and supplies set up a vicious circle: without ammunition there were no Madero victories, and without victories, morale and confidence among the irregulars dropped. Generals like Pascual Orozco were wont to expend a million rounds of rifle cartridges in one engagement; it cost $15,000 to

[19]Cline (1953, pp. 121–124).

replace them, and when, from shortage of funds, further supplies were not immediately forthcoming, the guerrillas suspected treachery and political transactions.

The inability of the Díaz government to quell these small revolutionary brush fires revealed the hollowness behind its impressive facade. For reasons best known to himself, Díaz had sent Bernardo Reyes and José Limantour to Europe into "honorable exile." Within the Mexican government all was disorder; Díaz, senile and drugged for a jaw infection, could himself give no coherent direction to affairs. There was little time with which to work. The army had proved to be mostly a myth—padded rosters showed 30,000 men, but half were fictitious; in a showdown Díaz had no power. By February 1911 the crisis had been prolonged for ten weeks but there was still hope for his survival in office. Though the government had not scattered the revolution, neither had the Maderistas gained significant victories.

At this point Díaz recalled Limantour. En route from Paris, the financial genius interviewed the Maderos and fellow revolutionists in New York. Despair had split their ranks; one clique, the Vasquex Gómez ex-Reyistas, were willing to settle on an amnesty basis, but the Maderos bluffed. They talked grandly and ambiguously about large resources being placed at their disposal by sympathizers in the United States; privately Gustavo was writing to Francisco at revolutionary headquarters in Texas that for want of a few cartridges and a little money the whole revolution was in jeopardy. Without the victories envisaged, the revolutionists had a poor bargaining position.

Limantour returned to Mexico City, where he took charge of the government. He promised changes, and sent word to Reyes to hurry home. Both the revolution and the government were losing prestige daily. As insurrectionists converged on Ciudad Juárez, across the border from El Paso, a serious international incident that could lead to United States intervention seemed a growing possibility. Neither side wished that. They started to haggle.

The negotiations at Ciudad Juárez were a failure but they paved the way for Díaz' final removal. The Maderistas demanded the resignation of the president, recognition of Francisco as provisional president, expulsion of *científicos* from Congress, eighteen state governorships, and payment of the expenses of the revolution to date, late April 1911. Limantour, whose agents were carrying on these talks, refused. The uneasy armistice between Federal forces and the revolutionary troops was broken after quarrels among the opposing forces led to sporadic shootings, then to a pitched battle. In it Orozco and Villa captured Ciudad Juárez for Madero by storm on May 10. Unconnected but important was Zapata's taking and sacking Cuautla on May 12; this town was a southern Federal stronghold. Success of this nature emboldened the lukewarm and wavering revolutionaries; at the very last moment, numerous small bands calling themselves Maderistas emerged to take over local and state governments.

The Díaz cause was lost. A treaty signed by the government (Limantour's agents) with the revolutionaries on May 21 ended the immediate fighting. In it both Díaz and Limantour agreed to resign. A somewhat colorless but powerful Catholic politician, Francisco de la Barra, was to assume the provisional presidency of Mexico until new elections (to replace the fraudulent ones of July 1910) were held.

Díaz was never fully aware of what Limantour's agents had done. When news of the treaty reached Mexico City on May 23 he attempted to disperse the mobs that formed to demand his immediate resignation. In the great square of Mexico loyal troops sprayed one demonstration with maching-gun fire; in a few moments two hundred Mexicans had been killed. Finally friends and relatives of the old Caudillo persuaded him that there was no alternative; early on the morning of May 25, 1911 Porfirio Díaz resigned. The Madero revolution was a military success . . .

Now that the stated object of the Madero uprising had been accomplished, Mexicans could and did stop to assess what had occurred. In the intoxicating atmosphere of "liberation" they paid the most concern to domestic aspects. The Iron Hand, so talked about in the propaganda of 1909 and 1910, had been lifted with the exile of Díaz.

Discussion

Cumberland (1952) seems to be quite alone in the view that "...no large segment of the military ever joined the revolutionary forces [p. 122]." Gruening (1928), Beals (1932), Parkes (1960), Prewitt (1941), Lieuwen (1958), and Andreski (1967) are among the sources who claim that the armed forces were disloyal, though most of these sources are very vague regarding the degree of disloyalty, the timing, and the proportion of the armed forces who were disloyal. This is evident from the quotations to follow. (The data most directly relevant to disloyalty are italicized.)

GRUENING: . . . in defense of the government and its system against a popular up-rising, *the enemy literally was not there. . . . The flesh and blood conscripts deserted in droves, tearing off their insignia as they jumped from troop trains and fled into the chaparral.* But the generals trafficked to the end. They did not take the rebellion seriously and wanted to prolong it. . . . From Paris the white-bearded and pompous *General Bernardo Reyes* announced that he was hurrying back to crush the Revolution. *By the time he reached Havana its progress led him instead to offer it his services . . .* [p. 302].

ANDRESKI: During the Mexican revolution *different sections of the regular army fought each other* [p. 247].

BEALS: Half the roster were straw men, paid, uniformed and fed at regular rates. . . . The rank and file was made up of criminals, conscripted political opponents, forced Indian levies. *Such troops had no stomach for real fighting. Nearly all General Luque's troops deserted* [p. 428].

PARKES: The army had been steadily weakened. Nominally thirty thousand, it actually contained only eighteen thousand men, *and these were unwilling conscripts . . .* [p. 320].

PREWITT (writing of the Díaz army) . . . this ornamental body *first disintegrated before the impact of the Madero movement and then went over to it . . .* [p. 612].

LIEUWEN: . . . when in 1910 a popular revolution broke out *the vaunted capabilities of the Díaz army and the asserted loyalty of his officer corps proved to be fictitious*. The army in reality proved to be but a fragile shell [p. 103].

And last, another quotation from Lieuwen—one of the few authors who gives some hint about the timing of the disloyalty:

> . . . [S]pontaneous   uprisings   began   in   scattered   areas.   When   the
> weakness of the regular army became apparent, the movement began to snowball. *An increasing number of officers deserted the regime and joined the revolutionary forces*, impressed by their power and by their popular support. Their object obviously was to emerge on the winning side. Thus, *with the help of the regulars, the Díaz regime was overthrown* and Francisco Madero assumed the presidency [*Ibid.*, p. 106].

With regard to the degree of disloyalty, these data suggest that troops who were disloyal were either neutral or fought on the rebels' side (that is, they were moderately or maximally disloyal according to my scale). The last quotation from Lieuwen suggests that this disloyal behavior started early in the rebellion, and together with the other sources, a picture of continuing and growing disloyalty develops. It is not easy to capture this picture in two expressions, but hopefully the situation is not too distorted by the following summary expressions.

A few (2–10%) of the armed forces fought on the side of the rebels from early in the rebellion (in the first 6–25% of the **duration**):

$$4_D \times 3_T \times 0.5_P = 6.$$

In addition, some (11–25%) of the armed forces fought on the side of the rebels from about halfway through the rebellion (in the middle 26–75% of the duration):

$$4_D \times 2_T \times 1_P = 8.$$

Hence, the *Disloyalty Score* for the Mexican Rebellion is 14.

8

Unsuccessful Rebellions and the
Behavior of the Armed Forces

This chapter, organized in the same way as Chapter Seven, is devoted to the description and analysis of the unsuccessful rebellions that were drawn in the random sample. These rebellions, too, will be presented in alphabetical order: Austria, Burma, Colombia, Cuba, Honduras, Italy, and Spain.

8. AUSTRIA—THE UNSUCCESSFUL REBELLION OF 1934

An interesting aspect of the Austrian case is that the rebels were responding defensively to a government-initiated attempt to disarm and suppress them. Hence Gedye's (1939) description: "February 1934 was not a socialist revolution, but a *Heimwehr* counter-revolution [p. 112]." (The *Heimwehr* was a Fascist army.) The definition of rebellion used in this study does not distinguish between offensive and defensive rebels, as long as both the rebels and the regime are violent. Nor does it give meaning to the word "counter-revolution." Nevertheless, these characteristics do make the Austrian case unlike many of the other rebellions drawn in the random sample.

Case Description[1]

Background

Political situation in January. At the beginning of 1934, Dr. Dollfuss [Austria's Chancellor] and his conservative Christian Socialist following held control of the government through an alliance with the even more reactionary Heimwehr (Home Guard), a private Fascist army led by Prince Ernst Rüdiger von Starhemberg. The Heimwehr looked to Fascist Italy for its inspiration and was reliably reported to have received financial aid and political guidance from Mussolini. In opposition to the government were the Social Democrats and the Nazis, who in turn were violently opposed to each other.

The rapid growth of the Nazi movement in Austria as a constituent part of Hitler's National Socialist movement in Germany had for its aim the long-sought Anschluss, or political union of the two German-speaking countries. When the opposition of the powers prevented the forcible incorporation of Austria into the Third Reich, the Nazis sought to achieve the same end by the more indirect method of establishing a nominally independent Nazi regime in Austria. To withstand this assault, Chancellor Dollfuss was obliged to join forces with either the Heimwehr or the Social Democrats. He chose the Heimwehr, partly because this choice was more in keeping with the political attitudes of his conservative following. More important, Italy's support of the Dollfuss regime as against Germany was apparently conditioned upon the destruction of the Socialist movement in Austria. Accordingly, when the Heimwehr leaders entered the Dollfuss Cabinet in September, 1933, the Socialists on the one hand and the government coalition on the other began preparations for the armed struggle which they saw was inevitable.

The Rebellion

The Socialist opposition would be a tougher problem [than the Nazis for the government] for nearly half the electors were its supporters. The blow against this party was struck in February 1934. Dollfuss had already stopped the grants-in-aid voted by Parliament towards the municipal expenses of Vienna; he now summarily ordered the dissolution of the Council and the disarming of the Schutzbund. The Schutzbund, descended from the "People's Guard" of 1918, was the armed portion of the Socialist Party.] The Mayor of Vienna, protesting against the suppression of the Council, was arrested and sent to jail. The search for arms among the haunts of the Schutzbund was resisted; fighting broke out, spreading rapidly throughout the city. Then the contest spread to the provinces; in Linz, Graz and Steyr there were sharp battles between Government troops, assisted by the Heimwehr, and the Socialist Schutzbund. For four days, from 12 February to 15 February, civil war raged in the streets of Vienna. The sides were fairly evenly matched, except in one important particular—the Government had artillery. Even against shell fire the Socialists held out in their workmen's dwellings; the new housing estates were turned into for-

---

[1]The section, "Background," is from *NIYB* (1934), and the section, "The Rebellion," is from Eugene L. Hasluck (1938, p. 42).

tresses. On the 15th the Government offered a free pardon to all who would surrender, excepting only the leaders. The Vienna Socialists were already almost beaten, and surrender followed. The official Government report gave the dead as 239, including both sides; the Socialists maintained that at least 1500 fell on their side alone. Most of the Socialist leaders escaped to Czecho-Slovakia, but in Vienna and the provinces the surrender was followed by eleven hangings and over a thousand commitments to prison, whilst several thousands more were sent to concentration camps. As a further sequel all Trade Unions throughout Austria were declared suppressed.

In April, to the general surprise, Dollfuss summoned Parliament to meet again. But it was a Parliament from which every Socialist member—nearly half the House—was excluded.

Discussion

Both the Government's armed forces and the *Heimwehr* (a previously private Fascist army which, shortly before the Socialist rebellion, Chancellor Dollfuss officially recognized as a kind of "auxilliary police," paying them and arming them to fight the Socialists) appear to have remained completely loyal to the Government. A careful search through all the sources (see the bibliography for all sources used for this case), some of which are detailed and first rate (see Gulick, 1948; Geyde, 1939), provided no hint of army, police, or *Heimwehr* disloyalty at even the minimal level of unwillingness to fight. Quite the contrary; all the evidence suggests a willingness on the part of the armed forces to be quite brutal in suppressing the rebels.

In an attempt to explain the defeat of the Socialists, Bauer specifically mentions "the loyalty of the army to the Government" as a factor (Bauer is cited in Gulick, 1948, p. 1348). And Braunthal (1945, p. 281), commenting on the outcome of the Austrian rebellion, maintains that the armed forces have to become unreliable to triumph in this kind of situation. To support this thesis, Braunthal mentions a few examples, including the Nazi rebellion that was to occur a few months later, about which he has this to say: "Their attempt, however, failed, because Dollfuss' grip upon the forces of the state was *still* firm, the troops accepted the orders of the Government [p. 282; italics added]."

Hence, the *Disloyalty Score* for the Austrian Rebellion is 0.

9. BURMA—THE UNSUCCESSFUL REBELLION OF 1953

The Burmese Rebellion is extraordinarily complex since a number of very different rebellions were going on at the same time. While it shares this quality with the Afghanistan rebellion, it differs from the latter in that a major rebellion in Burma—the revolt of the Karens—was separatist, and therefore disqualified from consideration in this study. (See the discussion of the distinction between civil war and mass rebellion in Chapter Four.) But it is impossible to ignore the Karen rebellion, since so many Karens were in the army, and their defection from it, albeit to fight in their own behalf, contributed to Burma's very high disloyalty score. So, while it is possible to ignore the rebellion when considering the scale of the rebellion (see Appendix III), it would clearly be a gross distortion to pretend that the Karens did not defect. Their defection obviously undermined the strength of the government forces, thereby strengthening the non-Karen rebels, which is relevant to the outcome of the non-Karen rebellion.

A further complication results from the fact that the remnants of the Chinese Kuomintang (KMT) armies took refuge in Burma following the Communist victory over Chiang Kai-shek. Hall (1960) actually argues that the Kuomintang (and the Karens) very much prolonged the rebellions of the Communists and the People's Voluntary Organization (PVO) in Burma.

The question of duration is also very difficult to decide in the Burmese case. While Hall (*Ibid.*, p. 180) states that the rebellions were finally crushed in 1954, more recent sources suggest that this was not the case. Yet the later sources cite no end to the rebellions, and it could even be argued that the end has not yet come. But for the purpose of this case analysis, we will accept Hall's date of 1954. Since the defections occurred very early in the rebellions, this decision does not significantly affect the disloyalty score.

Case Description[2]

After Independence—Disunity

Burma had won freedom as a result of World War II. It had chosen its leaders and by 1948 was prepared to move forward economically and politically. Its economy made a quick recovery; rice was available for export; the army was being reorganized; the young republic was on the march. The prime minister, however, had erred when he said on the first Independence Day that the people were united. A major part of the Burmese had a feeling of unity; but there were dissidents, and this made for trouble . . .

As a result of Moscow-directed international conferences, attended by Burmese Communists, a series of which were held in India during February–March 1948, the

---

[2]Sources: Hall (1960, pp. 178–180) and Frank N. Trager (1954, pp. 20–22). Trager, who was a Research Associate at the Center of International Studies at MIT at the time this book was published, is one of the foremost Western experts on Burma. The summary used here is written rather simplistically because it was written for the *Headline Series*—a series of books on foreign policy issues for the layman, intended to stimulate discussion and promote understanding among the United States population. Unfortunately, no better summary account could be found. The summary description begins with an extract from Trager's (1954) *Burma*.

Burmese Communist party adopted a "rule-or-ruin" position. Failing to gain control of the AFPFL [a "popular front" organization], they resorted to insurrectionary opposition in March 1948. A little later one sector of the wartime resistance army, known as the White Band People's Voluntary Organization (PVO), unable "to settle down" after the war and bereft of the unchallenged leadership of Bogyoke Aung San, also went into the opposition and at various times joined forces with, or was "taken over" by, the Communists.

The Karen Rebellion

All through 1948 the new government tried to woo, win or otherwise placate these insurrectionary groups, particularly because it feared the major uprising which actually came in January 1949, this time from the Karens. The latter group split into a section loyally supporting the government and an insurrectionary force determined to secede from the Union of Burma and set up a separate state. The Constitution of Burma had provided for a Karen constituent state within the Union. However, the opposition Karens, who had long enjoyed a preferred status under the British regime and had been the object of much Christian missionary attention, had too little confidence in the predominantly Burmese and Buddhist government.

Thus by February 1949 the fledgling government found itself menaced by the Communists, the People's Voluntary Organization army, and the Karen insurrections. Various rebel forces held much of the Irrawaddy Valley from Mandalay down to Insein—six miles north of Rangoon, the capital . . . . [In the following, Hall, 1960, is the source.]

Had it not been for the Karen rising the communist rebellion would have been for all practical purposes stamped out in 1949. But the Karen rising, formidable in itself, all the more so since it began at Insein close to Rangoon, gave new life to the communist struggle. Under the terms of their agreement the KNDOs (Karen National Defence Organization) were to control Lower Burma, the communists Upper Burma. In the critical year 1949, when communism triumphed in China, the rebels captured such key places as Mandalay, Meiktila, Bassein and Toungoo, and paralysed road, rail and river communications throughout most of the country.

But the government did not fall, and its determination to become master in its own house never wavered . . . .

It was a slow process winning back the country district by district, and opening up communications, with the rebels launching constant counterattacks and often regaining lost territory. Slowly the tide turned against the insurgents. In 1951, it was possible to hold the first general election after independence, though only on a regional basis . . . .

Again the rebellion was on the point of collapse, and again a complicating factor intervened to give it a fresh lease on life. In January 1950 the last Kuomintang division on the Asian mainland, under General Li Mi, was routed in southern Yunnan by the Chinese communists. Soon afterwards the remnant of its troops to the number of 10,000 in civilian dress, began to filter through the Burma border into the Wa states and Kengtung. Burmese troops attacked the KMTs but they escaped in small parties into northern Siam, and later returned. With most of their effective units engaged in dealing with their own rebels the Burmese found it impossible to deal effectively with Li Mi . . . .

Throughout 1952 Li Mi was building up his strength in defiance of Burma. Early in 1953 his units launched attacks across the Salween into the Shan State, the Kachin State and the Kayah State (Karenni). So, instead of completing the task of crushing her rebels, Burma had to use the major part of her armed forces in driving off the invaders. . . . The Burma army . . . launched a major offensive, 'Operation Bayinnaung,' which culminated in the capture of the KMT headquarters in March 1954. Even then, although a further evacuation was agreed upon, thousands of Li Mi's forces were never rounded up, and today still prey upon the hill villages of Kengtung.

It was the turn of the rebels next. In July 1954 a drive against the communists in central Burma destroyed them as an effective force, while another against the PVOs was equally successful.[3]

Discussion

When Burma became a republic on 4 January 1948, the Red Flag Communists (as distinct from the White Flag Communists, who were pro-Stalin) were already "in the field," according to Tinker (1967). But it was at the end of March 1948 that the major rebellion began, when the White Flag Communists, by far the larger group, turned to armed rebellion [*Ibid.;* see also Trager, 1966, p. 99].

On 16 June, nearly 3 months later, one battalion (the 6th Burma Rifles) mutinied, and, according to Tinker (1967), "some of its members went over to the Communists [p. 36]." Then on 29 July, 4 months after the White Flag Communists began a rebellion against the government, approximately 4000 armed members of the White Band People's Volunteer Organization (PVO) followed suit (Trager, 1966, p.107).[4]

Tinker (1967) writes, since the PVO was "formally a part of the Anti-Fascist People's Freedom League (AFPFL) coalition [p. 36]," that is, the government, it seems they have to be regarded as regime forces, even though not regular forces. It was only 2 weeks later, on 10 August, that

[3]Further information on the outcome of the Karen rebellion might be of interest. Hall (1960) has this to say:

> The Karen National Defence Organization was the toughest nut to crack. Determined operations against them in the Delta region and on the Siam border towards the end of 1953 broke the back of their resistence. The final blow, however, was not delivered until March 1955 when Papun their "capital" was captured. The rebellions now have all been crushed, but at the time of writing (Autumn 1955) lawlessness and dacoity still remain very serious problems [p. 180].

[4]Perhaps it would be helpful at this point to say a bit more about the PVO. The PVO was a paramilitary force organized and trained to fight the British. In fact, it never was used for this purpose. After independence was won, and the government sought to disband it, the majority group—the so-called White Band PVO, was unwilling to do so, whereas the minority Yellow Band PVO was willing to work out a compromise; the latter group did not go into active rebellion (Trager, 1966).

two more battalions of the regular army mutinied (the 1st and the 3rd Burma Rifles), both turning their military forces against the government (that is, showing the maximum degree of disloyalty). In addition, many units of the Union Military Police "went underground," so that 88 out of a total of 311 police stations were "in rebel hands [*Ibid.*]." According to Trager (1966, p. 107), there were at this point from 700–1400 army mutineers and about 3000 police and local militia who had defected. Most had done so in August, 4½ months after the major communist rebellion had begun, and 7½ months after independence, at which time a lesser communist rebellion was already in operation. By either of these starting points, then, the maximum degree of disloyalty (fighting against the government) occurred early in the rebellion. But more was to come.

In late December 1948 and early January 1949 all of the regular Karen battalions mutinied [Tinker (1967, p. 323) cites February 1949]. Prior to this, the Karens had "contributed the largest element in the fighting forces [*Ibid., p. 325*]" and included "some of the best troops and most of the professional leaders [p. 324]." In fact, Tinker writes that: "In consequence, the army lost most of its experienced officers and NCO's [*Ibid.*]." While the Karens mutinied to take part in a separatist Karen rebellion rather than to join the other rebels (as has already been mentioned), their defection still falls into the category of maximum disloyalty since they fought against the regime forces.

All the sources describe February 1949 as the real low point for the Government. Trager (1966, p. 107) estimates that there were 13,000 armed "leftists," plus Karens from six battalions and the police forces—a total of about 7000. In contrast, the total government defense forces, according to the Prime Minister, consisted of only "a few loyal army battalions [*Ibid.*]." While insisting that it is impossible to give a definite estimate, Tinker (1967, p. 326) puts the figure at six battalions, plus "about 15 military police battalions of lower quality, and thousands of hastily raised, undisciplined 'levies.' Numbers were on the rebels' side ... [p. 48]," he concludes. According to Trager (1966), there were approximately 700 men in a battalion, so six battalions totals just over 4000 (p. 107).

Hence, the total of the armed forces who had defected by February 1949, 11 months after the major communist rebellion had started, were: 4000 armed PVO's, 700–1400 army mutineers (the mean of 1050 will be used), 3000 police, and 7000 Karens from the police and the army. Thus, the total is: 15,050 defectors from the regime's armed forces.

It seems, then, that the majority (51–95%) of the Burmese armed forces defected to a maximal degree early on in the rebellion (in the first 6–25% of the duration). This is consistent with Trager's (1966) assessment. He writes: "Burma's trained fighting forces were sharply divided by the insurrection, and a *majority of them actually went over to the rebels* [p.116; italics added]."

$$4_D \times 3_T \times 3_P = 36.$$

Hence, the *Disloyalty Score* for the Burmese Rebellion is 36.

10. COLOMBIA—THE UNSUCCESSFUL REBELLION OF 1948

The Colombian rebellion of 1948 has become known as the *Bogotazo,* after the capital city, Bogotá, where the major upheaval occurred. It has also been variously described as "the riots," "the worst riot in Colombian history," a "revolt" and an "insurrection," an "uprising" and "rioting and revolution," and as a "social revolution."[5] Most upheavals that are called riots are much too small in scale to qualify as mass rebellions by the definition used in this study: the *Bogotazo,* however, qualifies easily. (See Appendix III for scale analysis.)

Case Description[6]

Lleras [the President, a Liberal] believed in 'national union'—coalition with the Conservative Party—as the only practical means of facing a situation verging on civil war. With three moderate Conservatives in his Cabinet and the support of the principal Liberals, he was successful in his policy initially. But a leftist had been gaining considerable power with the masses and attacking the coalition policy. This was Jorge Eliécer Gaitán, an able jurist and something of a demagogue. He was able also to capture and to hold the allegiance of certain of the intellectuals and idealists, some of the industrialists who believed that to give him his head would be the best protection against the inevitable pressure from below, and of the masses, who gave him almost fanatical allegiance as their saviour from conditions of life which were now becoming increasingly difficult. In the elections of 1946 Gaitán was put forward as the leftist Liberal candidate, while the centre of the party presented the moderate, Gabriel Turbay. Turbay polled 437,707 votes, Gaitán 360,263, and the Conservative Mariano Ospina Pérez was returned to power with 565,849 . . . .

Ospina endeavoured to rule by coalition and to continue the policy of 'national union,' giving the Liberals half the ten posts in his Cabinet and half the departmental governorships. But his coalition, after incessant internal wrangling, broke down finally in March 1948 with the resignation of all the Liberal members. Turbay had meanwhile died in Paris, leaving Gaitán as the undisputed leader of the party, almost certain to be elected for the next presidential term. While Santos, López, and Lleras supported collaboration, he violently and unceasingly attacked it. His

[5]Dix (1967, p. 104); *EB* (1967); *KA* (see Chapter Seven, note 1); *F-on-F* (Chapter Seven, note 1); Fluharty (1957, p. 107); and Galbraith (1966, p. 148), respectively.

[6]Galbraith (1966, pp. 145–148). In the words Galbraith uses ("mob," "savagery") and his attitude in general, he reveals a LeBon-like view of this rebellion.

sudden assassination in Bogotá on 9 April 1948 was the signal for a nation-wide outbreak of rioting and looting which reached its greatest height in the capital, where the Ninth Inter-American Conference was in session, attended by General Marshall. The mob went berserk, attacks on the presidential palace were beaten off only with the greatest difficulty by the handful of soldiers available, public buildings were burned and also those associated with the Conservative Party, such as that of El Siglo and Gómez's own estate near the city. Fortunately for the government, political motives were mostly forgotten by the mob in the first hours after the murder, and indiscriminate destruction and looting became the order of the day, particularly in the centre of Bogotá, where immense damage was done. The police deserted to the mob, and it was several days before the armed forces rushed to the city could restore order, and months before the declaration of a state of emergency could be relaxed.

The directorate of the Liberals presented itself at the Palace in the evening of 9 April with a demand for the President's resignation, which he steadfastly refused. After an all-night debate, he agreed to form a coalition government again, with Darío Echandía, Gaitán's natural successor to the leadership of the Liberals, as Minister of State, and with General Ocampo, another Liberal, as Minister of War.

It seems certain that the murder of Gaitán was a private affair and not related to his position as leader of the majority opposition party. (The conclusions of members of Scotland Yard specially summoned to the country to investigate the murder were never published. Their visit was part of the almost panic-stricken appeasement of popular opinion by the government in the days immediately following Gaitán's death.) Secondly, it is alleged—with some show of reason—that Gaitán was receiving material assistance from the Venezuelan government party, the Acción Democrática, in a plot to overthrow the government by force in June 1948. The Venezuelan exiles in Barranquilla from 1929 to 1936, who later became the leaders of this party, were then openly Communists and were planning the liberation from 'feudalism' of the Caribbean countries, a term later extended to cover Ecuador and Peru. The 'Barranquilla Plan' had on the whole progressed satisfactorily, and it was in accordance with it that Colombia should be assisted to overthrow the Conservative minority in power.

It was claimed later by the Colombian government that proof of Venezuelan intervention was discovered: the evidence was a large cheque from Rómulo Betancourt paid to Gaitán, and the broadcasting by Venezuelan radio stations of reports of certain events in Colombia before they actually took place, but these were soon diplomatically hushed up as dangerous statements about a man whom the mass of the people regarded as a martyred saint. It is certain, at all events, that the Venezuelan press and radio published a number of reports that Colombia had risen and 'thrown off tyranny,' and repeated cries were heard among the rioters in Bogotá that the Venezuelan army had crossed the frontier to help 'the people,' while Betancourt's name was loudly applauded as 'friend of the people.' [Even if this rather questionable evidence of Venezuelan intervention were accepted, it would not disqualify Columbia from my study because no one was actually sent from Venezuela to fight.] What little organization was discernible in the events of those April days—notably the immediate seizure of radio stations, beginning with the Radiodifusora Nacional, and some of the messages and exhortations which were broadcast before their recapture—is consonant with the existence of a plan made for the June revolution, which some of Gaitán's followers and fellow conspirators tried unsuccessfully to put into operation after his death. Though a certain number of Communists were in Bogotá to take part in a demonstration during the Inter-American Conference, and they and their local party were charged with organizing both the murder and the revolution, this theory is consistent neither with all the evidence nor with the course of events.

But the sacking of the centre of Bogotá and parallel events in many parts of the country were not actuated solely by the death of a man whom the mob looked upon as their saviour. They were the product of an unstable political and social situation which had been developing for years. What actually took place was a social revolution, and it is for that reason and not for their dramatic violence that those days will deserve the careful attention of historians of Colombia. Only lack of leadership, the unpreparedness of those who might have taken advantage of the situation, the alcoholic excesses of the mob in the capital, the firm stand taken by the President with admirable dignity, and the loyalty of the armed forces averted the overthrow of the government. Even the wildest political demagogue must have been alarmed to see, after nearly fifty years of peace, the appalling savagery of a mob whose feelings had been consistently exacerbated over a period of time by the preaching of doctrines above its standard of political education against a background of unsatisfactory living conditions.

Nor did the Church escape. All over the country, churches and clergy were attacked. Churches, convents, ecclesiastical colleges, schools, and institutions run by the Chuch were burned, and clergy were seized, killed, and in some cases horribly mutilated.

Discussion

According to most of the sources, the police defected very early in the rebellion, while the army did not. It is the more contemporary sources that are inconsistent with the others; in *F-on-F*, for example, it is reported that: "Troops and police, hesitant at first, soon struck back in Bogotá and other cities." And in *NIYB*, it is stated that the police were neutral, rather than that they fought on the side of the rebels: "It was later disclosed that nearly 600 policemen belonging to the Liberal Party remained neutral in the conflict . . . ." One of the noncontemporary sources, Fluharty (1957), actually suggests that some of the army were also disloyal: "The Bogotá garrison, though called out, refused to leave the barracks . . . [p. 101]." However, all the other authors state that at least in Bogotá, while the police defected very early, the army did not. Yet none of the admittedly scant data indicates that the army troops were unwilling fighters.

On the role of the police, Galbraith (1966) writes: "The police deserted to the mob . . . [p. 146]." Martz (1962): "Within an hour of the time Gaitán slumped to the concrete, the mobs were swollen with the addition of the national police, who had immediately gone over to the rioters [p. 56]." Fluharty (1957): "... the police everywhere were joining the rioters, even providing them with ammunition [p. 101]." And Hobsbawm (1963): the rebellion "was freely supported by the police of Bogotá [p. 248]." [Beaulac (1951, p. 244) presents similar information.]

Both Dix and Galbraith actually attribute the failure of the rebellion, at least in part, to the loyalty of the armed forces. For example, Dix (1967) writes: "Any prospect that the riots would turn into real revolution was eliminated by ... the attitude of the Conservative-dominated army ... [p. 104]." [See also Galbraith (1966, p. 148).]

A number of sources describe Bogotá as being seriously undermanned as far as soldiers were concerned. For example, Beaulac (1951) writes:

> We learned later why the army had delayed so long in going into action. Out of 10,000 soldiers spread thinly over Colombia's rugged terrain, only some 2,000 had any military training. ... Furthermore, of the 2,000 soldiers that should have been in the Bogotá area that day, 1,400 were outside the area engaged in military exercises [p. 250].

However, most sources agree that when the soldiers finally arrived, they fought in a "determined" way. Martz (1962) explains the enormous casualties as "in part a tribute to the army directives to shoot first, asking questions later [p. 57]." And Martz concludes: "There was never any question of army loyalty. True to its non-political tradition, the military defended the constitutional order ... [p. 61]." And finally, Beaulac (1951) states that: "While the army, or most of it, was ill trained, it also was loyal and, when it finally went into action, effective [p. 251]."

Since it appears that the police and the army acted very differently in this rebellion, it is important to know the sizes of these two branches in order to assess the percentage of the armed forces that were disloyal. According to *SY* (1948), the peace effective of the army varied betwen 12,000 and 15,000 men, and there were 10,000 national police. [Beaulac (1951, p. 250) states there were only 10,000 in the army, but *SY* is probably more accurate.] Since the evidence really relates only to the Bogotá police, my final estimate of the percentage of the armed forces who were disloyal is 11–25%.

In summary: some (11–25%) of the armed forces fought on the side of the rebels from the very beginning of the rebellion (in the first 5% of the duration):

$$4_D \times 4_T \times 1_P = 16.$$

Hence, the *Disloyalty Score for the Colombian rebellion is 16.*

11.   CUBA—THE UNSUCCESSFUL REBELLION OF 1912

The Cuban rebellion of 1912 is one of the three rebellions about which least is known of the cases drawn in the random sample. (The other two are the Honduran and Italian rebellions of 1933 and 1914, respectively.) The most outstanding characteristic of this Cuban rebellion is that all the rebels appear to have been black; thus, it is the only racial rebellion in the study. Perhaps it should be mentioned that, according to Wigdil (1912, p. 1352) the blacks, together with the "mulattoes," constituted about 75% of the voters.

Whereas an antiblack bias comes through strongly in most of the sources, Fitzgibbon (1935) is exceptional in not revealing this bias in *Cuba and the United States 1900–1935*. An excerpt from this book follows.

Case Description[7]

A far more serious movement was the "race war" of 1912. Disaffection among Cuban negroes extended as far back as 1897 and as early as the first intervention, efforts were made to organize a negro party. These attempts were successful in 1907 when Evaristo Estenoz, an insurrectionist general, organized the Independent Colored party. In the next few years it worked for greater recognition for negroes in the distribution of patronage and was especially opposed to the Morúa law which purported to forbid the organization of any political party on lines of race or color.

On the refusal of Estenoz and his colleagues to drop the word "Colored" from their party name Gómez declined to aid them in any way. The movement soon assumed a more serious form. On May 20, 1912, armed bands of negroes rose in Havana, Santa Clara, and Oriente. The government immediately sent troops to quell the uprising, but on May 23 the United States ordered marines sent to Guantánamo, most of the disturbance being in Oriente and much of it in the vicinity of Guantánamo and Santiago.[8]

The United States Senate on May 25 adopted a resolution authorizing an investigation to determine what legislation would be necessary to settle the time and manner of possible intervention, and other points. Nine United States warships were concentrated at Key West by the latter part of May and on the twenty-fifth of that

[7]Fitzgibbon was Professor of History and Political Science at Hanover College when he wrote this book. Since his interest was in the relation between Cuba and the United States, it is to be expected that this aspect of the rebellion will be highly emphasized. Note the lack of information on casualties, number of rebels, etc. (The material quoted is from Fitzgibbon, 1935, pp. 149–150.)

[8]This was the beginning of United States intervention. The question is whether the case should be disqualified on the grounds that Cuba was not then an autonomous political system. While the intervention was certainly substantial and important, United States troops were not actually used to fight against the rebels (or the regime). And since the operationalization of "autonomous political systems" stresses this factor above all others, the case was not disqualified.

month the State Department instructed Minister Beaupré to notify the Cuban government of the possible landing of United States forces to protect lives and property but, said Knox, "this is not intervention." Gómez himself replied that "in reality (such measures) do not seem anything else."

In view of the extraordinary activity of the Cuban government in putting over 3000 men in the field in four days against the negro rebels Gómez thought the United States action unjustified. Taft replied that "these ordinary measures of precaution were entirely disassociated from any question of intervention," and on May 28 a force of 700 marines landed at Guantánamo. As disorder continued to spread, Gómez, on June 5, 1912, suspended the constitutional guarantees in Oriente. The greatest difficulty confronting the Cuban government was the protection of foreign property, especially sugar interests, and on one occasion the British minister expressed surprise that the marines at Guantánamo were being used only for the protection of American and not of other foreign interests.

The disorder in Havana was more distinctly a race war and the situation was little less than panicky. Washington officials on June 9 ordered two warships from Key West to the Cuban capital and the following day Senator Bacon of Georgia introduced a bill authorizing the President to use the army and navy to subdue the rebellion either with or without the consent of Cuba; the Cuban government, however, was not to be displaced. United States intervention would have been greatly to the liking of Estenóz, but of course he would oppose support of the incumbent government.

The Cuban government protested the dispatch of war vessels to Havana and a few days later circulated a report that the ships had been ordered withdrawn, but this report the Department of State denied. Toward the end of June government forces began to gain the upper hand over the negro rebels and Estenóz was killed in battle June 27. This marked the virtual end of the rebellion. United States officals ordered the larger war vessels at Key West, Havana, and Guantánamo north near the end of June and the marines at Guantánamo were ordered home on July 25.

Discussion

Wigdil's (1912) article is the only source that suggests there was an unwillingness to fight on the part of the armed forces. Wigdil, an American, had been living in Cuba for 3 years when he wrote this article. In it he reveals enormous ethnocentrism and conservatism, and he fails to document what he says.[9] Hence, as data, his article will be ignored.

[9]For example, Wigdil (1912) asserts:

> The forces of the Cuban army have been in the field for several weeks, but have failed to do anything, because they are cowards. A Cuban won't fight, but he will stab any enemy in the back. The army moves in force and makes half-hearted endeavors to meet small bands of the insurgents, but the negroes, moving in much smaller numbers, always get away. If the Cuban officers had the backbone to scatter their forces in smaller units, they could meet the revolutionists on even terms and results could be accomplished. Don't become alarmed, however, it won't happen; it is too dangerous—someone might get hurt in such an encounter [p. 1356].

The other sources provide data on the armed forces—how many were sent to quell the rebels, how quickly they were dispatched, etc. [see the accounts of Johnson (1920, p. 307), Rowland (1926, pp. 72–92), Strode (1934, p. 235), and Fitzgibbon (1935, p. 150)]—but none suggests any disloyalty. Rowland, in particular, in his 20-page account of the rebellion has a great deal to say about the various engagements and the number and nature of the participants, but he never refers to any disloyal behavior on the part of the armed forces. This probably means that there was no disloyalty, or very little.

Hence, the *Disloyalty Score* for the Cuban Rebellion of 1912 is 0.

12.   HONDURAS—THE UNSUCCESSFUL REBELLION OF 1933

Sources on the little-known Honduran rebellion are scarcer than for any of the other cases. In fact, aside from 25 articles in *NYT*, and less than a page in *NIYB*, no other sources could be found.

As so often happens in Latin America, the Honduran rebellion was precipitated by the losers' dissatisfaction with the results of an election.

Case Description[10]

Dissatisfaction with the result of the election led to a much more serious uprising by the defeated Liberals in mid-November. [On June 8 there had been a small-scale rebellion in northern Honduras, which cost 51 lives (see *NIYB*, 1932).] The revolt broke out November 13, when insurgents captured the cities of San Pedro in the north and Nacaome, key to the southern district of Honduras. Numerous towns and villages in various parts of the republic were occupied by rebel bands, but government troops aided by Nationalists recaptured most of these points, in some cases after heavy fighting. Three hundred casualties were reported in a 12-hour battle for the possession of San Pedro on November 15. *Despite initial government victories, the insurrection gained strength by the successive desertions of units of government troops* [italics added in this paragraph]. *The garrison at Comayagua joined the revolt on November 24 and on December 11 the important garrison at Amapala under Gen. Andrés García espoused the cause of Gen. José María Reina, who returned from exile in Guatemala and proclaimed himself provisional president. Other prominent army officers joined Gen. María Reina's ranks. The latter, moving his forces from Amapala Island in the Gulf of Fonseca to the mainland, joined forces at Aceituno with another rebel contingent under Gen. José María Fonseca.* He then marched upon Tegucigalpa, but in the Curaren region about 50 miles southwest of the capital, he was confronted with government forces under his brother Gen. Camilo Reina. At the close of the year a decisive battle was believed to be impending.

[10]*NIYB*, 1932.

Government forces had succeeded in cutting the insurgent army's communications with Amapala.

The Honduran Congress was called in emergency session on December 15. It approved decrees declaring martial law throughout the republic and commandeering for military purposes all funds in special treasuries. During a second special session, Congress approved the issuance of a $500,000 war loan and decreed the provisional suspension of internal debt payments, diverting the funds for war purposes. Meanwhile the revolutionary disturbances and the general fear of looting had brought business almost to a standstill.[11]

The serious revolt which broke out in November, 1932, following the victory of Gen. Tiburcio Carías Andino in the Presidential election of Oct. 30, 1932, was crushed by government forces early in 1933. With the recapture from the rebels of the port of Amapala on Dec. 30, 1932, the insurrectionists menacing the capital retreated southward. Amapala was reopened to international navigation on January 4 and the following day the rebel leader, Gen. José María Reina, and a group of officers crossed into Nicaragua and delivered their arms to the Nicaraguan National Guard. The remaining rebel force under Gen. José Antonio Sánchez was defeated by government forces January 14 and General Sánchez in turn fled into Nicaragua.

Discussion

The information on the disloyalty of the armed forces to the Honduran regime was italicized in the case description of the Honduran rebellion. The picture of disloyalty that emerges from this source is confirmed by data from *NYT*. According to *NYT*, on 24 November 1932 "the garrison at Comayagua abandoned its barracks . . . taking all arms with it . . .." This was 10 or 11 days after the outbreak of the rebellion, that is, in the first 6–25% of the rebellion's duration. Then on December 11, "the garrison at Amapala under General Andrés García joined the revolt." This was almost exactly halfway through the rebellion. Again, near the end of December, "the garrisons stationed in the small port cities are understood to have gone over to the insurgents," though the two earlier defections seem to have been more significant. And *NYT* is quite explicit that it was the Liberals, not the military, who initiated the rebellion.

Regarding the degree of defection, it seems clear that the defectors fought on the side of the rebels; that is, they were maximally disloyal. However, the question of the percentage of the army defecting is much less clear— there is even no information on the number of men in a "garrison." According to both *SY* and a League of Nations (1933, p. 225) source, there were approximately 2500 men in the army; and 250 in the police force, making about 2750 in total (*Ibid.*, p. 226). If "a garrison" may be assumed

[11]From this point, *NIYB* (1933) is the source.

to consist of more than 55 men (2%), but less than 275 (10%), then the first summary statement of disloyalty would be: a few (2–10%) of the armed forces fought on the side of the rebels near the beginning of the rebellion (within the first 6–25% of the duration):

$$4_D \times 3_T \times 0.5_P = 6.$$

This estimate applies also to the proportion involved in disloyalty roughly halfway through the rebellion when "the garrison at Amapala" joined the revolt. Hence, a summary of the second constituent of the disloyalty score is as follows: a few more (2–10%) of the armed forces joined the rebels by fighting on their side about halfway through the rebellion (in the middle 25–75% of of the duration):

$$4_D \times 2_T \times 0.5_P = 4.$$

Hence, the *Disloyalty Score* for the Honduran Rebellion is 10.

13. ITALY—THE UNSUCCESSFUL REBELLION OF 1914

The degree to which the sources vary with regard to the importance attributed to this rebellion—"Red Week" as it is almost always called—is quite remarkable. On the one hand, Salomone (1945) writes in these terms: "When the nightmare of a social upheaval had finally spent its full force and violence . . . it was realized that the Italian Liberal state had passed successfully through one of the most dangerous moments in its history [p. 60]." And Mussolini's paper, *Avanti!* (quoted in Salomone, 1945) had this to say on 12 June 1914. "Armistice. The general strike that came to an end yesterday was the severest popular uprising that has shaken the Third Italy since 1870 [p. 60]." Salomone also claims that the great Liberal-Conservative newspapers agreed with this view of the rebellion. And Kirkpatrick (1964) concludes, similarly, that "it was the most serious insurrection United Italy had known [p. 55]."

On the other hand, about half of the historical works consulted make no mention of the rebellion at all, or pay it very scant attention. And nowhere did I find more than two consecutive pages on the event. In part this may be because World War I, coming so soon thereafter, overshadowed the Italian rebellion. But the neglect may also be due to the tendency for history to be written about the winners, not the losers.

Case Description[12]

Resentment for the Libyan war was obviously an ideal starting point for incitement to revolt, and of all the regions in Italy, none appeared more smoldering and sullen

---

[12]Hughes (1967, pp. 97–98). This source is not necessarily the best one; for Italy, there were about five sources that were more or less equivalent in length and quality.

in its hatred of Parliament and government than Romagna, the province from which Mussolini came. There one of his young Socialist friends, Pietro Nenni, was calling out to the *braccianti* for insurrection, for a socialist republic. His cry was echoed by the redoubtable anarchist Malatesta, back from England to try to do in the Marches what anarchists had failed to accomplish in Sicily and Milan.

The material these men were working with was extremely combustible, and in March 1914, with the outbreak of an anti-draft demonstration in Ancona, the long-awaited violence erupted. Throughout Romagna the cry went up for revolt against the war-mongering government, the lackey Parliament, the servile army and the exploiters of all classes. The violently revolutionary *braccianti*, who had nothing to lose, and the more conservative peasants took up arms against each other. [However, the rebellion was mainly antigovernment.] In the cities, paralyzed by a general strike, mobs looted and ransacked, and the royal insignia was stripped from virtually all government buildings and monuments. Some twenty years after the wild dream of Bakunin, the red flag of anarchy did fly above the City Hall in Bologna, the capital of the region. Ancona declared itself an independent commune, and Romagna, not to be outdone, declared itself an independent republic. For one week, *Settimana Rossa* or Red Week (the term referred to the anarchist origins of the upheaval, and had nothing to do with the still non-existent Communist movement), an entire region successfully defied the central government; and—the most heady symbol of success—the general sent to quell the insurrection was forced to hand the rebels his sword.

Against the threat of chaos, Salandra [the Premier], with the approval of Parliament and most Italians, who were terror-struck by the revolt, sent some 100,000 troops into the region, twice the number Crispi had sent to Sicily to quell the uprising of 1894. In a matter of days order was restored. Malatesta managed to escape the police and once more fled the country; Nenni was arrested and imprisoned. Mussolini, whose exhortations to revolt in *Avanti!* were considered by many, including himself, as major factors in the upheaval, was admonished and left free. The government did not consider his role important.

Discussion

None of the dozen or so works that mention the Italian rebellion even hint at any disloyalty on the part of the police or army. And there is some positive evidence that the armed forces were loyal to the regime. Kirkpatrick (1964), for example, states that "the Confederation of labor called off the strike, because it recognized that the movement could not succeed without the support of any armed forces [p. 55]." And, according to Kirkpatrick, Mussolini, who "believed that the Revolution had come [p. 57]," learned a lesson from "Red Week" that he apparently never forgot: "After his own experience of Red Week . . . he resolved not to involve himself in conflict with the army [p. 95]." And again, Kirkpatrick writes of Mussolini that: "Ever since his experience of Red Week he had doubted whether he could attain power by revolutionary action and he remained convinced that he could not do so unless the army were on his side or at least neutral [p. 108]." The obvious inference to be drawn from these quotations is that the armed forces were completely loyal to the regime.

Chorley (1943), in trying to explain the outcome of the Italian rebellion writes that: "The mass impetus seems to have been there . . ., but the attitude of the troops was never put to an ultimate test. Finally, the movement was suppressed by the Nationalist Party . . . [p. 77]." It is not clear what Chorley's "ultimate test" is, but it is clear that she is trying to explain the loyalty of the armed forces. And Hughes (1967) refers to "the servile army [p. 98]"—servile to the government—which he would hardly do if there had been disloyalty.[13]

Hence, the *Disloyalty Score* for the Italian Rebellion is 0.

14. SPAIN—THE UNSUCCESSFUL REBELLION OF 1934

The decision and rationale for excluding rebellions in which some of the armed forces came from another country, were discussed in Chapter Four. Briefly, it was argued that the factors relevant to an understanding of why a regime's own forces are loyal or disloyal to it are not likely to be the same when the forces are those of foreign powers. Hence, I chose not to deal with cases in which there was intervention by foreign troops. Spain provides a rather problematic case on this score, since some of the rebels were suppressed by the Foreign Legion and Moroccan soldiers (Morocco was a colony of Spain at that time). These soldiers were not in any way carrying out the orders of other powers—on the contrary, they were employed and instructed by Spanish generals. Nevertheless, loyalty might work differently in such a case. Yet to disqualify the case did not seem warranted, particularly since this study does not examine the *bases* of armed force loyalty and disloyalty.

Case Discription[14]

The October Revolt. When the Cortes reconvened on October 1 the Catholic leader, Gil Robles, immediately attacked Premier Samper's policy with respect to the Catalán land law as "weak and humiliating." He demanded that the central government assert its authority and protect the large Catalán landowners from expropriation. The Samper Cabinet resigned the same day, and President Alcalá Zamora called on Señor Leroux to form a new ministry. The announcement on

---

[13]It was also Louise Tilly's considered opinion that "neither army nor police fraternized with revolutionaries or took part in Red Week except as repressive forces. (Personal communication.)

[14]*NIYB*, 1934.

October 4 that the Lerroux Cabinet would contain three members of Gil Robles' *Acción Popular* precipitated the long-expected uprising of the proletariat.

On October 5 the parties of the Left issued a call for a general strike which was followed immediately by a revolutionary outbreak throughout the northern and central parts of Spain. For three days the fate of the government hung in the balance. There was desperate street fighting in Madrid and many other cities, outbreaks among the peasants, and separatist insurrections in Catalonia and the Basque Provinces. On October 6 Pres. Luis Companys of the Catalán Generalitat proclaimed Catalonia a "State within the Spanish Federal Republic." Decisive action by General Batet, commander of the central government's troops in Barcelona, crushed the revolt in that city on the same day after severe fighting. President Companys and the other Catalán leaders were arrested. By October 9 the Lerroux Cabinet had succeeded in stamping out the revolt practically everywhere except in Asturias and the Basque Provinces. Contrary to expectations of Left Leaders, the army remained loyal to the government.

It was several weeks before troops broke the stubborn resistance of the miners of Asturias. There some exceedingly severe fighting was reported, accompanied by atrocities on both sides, and Ovideo, the capital of the province, was a ruined city when the struggle ended. Casualties due to the revolution were estimated at 3500 killed and 10,000 wounded or injured and the property loss was placed at 4,000,000,000 pesetas (more than $500,000,000). The insurrectionists killed many priests and landlords and destroyed numerous churches and convents.

The victory of the government left the Left forces in Spain with scarcely a vestige of their previous power.

Discussion

All the evidence suggests that the armed forces were completely loyal to the government. Since there were three major areas of rebellion—Barcelona, Madrid, and Asturias—each will be treated separately.

Barcelona. The *NIYB* reports that: "Decisive action by General Batet, commander of the central government's troops in Barcelona, crushed the revolt in that city on the same day after severe fighting." Peers (1936) and others mention that the rebel President Luis Companys of the Catalán Generalitat "sent for General Batet . . . and called on him to transfer his allegiance to the new Federal Regime [p. 167]." The General refused, fighting followed, then rapid rebel defeat. Interestingly enough, it seems that the General took a little time to think over whether he would be loyal or not. (*Ibid.*; also *Bulletin of Spanish Studies*.)

Madrid. There is less information on Madrid, but sources do suggest that the armed forces were loyal. For example Smith (1959) writes: "Madrid had also experienced the terror of civil strife. Soldiers entered the crowded Puerta del Sol and fired without provocation at imaginary foes on roofs and into the apartments of inoffensive people [p. 448]."

Austurias.   For various reasons the regular armed forces were not used
to fight the miners of Asturias. Instead, contingents of Moorish (Moroccan)
soldiers and the Foreign Legion were sent to fight in Spain. Thomas (1971)
explains that: "The regular troops based in Asturias . . . were too few in
number to be able to conduct any more than a holding operation . . .," so
the government "sent for Generals Goded and . . . Franco to act as joint
Chiefs of Staff to direct the suppression of the rebellion [p. 81]." It was
Generals Goded and Franco, then, who called in the Moroccans and the
Foreign Legion, including what had been the "key corps in the conquest
of Morocco [*Ibid.*]." They did so, according to Thomas, "chiefly
because they doubted whether any other regular troops would be successful
[p. 83]." Jackson (1965) takes this further by suggesting that generals
Goded and Franco "feared to send in the regular army because of the strong
possibility that the Spanish conscripts would refuse to fire on the revolutionists—or even desert to them [p. 157]."

It seems, in short, that the government did at least fear disloyalty on the
part of the troops. According to *NIYB* the rebel leaders also expected disloyalty ("Contrary to expectations of Left leaders, the army remained loyal
to the government" *NIYB*). But all the data suggest that these fears and
expectations were not fulfilled. Peers (1936), for example, refers to "the
loyal troops in Asturias . . . [p. 170]." And Manuel (1938) writes:
"Such cannon and rifles as did fall into the hands of the workers were badly
manned; no trained army leaders presented themselves [p. 139]."

The accounts of the suppression of the uprising, rather than focusing on
the question of loyalty, focus on how brutal the armed forces were in the
way they suppressed the Asturian rebels. De Madariaga (1958) writes:
" . . . the military authorities, strong in their victory, were ruthless in
their punishment [p. 437]." And Carr (1966) argues that "with its
brutal repression by the Moroccan Army, the Asturias rising reached the
dimensions of a civil war . . . [p. 635]." Finally, several writers—Smith
(1965, p.447), Manuel (1938, p. 139), and Peers (1936, p. 169)—refer
to "barbaric atrocities," some sources insisting that both sides were guilty
of atrocities. The figures on casualties also make it appear that the armed
forces were eager to do a thorough job in squelching the rebels.

Hence, the *Disloyalty Score* for the Spanish rebellion is 0.

Appendix I

Operationalizing the Definition
of Mass Rebellion

In Chapter Four the definition of mass rebellion was developed element by element. I stated exactly what each element meant and presented the rationale for including them in the definition. But it is a long way from definition to putting each element in workable, operational form. Just as the usefulness of a model is limited by the rules of correspondence that tie it in with the empirical world, so is the usefulness of a definition limited by the same kind of rules. Yet even where these rules are entirely arbitrary, their reliability is enhanced by making them explicit.

Appendix I carries the process of operationalization begun in Chapter Four through the final, tedious, hair-splitting step, so that the reader can see exactly how the cases of successful and unsuccessful mass rebellions were selected from descriptive historical accounts, not written, unfortunately, with my analysis in mind; while words like "revolution," "coup," "civil war," "rebellion," "riot," "insurrection," and "guerrilla warfare" abound in the historical accounts of *EB* and *NIYB,* I could never assume that the terms were being used in the same way I defined them.

DEFINITIONS RESTATED

A reminder of the definitions is in order at this point.

Mass rebellion is a form of violent power struggle, occurring within an autonomous political system, in which the overthrow of the regime is threatened by means that include violence, and in which the participants are largely from the masses.

A *successful mass rebellion* is one in which the regime is overthrown, that is, the rebels or their chosen representatives subsequently take over the positions of power for at least 1 week.

An *unsuccessful mass rebellion* is one in which the overthrow of the regime is not achieved, that is, the rebels or their chosen representatives do not subsequently take over the positions of power, having suffered a decisive defeat after a substantial confrontation with the regime.

More precise meaning is given to each element in these definitions in the following order:

    I. *outcomes of mass rebellion;*
   II. *violent power struggles and "means" that include violence;*
  III. *autonomous political systems;*
  IV. *the overthrow of the regime is threatened;*
   V. *the participants are largely from the masses.*

I. OUTCOMES OF MASS REBELLION

If the rebels or their representatives gain power for at least 1 week before being overthrown by another faction, or by a foreign power, then the minimal criterion for a successful rebellion is met. If the period is less than 1 week, then the case is disqualified on the grounds that it had a marginal outcome.

Similarly, all rebellions whose outcomes do not fit my definition of successful and unsuccessful rebellion are regarded as having marginal outcomes and disqualified. This category, then, is simply residual. Before giving further examples of marginal outcomes, I shall clarify what constitutes a confrontation sufficiently substantial to warrant consideration as a possible case.

The resignation of a regime prior to substantial fighting between its forces and the rebels is regarded as an abdication, rather than a defeat. However, if the resignation follows within 1–2 weeks of a substantial amount of fighting, then it is regarded as a successful rebellion. Similarly, if the rebels give up their struggle before getting involved in a substantial amount of fighting with the regime forces, the event does not qualify as an unsuccessful rebellion. If, however, they give up their struggle after a substantial amount of fighting, then the event is regarded as an unsuccessful rebellion. The criteria for what constitutes substantial fighting are the same as the criteria used for estimating the scale of rebellion. If the minimal scale score of 1.1 is met (see Table III.1, page 155, for the method of assessing scale), then it is assumed that there was sufficient fighting to qualify.

Examples of Marginal Outcomes

(1) Displacement of those in power occurs, but neither the rebels nor their representatives take over these power positions.[1]

(2) Displacement of the premier only (not a whole government) is achieved.

(3) Displacement of those in power occurs, but the rebels and/or their representatives only take over these power positions after one or more intermediary regimes have been formed and dissolved. Often, particularly in Latin America, a military junta takes over until elections can be held, and the rebel leaders are then elected; that is, the means of gaining power become constitutional. The arbitrary rule was made that the rebels or their leaders have to take over power within 1 month after the displacement of those against whom they had rebelled. Cases in which quasi-democratic means of gaining power by election were used are disqualified.

(4) Cases in which the rebels stop rebelling violently after reforms are made or promised—without a transfer of power having occurred—are disqualified (even if the reforms are never actually made); for example, Russia, 1905 and Sudan, 1964. In such cases, the form of the upheaval is seen to have changed from a mass rebellion to a mass reform movement. And since no regime overthrow is achieved, the rebellion is not regarded as successful. Similarly, cases in which the rebels give up, on being offered amnesty by the regime are disqualified on the grounds that the outcome is marginal.

(5) If a new regime is set up by the rebels without overthrowing the old one, the case is disqualified; for example, China, 1917.

[1]It could be that the rebels did not want to take over the positions of power, for example, they may have been anarchists. Or they may have cared about the process by which the leadership was chosen, and not who the leaders were per se. But for operational reasons it was necessary to exclude such cases, otherwise all the occasions in which demonstrations, etc., led to regime change and resignations (much more plentiful even than coups) would have become eligible for consideration. Since many of these upheavals would have been much too small in scale to qualify anyhow, this rule also served to eliminate recording events that would later be discarded as too insignificant.

II.   VIOLENT POWER STRUGGLES AND "MEANS"
THAT INCLUDE VIOLENCE

There have to be at least 50 deaths for the upheaval to qualify, and casualties have to be suffered by both regime and rebel forces. Furthermore, the decisive confrontation between rebels and regime that culminates in defeat or success has to be violent; that is, in the case of successful overthrow a violent confrontation has to precede the transfer of power to the rebels or their representatives by no more than 2–3 weeks. This rule disqualifies cases like Egypt, 1952, where the violent protests and the coup were unrelated organizationally and in terms of personnel.

Since it is rather rare for *EB* or *NIYB,* as well as most historical works, to give the specific information required by these rules, assessments often have to be made on the basis of such qualitative data as are available. For example, words and phrases like "battles," "engagements," and "a civil war broke out," "heavy casualties were suffered," "a bloody struggle ensued," are suggestive of violence at a level that would qualify. These words and phrases also suggest both rebels and regime are likely to have suffered casualties.

Evidence that rebels are armed, that there is substantial property damage, that direct action tactics are used, etc., are examples of information less suggestive that violence has occurred at a large enough scale to qualify, but they still warrant further investigation. However, when the event is described as "bloodless," "virtually nonviolent," "only five dead," etc., then it is excluded from consideration as a possible case.

The rule is that errors should always be made in the direction of inclusion, as it is easy enough to disqualify cases at a later stage. Exclusion is always final, inclusion, always tentative. As more reliable information is obtained, the case can be excluded at any stage prior to the final analysis of the results.

III.   AUTONOMOUS POLITICAL SYSTEMS

Mass rebellions that are local in character, that is, where it is not the central government that is threatened, but tribal or provincial authorities, are excluded from consideration. The assumption is that a nation constitutes an autonomous political system except in the following conditions:

(1) *The nation has not yet achieved independence.* Of course the official status of independence sometimes has little substance; for example, Cuba gained formal independence from Spain, but in fact this was followed by American occupation; Morocco became independent from France and Spain

in 1956, but foreign troops were not withdrawn for some time. In contrast, there are examples where "the substance of autonomy" is present before formal independence, as was the case for New Zealand. In such cases, the lack of formal independence is ignored. Except in the latter kind of case, the history of a country is combed for rebellions after the formal date of independence. Cases are then disqualified if it turns out that the country was independent in a formal sense only.

(2) *The nation is conquered or occupied by a foreign power.* Nations that have been occupied or conquered by a foreign power for more than 10 years, are treated as autonomous unless the conqueror is controlled by, or representative of, a foreign power. In this case, they are regarded as more similar to countries in colonial situations. If the nation is occupied only by the military forces of another country or an international organization, like the United Nations, but such troops play no part (or only a minimal one) in helping either the rebels or the regime, then the case qualifies. If such troops play a significant part in the rebellion, then the case is disqualified.

(3) *The nation has no real central government.* To qualify, the power struggle has to be between a regime and rebels. When it is between two groups of rebels or two regimes, this is often a clue to there being no real central government; for example, China, 1912–1927. Or, if there are two fighting factions and it is difficult to decide which constitutes the regime and which the rebels, this provides another clue that there might be no real central government.

In addition, the following types of power struggles are excluded, since they are not consistent with an autonomous political system:

(i) *Power struggles in which there is substantial external intervention.* If more than 500 people from another country fight on behalf of rebels or regime, the case is excluded. When actual figures are lacking, qualitative data are used to reach an assessment. When the people from another country are actually natives of the country they invade, the case is not necessarily disqualified (the Bay of Pigs involved much more than this, and consequently did not qualify). When they are mercanaries, the case is disqualified, for example, the Congo.

When an external power (or powers) directly influences the outcome of the rebellion by playing a formal mediatory role, the case is disqualified. This applies to an increasingly common kind of intervention by international organizations like the United Nations, or ad hoc groups of national representatives formed to mediate in civil power struggles (this is quite common in Latin America). Other forms of intervention do not disqualify the case. For example, it is acceptable if another country (or more than one) intervenes by giving arms, money, other supplies, training, expertise, or support by propaganda, to either the rebels or the regime. In addition, if asylum is provided the rebels, or if they are given territory so that they can organize their forces, have a safe retreat, or launch an invasion, such aid does not warrant disqualifying the case.

(ii) *Power struggles that take the form of civil wars.* Where it is "self-determination," "autonomy," "secession," that is being fought over, not the overthrow of the regime, the case is disqualified; for example, if instead of the regime-versus-rebels conflict of the mass rebellion, there is a regime-and-rebels versus a-second-regime-and-rebels conflict; or when each side has its own regime that enjoys a near monopoly of the means of coercion in certain fairly distinct geographical areas. These struggles are regarded as civil wars. This term is often used more generally to describe other types of upheaval, such as conflicts of very long duration or situations in which the inhabitants of the whole country are "forced" to take one side or the other. I do not use the term as loosely.

(iii) *Power struggles that occur between two different nation states.* These are regarded as wars.

IV.   OVERTHROW OF THE REGIME IS THREATENED

It is assumed that the overthrow of the regime is threatened when the violent confrontation between rebels and regime is "substantial." The criteria for deciding whether it is substantial or not are based on the amount of violence, the number of active rebels, the social–geographical area involved, and the duration of the rebellion. (The index for evaluating the scale of the mass rebellion was presented in Chapter Four.)

V.   THE PARTICIPANTS ARE LARGELY FROM THE MASSES

The "masses" include students, peasants, workers, bourgeoisie, minority groups, or a combination of these. The term excludes cases in which the rebellion is initiated or led by members of either the elite or the armed forces. Hence, the following kinds of power struggles are excluded:

(1) Those between individuals or groups within the elite; for example, the cabinet shuffles and personnel changes that often occur in response to a serious threat, but which should not be mistaken for mass rebellion.

(2) Various types of military rebellions.

     (a) It is quite common in Latin America, for example, for the army to intervene in opposition to the regime after a mass rebellion has begun. Often a military junta results, in which the rebels are quite unrepresented. Such cases are disqualified on the grounds that they are led by the army. Even when civilian rebel leaders do gain positions of power, it is only when the rebellion has not been led by the leaders of the military that the case is included. Nasser's victory in Egypt in 1952 had to be disqualified on these grounds (among others).

(b) In some cases, for example, Iraq, 1958, there appears to have been considerable mass support for the armed-force initiators of "the revolution," but even so, the rule outlined above was followed.

(c) In some cases, civilian and military leadership are combined. Such joint military and civilian initiative is acceptable, just as long as it is clear that it was not the military who really took the initiative. Of course, the military might "initiate" the rebellion by firing on a crowd, but only if they initiate the fight *against* the regime, not for it, is the case disqualified.

If the military is undividedly active on the side of the rebels, the case is disqualified due to the requirement that both regime and rebel violence must occur.

CASE-SELECTION RULES

In order that the findings not be overinfluenced by the upheavals of two or three countries, a maximum of two successful and two unsuccessful rebellions can be contributed to the universe of cases by a single country. When this maximum is exceeded, then scale is used as the selecting criterion: large rebellions are given priority over smaller rebellions.

Since a period of great upheaval typically follows a successful mass rebellion, due to the crisis of legitimacy, or the conflict between the old and new forces (as occurred for example in Mexico after 1911, and in the U.S.S.R. after 1917), and since this constitutes such a very special social context, successful and unsuccessful rebellions that occur in the wake of successful mass rebellions are disqualified. More specifically, if a successful rebellion qualifies for inclusion, no other case can be included for at least the next 5 years. If, however, the first overthrow is excluded because, for example, it is is too small-scale, or because it is initiated by the military, the next rebellion that qualifies can be selected, even though it may have occurred in the wake of a successful rebellion. There are very few cases like this.

The rule disqualifying mass rebellions that occur within 5 years of a successful mass rebellion does not apply to those that occur in the wake of an unsuccessful rebellion. While this may be a special social context, too, it is not nearly as special, since the old power block has not been overthrown.

Appendix II

Diagrams of Case Selection Procedure

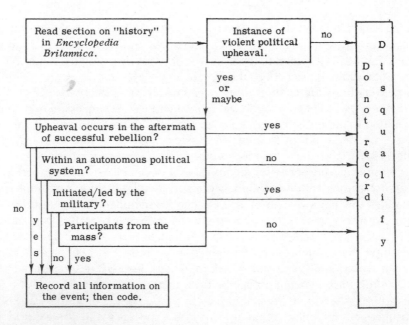

Figure 1. Case-selection procedure: Stage 1. All information on the events that did not reach the criteria set were recorded as insufficient information and then coded.

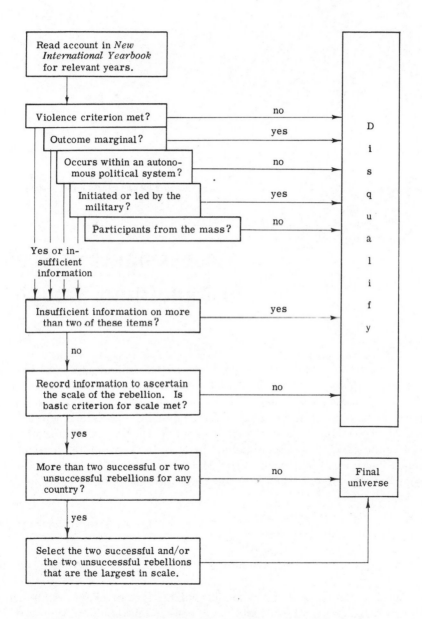

Figure 2. Case-selection procedure: Stage 2.

Appendix III

Assessments of Scale
of Rebellions Sampled

This appendix contains the assessments of the scale of each rebellion in the samples. The reader can thus see the bases for scoring each rebellion as of sufficient scale to be included in the study. For the reader's convenience, the index for evaluating the scale of mass rebellions is presented here as well as in Chapter Four. The mean of the four scores that contributed to the evaluation of the scale of the rebellion had to be at least 1.1 for the rebellion to qualify for inclusion in the study. The score for each of the contributing elements appears enclosed in a square at the beginning of each section.

1. AFGHANISTAN (1929)

(i) Amount of Violence $\boxed{1}$ 151–500 deaths

There is no information on casualties in *EB*, *NIYB,* or *AR*, nor in the better historical sources, on the amount of violence in this rebellion. Wild (1933), a rather poor source, is the closest we have to precise information. According to Wild: "There are no figures of the casualties on either side. It is

154

TABLE III.1

Index for Evaluating the Scale of Mass Rebellion

---

a. *Amount of violence*
    0 = minimal (<150 deaths)
    1 = some (151–500 deaths)
    2 = considerable (501 + deaths)
b. *Number of active rebels*
    0 = few (500)
    1 = some (501–1000)
    2 = considerable (1001 +)
c. *Social-geographical area involved*
    0 = a disturbance of a local character in a rural county or similar limited area; a similar
        limited area; a similar disturbance in several rural counties, or in a small town; a
        disturbance in a larger town; a disturbance in several towns of medium size, or in
        one important city, or in a small province
    1 = a disturbance in a larger province, or in a part of capital city; a disturbance in
        several large provinces, or in the whole capital city
    2 = a disturbance in the capital city and spread over several provinces; a disturbance
        where almost the whole country is involved; a disturbance in the entire country
d. *Duration of the event*
    0 = < 1 week
    1 = 1 week–6 months
    2 = 6 months +

NOTE: If the only information available cites figures of dead and wounded or "casualties"
(which presumably includes wounded, as well as dead), the number of dead are calculated
by Bodart's formula (Richardson, 1960, p. 10):

$$\text{Dead} = \frac{(k + w)}{3}, \text{ where } k = \text{killed}, w = \text{wounded}.$$

fair to assume that they did not reach any startling number. Eye-witnesses
have said, however, that the streets were foul with dead bodies . . .
[p. 217]." And earlier, when describing a particular battle at which there
were 2000 troops, Wild writes that, "800 lay dead the next morning
[p. 206]." Elsewhere, only vague statements like the following are forthcoming. Fraser-Tytler (1967): "For the next few days fierce fighting took
place . . . [p. 215]." Shah (1933): "Vigorous attacks and defense
continued, during which many Royalists were killed [p. 155]." Given
the number of participants and the duration of the rebellion, my estimate of
151–500 deaths errs, I think, on the side of underestimation.

(ii) Number of Active Rebels   2   1001+

When a figure is given for the number of rebels in the Afghanistan rebellion,
it is usually in the thousands. For example, early on in the rebellion, Shah

(1933) writes: "Soon the entire clan of Shinwar was bestirred; *thousands* gathered in battle array [p.151; italics added]." And Fletcher (1965) states that: "The Khugianis and Safia ... now joined in the rising, and a lashkar containing *several thousand* tribesmen moved against the city of Jalalabad [p. 216; italics added]."

When Habibullah Khan, later to become King, first attacked the capital, he had only 300 men, according to Fletcher (*Ibid.*, p. 217) and Shah (1933, p. 153), although Sykes (1940, pp. 312–313) claims that he had 2000 men! Whatever the number was at this point, Habibullah Khan had to withdraw: "But," Fletcher (1965) writes, "now the defenders of Kabul ... made the mistake of pursuing the Bachha (another name for Habibullah) into his snow-covered homeland. Here they found *thousands* of Kohistanis flocking to join the local hero ... [p. 217; italics added]." In general, with all the different tribes that participated, it is clear that there were more than 1000 rebels.

(iii) Social–Geographical Area ⟨2⟩

The rebellion started in the Eastern Province. Later, Habibullah Khan attacked the capital, Kabul. And since he was from the north, this area became involved, too. In addition, according to Shah (1933), "the Southern Province was with the rebels [p. 156]," and finally the Western Province of Herat joined them (p. 161). Thus, the whole country was involved.

(iv) Duration ⟨1⟩ 1 week–6 months

The rebellion lasted 2 months, starting on 14 November 1928 (Fraser-Tytler, 1967, p. 214) and ending with Habibullah Khan assuming power on 17 January 1929 [this is the date in *NIYB* and Shah (1933, p. 166); Fletcher (1965, p. 218) cites January 27].

Scale Score: 1.5

2. ALBANIA (1924)

(i) Amount of Violence ⟨0⟩ <150 deaths

While the descriptions of the Albanian rebellion contain many words, phrases, and sentences indicative that battles and fights occurred, Swire

(1929) claims that "there seems to have been, on both sides, except in isolated cases, a reluctance to shed blood [p. 432]." The only source that gives a figure is *NIYB*, according to which: "After scattered fighting resulting in about 200 casualties the insurgents entered the capital . . . ." But it cannot be assumed that casualties mean deaths; using Bodart's formula to estimate the number of deaths, the figure arrived at is only 66 dead, which produces a score of zero. (See Table III.1 for Bodart's formula.)

(ii) Number of Active Rebels   2   1001+

According to Swire, ". . . contemporary reports indicate that, at most, 12,000 Democrats and 4,000 government supporters took part in the struggle [*Ibid.*, p. 432]."

(iii) Social–Geographical Area   2

The rebellion started in the north from where the northern insurgent forces advanced upon the capital, Tirana. Members of the opposition in the south became active rebels soon afterward. Central Albania (approximately one-third of the country) remained loyal according to Swire (*Ibid.*, pp. 430–431) and Mousset (1930, p. 54), but this still means that most of the country was involved.

(iv) Duration   .5

The sources are somewhat inconsistent regarding duration. According to some, the rebellion lasted less than a week, and according to others, more. Mousset (1930, pp. 53–54) suggests it lasted approximately June 1–9, when Noli was proclaimed President, that is, more than 1 week; the *NIYB* places the beginning at approximately June 6, and the end at June 12 when the new provisional government was set up; that is, less than one week. According to *AR*, it was on June 16 that Noli formed a new government. Swire does not cite a specific date for the beginning; however, he places Zogu's retirement at July 10 and mentions that the new cabinet took office on July 17. It seems most appropriate to score the duration of the rebellion as between the "less than 1 week" and the "1 week to 6 months" categories.

Scale Score: 1.1

3. BOLIVIA (1952)

(i) Amount of Violence   2 501+ deaths

With the exception of Patch (1961), who states that "there was little loss of life [p. 127]," there is considerable agreement that the number of dead in this rebellion is well over 500, the figures ranging from 850 to 3000. For example: according to *HAR*, more than 1000, and up to 3000, persons were killed (Vol. 5, 1952, p. 34); NIYB records 3,000 "casualties" (that is, about 1000 dead, according to Bodart's formula); *F-on-F* reports 850–1500 persons killed, and over 1500 wounded (that is, about 1675 deaths, according to Bodart's formula); and the *Bulletin of Hispanic Studies* vaguely claims that "thousands were killed [Vol. 30, 1953, p. 103]."

(ii) Number of Active Rebels   2 1001+

I could not find any precise figures on the number of active rebels. Malloy (1970) writes that on the first day "the uprising involved relatively few people [p. 157]," but that by the second day "the rebellion had caught on and was spreading [*Ibid.*]." Besides the members of the MNR who initiated the rebellion, the entire police force was involved, together with factory workers and miners. It seems safe to assume, then, that the number of active rebels was over 1000.

(iii) Social–Geographical Area   2

The *HAR* reports that the rebellion "broke out simultaneously in La Paz, Oruro, Cochabamba, Potosí, Trinidad, Sucre, and Santa Cruz." In contrast, Patch (1961) states that "there was little fighting outside La Paz [p. 217]" (the capital). According to Malloy (1970), the uprising was restricted to La Paz on the first day, but by the second, "heavy action" occurred in Cochabamba, Oruro, and Potosí [p. 157]." Since Malloy's description is more consistent with that of *HAR*, and since his whole account is much more thorough and detailed than Patch's, Malloy's facts are accepted here.

(iv) Duration   0 1 week

There is consensus that the rebellion lasted only 3 days, from the morning of April 9 until April 11 (*F-on-F; HAR;* Malloy, 1970; *NIYB;* and Osborne, 1964).
Scale Score: 1.5

4. BRAZIL (1930)

(i) Amount of Violence   0 <150 deaths

Skidmore (1967) gives no information on casualties. Dulles (1967, p. 68), however, informs us that there were 20 deaths by the night of the first day; and that 16 soldiers were killed the next day—October 4. A little later, Dulles mentions 8 more deaths, and then that 35 more were killed, without in any way giving the impression that he is trying to provide exhaustive information on casualties *(Ibid.,* p. 69). Camacho's (1952) description of the event is that: "It was in fact practically a bloodless revolution . . . [p. 46]." However, Bello (1966), asserts that the "delaying" actions of the government "took the lives of many men loyal to the Union [p. 273]." The *NIYB* reports that: "The *coup d'etat* in Rio de Janeiro was accompanied by lively street fighting and a brief counter-revolutionary outbreak, but casualties were slight." And earlier *NIYB* refers to "ten days of fighting," and that the rebels' "triumphant advance from the South against São Paulo and from the North against Rio de Janeiro was retarded by the increasing opposition of government forces."

From these unfortunately vague statements, I think we may conclude that there were fewer than 150 deaths in the Brazilian rebellion. Since some of the accounts of the 1930 rebellion are quite lengthy—the very absence of data on casualties would thus seem to indicate that there were in fact not many deaths.

(ii) Number of Active Rebels   2 1001+

Two sources cite figures on the number of rebels. Young (1967) writes that on the third day: "The number of rebel troops in the field was estimated at from 20–30,000 [p. 63]." Bello (1966) seems skeptical that there were so many: "According to the undoubtedly exaggerated statement of the revolutionists' high command, 30,000 men . . . had moved up from the South [p. 273]." Even if Bello's skepticism is justified, it seems certain that there were more than 1000 rebels.

(iii) Social–Geographical Area   2

Skidmore (1967) writes that "the rebels marched on Rio de Janeiro from South (Rio Grande do Sul), North (Paraíba), and West (Minas Gerais)," and that a "formidable armed oposition" developed "in the states of Rio Grande do Sul, Santa Catarina, and Paraná [p. 5]."

The *NIYB* for 1930 makes the social-geographical area sound greater yet: "The revolt broke out October 3 in the Southern states of Rio Grande do Sul and Minas Gerais and simultaneously in the extreme north of the Republic. Ten days of fighting gave the rebels control of 10 of the 20 states of the federation." Later, *NIYB* describes the "lively street fighting" in Rio de Janeiro. It seems clear, then, that a large portion of the country was involved in the rebellion.

(iv) Duration   [1]   1 week–6 months

All sources are in agreement that the rebellion broke out 3 October 1930 (Young, 1967, p. 54). Bello (1966) cites 24 October 1930 as the date that "the junta delivered the government to Getúlio Vargas ... [p. 274]." On the other hand, according to Skidmore (1967): "The Junta ruled Rio de Janeiro in its own right for ten days before finally delivering power on November 4 to Getúlio Vargas ... [p. 6]." The *NIYB* account agrees with Skidmore, except that it gives November 3 as the day on which Vargas, the leader of the rebellion, was inaugurated. However, this disagreement does not bear on coding categories.

Scale Score: 1.25

5.   CHINA (1927–1949)

(i) Amount of Violence   [2]   501+ deaths

According to Rigg (1951, p. 274), the Chinese Communists admitted having suffered 1,432,500 casualties from 1 July 1946 until their victory in 1949. O'Ballance (1962) also mentions 1½ million as the figure the Communists cited, but states that: ". . . [I]t is quite probable that the Reds had lost at least 2 million killed in four and one half years of civil war since August 1945 [p. 186]." Gittings (1967, p. 304), who appears to be the best source on casualties, provides many sources for his calculations of 1,522,500 casualties over the 1946–1950 period. For once, there is considerable agreement among the sources.

The Communists claimed 1,711,110 Nationalist casualties from 1 July 1946 to 30 June 1950 (Rigg, 1951, p. 255). (There are enormous figures for casualties during the Sino-Japanese war, but this period is not analyzed here.) Since the numbers are so much in excess of the maximum criterion, it seems unnecessary to consider the less accessible figures for the 1927–1937 period.

(ii)   Number of Active Rebels   2   1001+

Gittings (1967, p. 304) and the Communist sources (Liu, 1956, p. 254) both cite the following figures for Communist guerrilla and regular strength combined. June 1945: 1,950,000; June 1946: 1,278,000; June 1948: 2,800,000; June 1949: 4,000,000; June 1950: 5,000,000. The only difference between the two sources is that Liu gives no figure for June 1950; and for June 1946, he cites 1,200,000.

(iii)   Social–Geographical Area   2

By early 1949, Fitzgerald (1952) reports that the Communists "controlled all China north of the Yangtze [p. 115]," while the Kuomintang still held the South and West. Even though the Communists had never controlled many parts of the country before the Nationalist regime was overthrown, this does not mean that the areas that were not controlled by them were not heavily involved in the struggle. Therefore, there is no question that the social-geographical area easily reaches the maximal scale criterion used in this study.

(iv)   Duration   2   6 months +

For a number of reasons I decided to regard 12 April 1927 as the date on which the Chinese rebellion started. Since this date is not generally accepted as the beginning of the rebellion, my decision requires explanation. O'Ballance (1962) reports that the uneasy alliance between the Communists and the supporters of Chiang Kai-shek, who fought together in the Nationalist Army for a united China, finally came to an end on 12 April 1927, when Chiang Kai-shek, supported by his Military Council, "struck hard at the Communists in Shanghai...[p. 35]." O'Ballance continues: "At the end of three days it is believed that he [Chiang Kai-shek] had killed at least 5,000 Communists in this purge. All suspected of Communist sympathies were removed from any position of authority, whilst known Communists were either killed or driven underground. ... Throughout May and June this blood bath continued [Ibid.]." O'Ballance's data reveal, then, that it was not just a violent struggle within the armed forces; nor was it simply a massacre of the Communists: "... in places where the Communists were in control, or were able to do so, they massacred any KMT members suspected of right wing sympathies. There was a pause and then in desperation they reacted, instigating a peasant rising in Hunan [Ibid.]."

On the basis of these data, it seems that 12 April 1927 should be regarded as the date on which the rebellion began. It was 1 October 1949, over 20 years later, that Mao Tse-tung proclaimed the People's Republic of China. Excluding the period of the Sino-Japanese War (for reasons discussed in Chapter Seven), the total duration was about 14 years.

Scale Score: 2

6.   CUBA (1953–1959)

(i) Amount of Violence   2   501 + deaths

Of the major battle of Santa Clara, which occurred near the end of the rebellion, *HAR* writes that "an estimated 3,000 casualties were reported after a few days of fighting (Vol. 12, Nov. 1958, p. 668). And shortly after the rebellion had succeeded, *HAR* reports an "estimated cost of $100 million and some 8,000 lives, excluding victims of Batista's tortures," as the final toll (Vol. 12, Jan. 1959, p. 21). On the other hand, Macgaffey and Barnett (1965) mention, with no disclaimer, that "estimates of fatalities in the struggle against Batista totaled 1,000 in the mountains, 19,000 in the cities [p. 288]." These are the figures quoted by other less careful works, too (for example, Sartre, 1961, p. 56). However, Goldenberg (1965)—one of the better sources on the Cuban rebellion—brings the following light to bear on the question of casualties:

> The official legend speaks of 20,000 dead. But this is a deliberately exaggerated figure: against such a black background the terrorist acts of the revolutionaries themselves will seem negligible. *Nobody* knows the real number of victims. A special edition of Bohemia published soon after the victory of the revolution, contained a long list of the dead of recent years. There were just over 1,000 names. . . . The actual military operation did not cause heavy losses—certainly less than a thousand altogether. But many people were assassinated or became victims of the terror. The police tortured and murdered, the army competed with the police, and pro-Batista armed bands . . . vied with both. . . . Nevertheless there can be no question of anything like 20,000 victims [p. 144].

Although the disagreement between the sources is considerable, there is at least no doubt that there were more than 500 deaths.

(ii) Number of Active Rebels   2   1001 +

On 26 July 1953—the day after which the movement is named—about 163 rebels attempted to overcome Batista's soldiers at the Moncada barracks

(Thomas, 1971). According to Castro, by May 1958, when Batista announced an all-out campaign to crush the guerrillas in the Sierra Maestra, there were fewer than 300 men (*Ibid.,* p. 997). However, other groups were larger: For example, by midsummer of 1958, "there were perhaps 1,000 ex-bandits or free rebels over whom Raúl Castro had more or less established his leadership [p. 994]."

By the end of the rebellion, most sources seem to settle on a figure of around 1000 rebels—more or less. For example, Draper (1962) writes: "The true number was probably closer to 1,000 than to 3,000 [p. 13]." And Goldenberg (1965) states that "reliable sources say that on the day of victory the whole Castro army consisted of 803 men, which together with all other groups made up a force of 1,000 to 1,500 [p. 159]." Macgaffey and Barnett (1965), however, claim that there was "a much larger urban resistance movement . . . [p. 288]." And as I have already noted, they estimate that there were 19,000 casualties in the cities. Even if this figure is a gross overestimation, it is still likely that there were many more rebels than there were casualties, and it seems that there were definitely over 1000 deaths. Most of the sources, however, ignore the urban resistance—perhaps because they so much want to believe that a very small David really can beat Goliath. At any rate Lieuwen (1961) is another source that confirms the view that the number of rebels is much higher than the earlier sources quoted above. According to him: "The final drive occurred in late December as the guerrillas, now 8,000 strong and overwhelmingly supported by the civilian populace, descended from their mountain fortresses and attacked the cities . . . [p. 265]."

(iii) Social–Geographical Area $\boxed{2}$

The Sierra Maestra mountains in the eastern part of Cuba, in Oriente province, was the major locale of the Castro-led rebels during most of the rebellion. Other guerrilla groups were in Las Villas province, and the naval revolt occurred in Cienfuegoes, which is also in Las Villas. There was a large urban resistance movement in the cities: "Throughout the island," write Macgaffey and Barnett (1965), "underground cells of the 26th of July organization and of the closely allied Civic Resistance Movement conducted terrorist activity, distributed propaganda, and brought thousands of persons into participation in the opposition [p. 288]." Santa Clara, a city in Las Villas province, was the locale of the final engagement. The maximum score for social–geographical area is therefore easily met.

(iv) Duration   2   6 months+

There is some consensus that the rebellion had its beginning on 26 July 1953, with the assault on the Moncada barracks. (However, to arrive at a disloyalty score, it seemed more reasonable to consider the date of the invasion, 1 December 1956, as the beginning of the rebellion; see Chapter Seven.) And in early January 1959, Castro became the new ruler of Cuba.

Scale Score: 2

7. MEXICO (1910–1911)

(i) Amount of Violence   2   500+ deaths

The sources examined avoid citing specific figures on casualties, except in the case of Díaz's last-ditch effort to remain in power by "dispersing" the people who had gathered to demand his resignation on 23 May 1911. According to Callcott: "Published accounts admitted seven killed and forty wounded," but, "a better estimate is thirty times those numbers," that is, approximately 210 killed and 1200 wounded. (Callcott presents two sources as references for these figures.) Cline also gives the figure of 200 deaths for this event (see the case description in Chapter Seven).

It is probably because of the way in which the rebellion was conducted that even sources that are quite specific and quantitative when it comes to other aspects of the rebellion, are not quantitative regarding total casualties. Tannenbaum (1933) suggests that it was not the kind of rebellion for which the number of casualties could really be known:

> It was not a revolution that was fought by large armies. There were, it is true, some fairly large battles during the Revolution, but over the whole period these represent only incidents in the way of military history. The real battles of the movement were fought anonymously by little bands of peasants and soldiers to vindicate their right to overthrow the government. Small groups of Indians under anonymous leaders were the Revolution. If the leader was successful, if he was shrewd and quick, and if luck was on his side, he won many skirmishes and escaped with his life. His little band grew after every successful battle. New elements joined in. He acquired more ammunition, more arms, more horses. If he was defeated or killed his little army melted away . . . [p. 119].

However, the number of casualties that occurred on the one occasion mentioned at the beginning of this section, suggests that over the 6-month period, there certainly must have been more than 500.

(ii) Number of Active Rebels | 2 | 1001 + deaths

Cline (1953) indicates that there were approximately 17,200 rebels (p. 122). Ross (1956) more vaguely states that: "The number of fighting effectives of the Maderista movement probably never exceeded twenty thousand ... [p. 152]." Cumberland (1952), on the other hand, while arguing that "it has been impossible to ascertain the exact number of men under arms ...," goes on to quote, without further qualification, that "... the Minister of Governación under the ad interim government reported that there had been approximately seventy thousand [p. 145]." Considerable as this disagreement is, we can at least be sure that there were more than 1000 rebels.

(iii)   Social–Geographical Area | 2 |

Cline (1953) stresses "how small and regionalized was the affair, even at its apogee in May 1911. More than three-quarters (76.8%) of the total fighting strength of the Madero revolution was concentrated in the western and northern states of Mexico [p. 122]." Cumberland's (1952) data, however, suggest a greater social-geographical spread. He writes that: "Armed activity accelerated in March, and within less than two months the Madero forces occupied a respectable portion of the national territory, including many cities [p. 137]." Later Cumberland goes on to say that "hundreds of small groups were under arms in every state ... By May 24 a large number of towns and cities were in revolutionary hands ... [pp. 144–145]." Ross's (1955) description somehow manages to support both Cline and Cumberland. On the one hand he writes that: " ... at least 60 percent of these [the rebels] were concentrated in the northern tier of the states [p. 152]," supporting the regional view. On the other hand, a little later, Ross describes the social–geographical area as follows:

> The revolutionary flame had spread like a prairie fire throughout the republic. ... Only five of the thirty-one territorial entities were untouched by the revolution, and in most of the others the insurgents dominated the major portions. In many states effective federal control was limited to the capital and a few principal cities which, in most instances, were besieged by the rebels. Ambassador Wilson reported that by the time the definitive treaty of peace was signed the revolutionists controlled two-thirds of the country and the remaining one-third was rapidly tending to the same direction [p. 166].

In any of these descriptions, the Mexican rebellion easily meets the maximum score on this dimension.

(iv) Duration   2 6 months+

Cline (1953) writes that: "Premature outbreaks occurred on November 18, 1910... [p. 121]." And elsewhere Cline (1962) says of 20 November 1910 that: "The Revolution officially started on that day... [p. 121]."

Regarding the end of the Mexican rebellion, Cline (1953) writes: "Early on the morning of May 25, 1911 Porfirio Díaz resigned ... [p. 124]." This makes the duration just over 6 months.

Scale Score: 2

8. AUSTRIA (1934)

(i) Amount of Violence   2 501+ deaths

There appear to be at least two sets of figures attributed to official government sources: according to Braunthal (1945, p. 101), he and Hasluck (1938) are in agreement that there were officially 239 dead on both sides and 718 wounded (p. 42). Gulick (1948, p. 1290) and Gregory (1935, p. 264) read the official figures as 314 dead and 805 wounded. Applying Bodart's formula, even the lower estimate would approach 501 deaths. In addition, most students of the Austrian rebellion stress that unofficial sources claimed many more casualties. Hasluck (1938) writes that "the Socialists maintained that at least 1500 fell on their side alone [p. 42]." Deutsch (1924), commander of the Schutzbund, claims that: "The government, to calm down foreign opinion, gave out clearly false figures when it spoke of 300 dead. Unfortunately this number must be multiplied many times. ... The civil war in Austria was one of the bloodiest in the history of the last century [p. 78]." Bauer (1934, p. 6), another leader of the Schutzbund, makes a similar assertion. Gregory (1935), on the other hand, a partisan in the other direction, accepts one of the official figures with the qualification that " ... it is possible that, owing to their tactics of escape, a number of the rebel losses remained officially unaccounted for. But for a three days' civil war nobody can pretend that these losses ... were excessive [p. 264]." In the first-hand account of Gedye, the Central European correspondent of *The Times,* he estimates 1500–2000 Socialists dead, "including a high proportion of women and children," and 5000 wounded (Gulick 1948, p. 1290). This seems to me to be closer to the truth. Since official figures usually do underestimate casualties, especially when the rebellion has been unsuccessful, and since Hasluck is only a secondary source, and all the others are very partisan, I think Gedye provides the most reliable information on this matter.

(ii) Number of Active Rebels $\boxed{2}$ 1001+

Hasluck (1938, p. 42) points out that nearly half the electors were supporters of the Socialist opposition. But obviously this does not mean they were all active participants in the rebellion. Indeed, according to Gulick (1948): "Though all figures on actual participants and active supporters . . . are only guesses, it is certainly true that in the aggregate they were a very small minority of those who might conceivably have joined in a mass revolt [p. 1346]."

The closest there is to specific information on the number of rebels who *were* active in this rebellion comes from Gregory (1935), who writes that: "In actual numbers in Vienna, the Schutzbund, in spite of its suppression, could mobilize about 12,000 armed men [p. 257]." It seems clear from this material, as well as from the data on casualties, that there were more than 1000 rebels.

(iii) Social–Geographical Area $\boxed{2}$

Vienna was the main locale of the rebellion, but battles also occurred in Upper Austria, and, according to Gulick (1948), the best source on this rebellion, ". . . the most significant conflicts outside of Vienna took place in Styria. From various accounts it is clear that something like twenty communities, including suburbs of Graz, were the scenes of clashes [p. 1289]." Hasluck describes the social-geographical area covered as follows: "[F]ighting broke out, spreading rapidly throughout the city. Then the contest spread to the provinces; in Linz, Graz and Steyr there were sharp battles . . . [p. 42]." While there are other data on social–geographical area, it is already evident that the maximum scale criterion is met.

(iv) Duration $\boxed{0}$ < 1 week

The sources (Hasluck, 1938; Bauer, 1924, p. 6; Gregory, 1935, p. 262) are in agreement that the rebellion lasted February 12–15, when "the Government offered a free pardon to all who would surrender, excepting only the leaders. The Vienna Socialists were already beaten, and surrender followed."

Scale Score: 1.5

9. BURMA (1948–1953)

(i) Amount of Violence   [2] 501 + deaths

Tinker (1967), using *The Nation,* 16 September 1952, as his source, reports that government "casualties" were: "3,424 dead, including 1,342 army personnel [p. 50]." Including both rebel and government forces, Trager (1966) claims 3 years later that: "By the end of 1955, nearly 28,000 soldiers and civilians had been killed ... [p. 118]." Such figures leave no doubts as to how the amount of violence should be scored, even if a large proportion of these casualties were to be Karens (the group that has to be ignored for purposes of evaluating the scale of the rebellion).

(ii) Number of Active Rebels   [2] 1001 +

Estimates of the number of rebels vary enormously. Trager (1966) writes that:

> There are no reliable estimates of the number of insurgents involved in the fighting, and the following figures for 1948–1949 represent at best a mere guess. The two groups of Communists, the BCP and CPB, had approximately 5,000 armed members in all. They were joined by approximately 4,000 armed PVO's, 700–1400 army mutineers, and 3,000 police and local militia (situandans). Thus there were approximately 13,000 armed leftists [p. 107].

However, other sources disagree greatly with some of these figures. In contrast to Trager's (1966) estimate of 4000 PVO's, Tinker (1967, p. 34) cites a figure of 300,000 for this group. (This figure, for which Furnivall is the source, is "much higher than any other estimate," according to Tinker, 1967, p. 34). And, at the start of the rebellion in 1945, Tinker claims that the Communists had 25,000 "active supporters in arms" as compared with Trager's (1966, p. 35) 5,000. In 1949, U Nu, the Premier, estimated that there were 10,000 rebellious Communists (*Ibid.,* p. 47).

Still other estimates are given by other sources, and there are figures on the fluctuations over time. But for the purposes of ascertaining scale of rebellion, it is quite clear that the non-Karen rebellion was of a very large scale according to this criterion.

(iii) Social–Geographical Area   [2]

Tinker (1967) provides a map on which he indicates the areas dominated by the rebels February–May 1949, and beside which he lists the number of towns captured by the different rebel groups in 1949 (pp. 44–45). The Communists captured Tharrawaddy, Pyinmana, Yamethin, Myingyan, Pakokku, and Henzada, the last one together with the PVO; and the PVO army mutineers captured Prome, Thayetmyo, Magwe, Minbu, Yenangyaung, Chank, Sandoway, and Kyaukpyu *(Ibid.)*. Most of these towns are in central and western Burma. Fifteen towns are mentioned as captured by the Karens, two of these in cooperation with the Communists, but this group is not relevent here.

There can be no doubt that this case reaches the large scale criterion on social-geographical area.

(iv) Duration ☐2 6 months+

At the time Burma became a republic, 4 January 1948, some Communist rebels were already in rebellion. But the major rebellion began at the end of March 1948 (Tinker, 1967, p. 35; Trager, 1966, p. 99).

Regarding when the rebellion ended, there is much less consensus, as was discussed in the remarks introductory to this case. In Chapter Eight I explained why I decided to follow Hall's judgment that the rebellion was crushed in 1954.

Scale Score: 2

10. COLOMBIA (1948)

(i) Amount of Violence ☐2 501+ deaths

The assessments of the numbers killed vary enormously for the Colombian rebellion. The contemporary reports give much the lowest figures, for example, *F-on-F* reports 300 casualties; *Newsweek*, that "the director of the city morgue reported 300 dead"; and "Foreign correspondents put the number of dead alone at over 500 . . . ." According to Beaulac (1951), the American Ambassador at that time: "The government estimated that 1,000 persons were killed throughout the country [p. 251]." These figures are much lower than those given by the two best sources. Dix (1967) states that there were "several thousand deaths [pp. 103–104]," and Martz (1962), that: "Several thousand died before nightfall, and countless more in the dark hours that followed [p. 56]." Of course it is usual for governments to underestimate casualties, at least, when they win; moreover, it is known that censorship was imposed, which might account for the low estimates in the more contemporary accounts. In any event, the discrepancy among figures is still enormous. Since I have most confidence in the assessments of Martz and Dix, as their work seems to be the most careful, the amount of violence easily meets the maximum for this criterion.

(ii) Number of Active Rebels   2 1001+

None of the sources provides even an estimate of the number of rebels. The only figures available are for the number of Gaitán supporters (Gaitán was the charismatic leader of the masses whose assassination was the precipitant of the rebellion). In 1946, Gaitán received 340,000 votes, according to Bernstein (1964, p. 138), or 360,263, according to Galbraith (1966, p. 146). But this is not really a satisfactory indicator of the number of rebels. Fluharty (1957, p. 100) writes of one event that "a crowd of hundreds" went to burn and loot the President's home; again this informaton is rather minimal and vague.

While the data are unsatisfactory, it seems reasonable to estimate that there must have been over 1000 rebels, from the general descriptions of the upheaval (see Chapter Eight), from the casualties, and from the social–geographical area.

(iii)   Social–Geographical Area   2

Galbraith (1966) describes the upheaval as a "nation-wide outbreak of rioting and looting which reached its greatest height in the capital [p. 146]." Similar descriptions are given by Bernstein (1964, p. 139), Fluharty (1957, p. 108), Beaulac (1951 p. 251, and *NIYB* (1948). Martz (1962) goes into rather more detail than some of the other reports:

> As the capital quieted down, the outburst of pent-up emotion and resentment spread across the nation. For at least a month there was serious fighting in rural areas . . . . The worst outbreak triggered by the Bogotá holocaust took place in Cali and the surrounding region. In the capital of Valle del Cauca the rebels temporarily triumphed [p. 58].

Other cities specifically mentioned as areas of rebellion by Martz and *KA* are Cartagena, Barranquilla, Puerto Tejada, and "virtually all of the Cauca Valley [*Ibid.,* p. 60]."

(iv) Duration   1   1 week–6 months

According to Beaulac (1951), ". . . it was two weeks before all snipers were eliminated [p. 251]." Fluharty (1957) states that: "Revolutionaries

held out against the army in some towns for as long as a month [p. 108]."
And Martz, quoted above, reports that there was serious fighting "for at
least a month [p. 58]." Hence, the Colombian rebellion falls into the
middle duration category.

Scale Score: 1.75

11. CUBA (1912)

(i) Amount of Violence   2   501+ deaths

Rowland (1926, p. 85) mentions that 800 rebels surrendered "while the
rebellion was still in progress," and 600 more later. This information is
followed by the broad statement that: "In the period between the death of
Estenoz [on June 27] and that of Ivonet [July 18] most of the insurrectionists
had been killed, captured or had surrendered [p. 86]." Despite the fact
that Rowland's account of the rebellion is quite detailed, he gives no more
specific information on the amount of violence than this. The *NIYB* simply
states that the rebels "suffered heavy losses"; and *EB* reports that "thousands lost their lives." Chapman (1927, p. 312), Beals (1933, p. 62),
and Strode (1934, p. 235) all agree that 3000 blacks were killed, though I
suspect Chapman is the source for Beals and Strode. (Beal's book, published after Chapman's, is replete with phrases and sentences that are
nearly identical to some of those found in Chapman.) It seems likely, then,
that there were more than 500 deaths.

(ii) Number of Active Rebels   2   1001+

Rowland (1926) writes that: "There were various estimates of the forces
. . . ranging from about twenty-five hundred to over four thousand, at the
height of the revolt [p. 75]." Chapman (p. 312), Beals (p. 62), and
Kennedy (1913, p. 467) are all also in agreement that about 4000 blacks
were active rebels.

(iii)   Social–Geographical Area   2

Fitzgibbon (1935) writes that on a particular day "armed bands of negroes
rose in Havana, Santa Clara, and Oriente [p. 146]." Chapman (1927,
p. 310) states that it ". . . was soon well in hand everywhere but the
Oriente, especially in the section running from the neighborhood of

Guantánamo to San Luis . . .," but he fails to explain further where "everywhere" was.

According to the most detailed source, Rowland (1926), the first outbreak occurred in Santa Clara province, where there were several local outbreaks (p. 73), but Oriente was "the main scene of operations [p. 72]." Only about 30 or 40 rebels "took the field" in the provinces of Matanzas, Pinar del Rio, Havana, and Camagüey *(Ibid.)*. At one point the rebels controlled several cities in the Oriente: "Santiago de Cuba, El Caney, El Cristo, San Luis, Songo, La Maya, Sampré, Tiguabos, Guantánamo and Daiquiri [p. 75]." It seems clear that the maximum criterion for social–geographical area is met.

(iv) Duration   1 1 week–6 months

Fitzgibbon (1935, p. 149) and Chapman (1927, p. 310) assert that the rebellion started May 20; *NIYB*, Johnson (1920, Vol. IV, p. 306), and Strode (1934, p. 235) cite May 22 as the date, and Rowland (1926, p. 72), May 18. Chapman (p. 313), Strode (p. 235), and Rowland (p. 86) agree that "by July 18 the last body of rebels had been cut to pieces or taken." Fitzgibbon (1935) cites June 27, the day that one of the leaders, Estenoz, was killed, as "the virtual end of the rebellion [p. 150]." Either way, the duration of the Cuban rebellion falls within the 1 week–6 months category.

Scale Score: 1.75

12. HONDURAS (1933)

(i) Amount of Violence   1 151–500 deaths

Three hundred men are reported killed or wounded after the opening 12-hour battle of the Honduran rebellion, November 15 (*NYT*, Nov. 16; *NIYB*, 1932). On November 30, there is mention of "heavy fighting," and that "Red Cross workers hurriedly left the city toward the battlefront" to treat the wounded, but no figures are given for this battle (*NYT*, Nov. 30). "Numerous casualties" are reported for another battle, and regarding yet another: "15 rebels were killed and many wounded . . . [*Ibid.*]." For a 15-hour battle on December 6, "the total casualties were not given but it was reported that at least 150 rebels were killed [NYT, Dec. 7]." On December 24, "two nationalist fores attacked rebels near Langue. The fighting lasted 2½ hours, during which airplane bombing killed many rebels [*NYT*, Dec. 25]." In another region near Pespire, "53 rebels were killed any many wounded . . . in a 3 hour fight [*Ibid.*]."

Stokes (1950), who gives this rebellion only two or three sentences worth of attention in his book on Honduras, writes that the "uprising" was "put down only after considerable loss of life and destruction of property [p. 56]." Erring, then, on the side of underestimation, the number of deaths is estimated to fall within the 151–500 category.

(ii) Number of Active Rebels $\boxed{2}$ 1001+

In addition to the figures on number of dead and wounded above, it is known that the rebels came from the party of the Liberals, who were defeated in a recent election; that is, the rebels belonged to one of the two major political groups. This suggests that there was, at least, a great deal of potential support for the rebels. We are also told that 1500 federal troops were used to try to take back Santa Rosa from the rebels. In addition, an unspecified number of Curaren Indians joined the insurgents. Figures for at least one battle are given as 600 rebels and 900 government troops. Hence, it seems reasonable to estimate the total number of rebels at over 1000.

(iii) Social-Geographical Area $\boxed{2}$

As *NIYB* reports: "Numerous towns and villages in various parts of the republic were occupied by rebel bands . . . ." In some of the 25 reports on the Honduran rebellion published in the *New York Times*, many of the towns where disturbances occurred are named; for example, San Pedro, Nacaome, Trujillo, La Ceiba, La Esperanza, Puerto Cortes, Santa Barbara, Nacaomi, Pespire, Santa Rosa, Gracias, Aceituno, Curaren, Labrea, Langue, San Marcos, San Lorenso, Amapala, and several others. It seems clear, then, that the maximum criterion is reached for social-geographical area.

(iv) Duration $\boxed{1}$ 1 week–6 months

The rebellion started on 14 November 1932, according to *The New York Times,* and November 13 according to *NIYB.* The *NYT* account has it that the rebels were finally defeated 14 January 1933; thus, the rebellion was almost exactly 2 months in duration. Stokes (1950), on the other hand, writes that: "The revolution was quelled by April, 1933 [p. 56]." However, this difference does not alter the assessment that the rebellion lasted less than 6 months.

Scale Score: 1.5

13. ITALY (1914)

(i) **Amount of Violence**   ☐ number of deaths
                                                      unknown

Numerous qualitative statements are made about violence in the Italian rebellion. For example: Horowitz (1963) states that: ". . . violence became the order of the day in those areas"—Marche and Romagna; Italy had "the appearance of a country in the midst of civil war"; and "violent clashes took place in many rural areas [p. 93]." According to Chorley (1943): "There was a good deal of violence; for days the towns were held by the people, soldiers were beseiged in their barracks . . . [p. 76]." Finer (1935) mentions that: "There was considerable violence [p. 57]." However, the only source to give any quantitative information is *NIYB* (in the section under "Syndicalism"): "According to the statement of Premier Salandra, more than 100 soldiers and police were wounded, many fatally."

It seems to me that the qualitative statements suggest there were many more than 100 casualties; after all, the Premier mobilized 100,000 soldiers to suppress the rebellion (Hughes, 1967, p. 98; Smith 1959, p. 291). Yet, in the absence of any quantitative data beyond the *NIYB* report, it seems most reasonable to leave this figure as an unknown, especially since some sources suggest that the armed forces were used with restraint. For example, Horowitz (1963) writes: "The government, exercising fore-bearance, did not bring to bear the full weight of its police and military forces, but waited for the storm to spend itself [p. 93]."

(ii) **Number of Active Rebels**   ☐ 2 1001 +

Once again, the sources seem shy of figures, except for *NIYB*, which mentions that 15,000 employees of the state railways participated "in the revolutionary movement." But here I think it *is* possible to make an estimate. For it seems unlikely that an army of 100,000 would be used to quell fewer than 1,000 rebels, particularly since the total peace strength of the regular army was 305,000, that is one-third of the army was mobi-lized to deal with the rebellion (U.S., Department of War, 1916, p. 66). I also doubt that fewer than 1000 rebels could cover the social-geographical area, about which there are more specific data.

(iii) **Social–Geographical Area**   ☐ 2

All sources are in agreement that the disturbances were most serious in Romagna and the Marches (see *NIYB*, Syndicalism). However, many other areas were also involved. According to Seton-Watson (1967):

> A wave of disorder spread across Italy. . . . There were riotous demonstrations and
> barricades in Rome and the great cities. The climax was reached in Emilie and the
> Marches where authority virtually collapsed. . . . Ancona itself was held by the
> rebels for a week. In Milan the syndicalists rioted under Corridoni [p. 394].

Salomone (1945) likewise describes the rebellion as very widespread. After
its beginning in Ancona, "Red Week had grown into an insurrection
spreading over all Italy from the 'red' strongholds of the Romagna and the
Marches [p. 60]." The maximal criterion for social–geographical area,
then, appears to have been met.

(iv) Duration ☐1 1 week–6 months

Nearly all the sources refer to the rebellion as "Red Week," yet several
descriptions suggest it lasted somewhat longer. For example: Seton-Watson
(1967) writes that in Emilia "restoration of order took 10 days [p. 394]."
And Sprigge (1944) writes that: "The restoration of order in the Romagna
caused Salandra no great trouble. The powers of the State were able, in a
few brief weeks, to put an end to the petty outbreaks of the agrarian ex-
tremists [p. 110]." And Croce (1963) actually claims that: "By the end
of July peace had been restored [p. 269]"; since it began in the first week
of June, this would make the duration considerably longer than 1 week. It
seems reasonable, then, to regard the event as lasting from 1 week to 6
months.

Scale Score: 1.7

14. SPAIN (1934)

(i) Amount of Violence ☐2 501+ deaths

The official figures, published by the government months after the rebellion
[see Peers (1936)], showed a total of "1,335 killed, of whom 1,051
were civilians, 100 officers and men of the civil guard, 98 soldiers and 86
police and excise officers. The wounded numbered 2,951, rather more
than two-thirds of whom were civilians [p. 171]." Smith (1965, p.
448) and Thomas (1961, p. 84) cite similar overall figures. However,
Thomas points out that: "Such figures are likely to be over modest, though
it is doubtful whether they reached the number of 5,000 later claimed by the
victims of the repression [*Ibid.*, p. 84]." The *NIYB* reports figures in
between the official and rebel estimates—3,500 killed and 10,000 wounded.

(ii) **Number of Active Rebels**   2   1001+

Once again, there are large discrepancies in the figures cited for the number of rebels. Peers (1936, p. 170) and Smith (1965, p. 447) write that there were 6000 rebels in Asturias—by far the most important locale of the rebellion. Thomas (1961), on the other hand, claims that: "Thirty thousand workers had been mobilized for battle within ten days [p. 80]." In support of this figure, Thomas reports another writer, Grossi, as stating that there were 50,000 miners under arms *(Ibid.)*. Jackson (1965, p. 153) quotes Brenan as giving the figure of 70,000, and two other sources as etimating 20–30,000. Estimates that range 6,000–70,000 are most unsatisfactory; nevertheless the maximum scale criterion of 1000 is certainly met.

(iii) **Social–Geographical Area**   2

De Madariaga (1958) writes that: "A general strike paralyzed Madrid, Barcelona, Valencia, Seville, Cordoba, San Sebastian, Bilbao and Santander [p. 433]." But the sources agree that: "The rebellion soon revealed three centers: Oviedo, Barcelona, Madrid [*Ibid.*]." According to Thomas (1961), the "other outbursts in the rest of Spain [p. 79]" were of much less importance. Oviedo, capital of the Province of Asturias, was the site where the rebellion was by far the most severe. In any case, the maximum social-geographical criterion is easily met.

(iv) **Duration**   1   1 week–6 months

5 October 1934 is the date of the rebellious outbreak. On October 10, the *Bulletin of Spanish Studies* (Vol. II, p. 13) reported that practically the whole of Spain had been "tranquilized"—except Asturias. Then according to Thomas (1961), "after fifteen days of war and revolution . . . the rebels finally surrendered [pp. 83–84]." Manuel (1938) and most of the other sources give a similar time estimate, though Manuel adds: "The anarchists fought on for days after the official surrender [p. 140]." The *NIYB* makes the duration appear to be somewhat longer: "It was seveal weeks before troops broke the stubborn resistance of the miners of Asturias." Fortunately this disagreement is not relevant given my coding categories for this variable, as the duration was clearly less than 6 months and longer than 1 week.

Scale Score: 1.75

Bibliography

The bibliography is arranged to indicate:

1. General Sources: These are the works, cited or consulted, that were relevant to the preparation of the volume as a whole. A more comprehensive bibliography on the general topic of rebellion and political upheaval may be found in Gurr (1970a).
2. Sources Used in Obtaining a Universe of Mass Rebellions.
3. Case Study Sources: These are all the cited and some of the consulted works for each of the 14 successful and unsuccessful mass rebellions. The case study sources are listed by case study in alphabetical order for the reader's convenience.*

To prevent the bibliography from becoming unwieldy, I have omitted most references to revolutions and rebellions that were not drawn in the random samples, unless they were cited in the text.

* See Adam (1971a, b) for more comprehensive bibliographies on South Africa.

GENERAL SOURCES

Adam, Heribert
  1971a (Editor) *South Africa: Sociological Perspectives.* London and New York: Oxford
      Univ. Press.
  1971b *Modernizing racial domination.* Berkeley: Univ. of California Press.
Ahmad, Eqbal
  1965 "Revolutionary warfare: How to tell when the rebels have won. *Nation,* **201.**
Alexander, Robert J.
  1958 *The Bolivian national revolution.* New Brunswick, New Jersey: Rutgers Univ. Press.
Alker, Hayward R., Jr., and Bruce M. Russett
  1964 On measuring inequality. *Behavioral Science,* **9.**
AlRoy, Gil Carl
  1965 The meaning of "peasant revolution": The Cuban case. *International Review of
      History and Political Science,* **2.**
  1966 *The involvement of peasants in internal war.* Princeton, New Jersey: Center of Inter-
      national Studies, Princeton University, Research Monograph No. 24.
  1967 Revolutionary conditions in Latin America. *Review of Politics,* **19.**
Amann, Peter
  1962 Revolution: A redefinition. *Political science quarterly,* **87.**
Andreski, Stanislav
  1967 *Parasitism and subversion: The case of Latin America.* New York: Pantheon.
  1968 *Military organization and society.* Berkeley, California: Univ. of California Press.
Arendt, Hannah
  1938–1967 Armies of the world. *Britannica book of the year.*
  1958 *The origins of totalitarianism.* New York: Meridian.
  1960 Revolution and public happiness. *Commentary,* **30.**
  1962 The International Commission of Jurists reports.
  1963 *On revolution.* New York: Viking Press.
  1968 *Military organization and society.* Berkeley, California: Univ. of California Press.
  1968 Towards a praxeological theory of conflict. *Orbis,* **11,** Winter.
  1969 *On Violence,* N.Y.: Harcourt.
Baechler, Jean
  1970 *Les phénomènes révolutionnaires.* Paris: Presses Universitaires de France.
Bailey, Norman A.
  1968 Towards a praxeological theory of conflict. *Orbis,* **11.**
Barker, Ernest (Ed., Trans.)
  1962 *The politics of Aristotle.* New York and London: Oxford Univ. Press.
Beaulac, Willard L.
  1951 *Career ambassador.* New York: Macmillan.
Beals, Carleton
  1932 *Porfirio Díaz.* Philadelphia: Lippincott.
Bello, José M.
  1966 *A history of modern Brazil, 1889–1964,* trans. by J. L. Taylor. Stanford, California:
      Stanford Univ. Press.

Beqiraj, Mehmet
  1966   *Peasantry in revolution*. Ithaca, New York: Center for International Studies, Cornell
        Univ.
Berger, Peter L., and Richard J. Neuhaus
  1970   *Movement and revolution*. Garden City, New York: Doubleday.
Bernstein, Harry
  1964   *Venezuela and Columbia*. New Jersey: Prentice-Hall.
Bienen, Henry
  1968a   (Editor) *The military intervenes: Case studies in political development*. New York:
         Russell Sage.
  1968b *Violence and social change*. Chicago: Univ. of Chicago Press.
Billington, James H.
  1966   Six views of the Russian revolution. *World Politics,* **18,** April.
Binkley, Robert C.
  1934   An anatomy of revolution. *The Virginia Quarterly Review,* **10,** October.
Blake, J. A.
  1970   The organization as instrument of violence: The military case. *Sociological Quarter-
        ly,* **11,** Summer.
Blanksten, George I.
  1958   Revolutions. In H. E. Davis (Ed.), *Government and politics in Latin America*.
          New York: Ronald Press.
Blasier, Cole
  1967   Studies of social revolution: Origins in Mexico, Bolivia and Cuba. *Latin American
        Research Review,* **2,** Summer.
Bodart, Gaston
  1916   *Losses of life in modern wars*. Oxford: Clarendon Press.
Bordua, David J. (Ed.)
  1967   *The police; Six sociological essays*. New York: Wiley.
Borkenau, Frantz
  1962   *World communism*. Ann Arbor, Michigan: Univ. of Michigan Press.
Braunthal, Julius
  1945   *In search of the millennium*. London: Victor Gollancz.
Brennan, Ray
  1959   *Castro, Cuba, and justice*. Garden City, New York: Doubleday.
Brinton, Crane
  1930   *The Jacobins: An essay in the new history*. New York: Macmillan.
  1937   Social-astrology. *The Southern Review,* **3.**
  1952   *The anatomy of revolution*. New York: Knopf.
Brogan, Dennis W.
  1951   *The price of revolution*. New York: Harper.
Bunting, Brian
  1964   *The rise of the South African reich*. London: Penguin.
Calvert, Peter
  1967   Revolution: The politics of violence. *Political Studies,* **15,** February.
Calvert, Peter
  1970a   *A study of revolution*. Oxford: Clarendon Press.

Calvert, Peter
   1970b *Revolution.* New York: Praeger.
Camacho, Jorge A.
   1952 *Brazil: An interim assessment.* London: Royal Institute of International Affairs.
Cantril, Hadley
   1941 *The psychology of social movements.* New York: Wiley.
Carr, E. H.
   1964 *Studies in revolution.* New York: Grosset and Dunlap.
Carstens, Kenneth
   1973 Economic conditions of Africans in South Africa (unpublished manuscript), Harvard
          Divinity School, January.
Chapelle, Dickey
   1962 How Castro won. In F. M. Osanka (Ed.), *Modern guerrilla war: Fighting communist
          movements, 1941–1961.* New York: Free Press.
Chorley, Katherine
   1943 *Armies and the art of revolution.* London: Faber and Faber.
Clausewitz, Carl Von
   1918 *On war,* Vols. I–III. London: Kegan Paul.
Cobb, Richard
   1970 *The police and the people.* Oxford: Clarendon Press.
Cohn, Norman R. C.
   1957 *The pursuit of the millennium.* London: Martin Secker and Warburg.
Conner, James E. (Ed.)
   1968 *Lenin, on politics and revolution; Selected writings.* New York: Western.
Connery, Robert H. (Ed.)
   1968 Urban riots: Violence and social change. *Proceedings of the Academy of Political
          Science.* **29,** July.
Coser, Lewis
   1956 *The functions of social conflict.* Glencoe, Illinois: Free Press.
   1961 The termination of conflict. *Journal of conflict Resolution,* **5,** December.
Cross, James Eliot
   1963 *Conflict in the shadows: The nature and politics of guerrilla war.* Garden City, New
          York: Doubleday.
Crozier, Brian
   1960 *The rebels: A study of post-war insurrections.* London: Chatto and Windus.
Cumberland, Charles C.
   1952 *Mexican revolution.* Austin, Texas: Univ. of Texas Press.
Dahrendorf, Ralf
   1959 *Class and class conflict in industrial society.* Stanford, California: Stanford Univ.
          Press.
Davies, James C.
   1962 Toward a theory of revolution. *American Sociological Review.* **27.**
   1967 The circumstances and causes of revolution: A review. *Journal of Conflict Resolu-
          tion,* **11,** June.
   1969 The J-curve of rising and declining satisfactions as a cause of some great revolutions
          and a contained rebellion. In H. D. Graham and T. R. Gurr (Eds.), *Violence in
          America; Historical and comparative perspectives.* Washington D.C.: U.S.
          Government Printing Office.
   1971 (Editor) *When men revolt and why.* New York: Free Press.

DeBray, Régis
    1967   *Revolution in the revolution? Armed struggle and political struggle in Latin America,*
            Translated by Bobbye Ortiz. New York: Grove Press.
DeGrazia, Sebastian, and Livio C. Stecchini
    1965   *The coup d'etat: Past significance and modern technique.* China Lake, California:
            U.S. Ordinance Test Station.
De Tocqueville, Alexis
    1955   *The old regime and the French revolution,* Translated by Stuart Gilbert. Garden City,
            New York: Doubleday.
Deutsch, Karl
    1953   *Nationalism and social communication.* Cambridge, Massachusetts: Massachusetts
            Institute of Technology Press.
    1964   External involvement in internal war. In H. Eckstein (Ed.), *Internal war.* New York:
            Free Press.
Douglas, William O.
    1969   *Points of rebellion.* New York: Random House.
Draper, Theodore
    1962   *Castro's revolution. Myths and realities.* New York: Praeger.
Echeverria, Rafael Otero
    1959   Reportaje a una revolucíon de Batista á Fidel Castro. Santiago de Chile: Editorial
            del Pacifico South America.
Eckstein, Harry (Ed.)
    1964   *Internal war: Problems and approaches.* New York: Free Press.
Eckstein, Harry
    1965   On the etiology of internal wars. *History and Theory,* **4.**
Eckstein, Harry, and David Ernest Apter (Eds.)
    1963   *Comparative politics; A reader.* New York: Free Press.
Edwards, Lyford P.
    1927   *The natural history of revolution.* Chicago: Univ. of Chicago Press.
Eisenstadt, S. N.
    1963   *The political systems of empires.* Glencoe, Illinois: Free Press.
Ellwood, Charles A.
    1905–1906   A psychological theory of revolution. *American Journal of Sociology,* **11.**
Fagg, John Edwin
    1965   *Cuba, Haiti, and the Dominican Republic.* Englewood Cliffs, New Jersey: Prentice-
            Hall.
Fall, Bernard B. (Ed.)
    1967   *Ho Chi Minh on revolution; Selected writings, 1920–1966.* New York: Praeger.
Fanon, Frantz
    1965   *A dying colonialism.* New York: Grove Press.
    1966   *The wretched of the earth.* New York: Grove Press.
    1967   *Towards the African revolution; Political essays,* translated by Haakon Chevalier.
            New York: Grove Press.
Feierabend, Ivo K.
    1962   Exploring political stability: A note on the comparative method. *Western Political
            Quarterly,* **15,** September.
Feierabend, Ivo K., and Rosalind L. Feierabend
    1966   Aggressive behaviors within polities, 1948–1962: A cross-national study. *Journal
            of Conflict Resolution,* **10.**

Feierabend, Ivo K., Feierabend, Rosalind L., and Nesvold, Betty A.
   1969   Social change and political violence: Cross-national patterns. In H. D. Graham
          and T. R. Gurr (Eds.), *Violence in America*. Washington, D.C.: U.S. Govern-
          ment Printing Office.
Feldberg, Roslyn L.
   1970   Political systems and the role of the military. *Sociological Quarterly*, **11,** Spring.
Feldman, Arnold S.
   1964   Violence and volatility: The likelihood of revolution. In H. Eckstein (Ed.), *Internal
          war: Problems and approaches*. New York: Free Press.
Ferguson, J. Halcro
   1963   *The revolutions of Latin America*. London: Thames and Hudson.
Finer, S. E.
   1962   *The man on horseback; The role of the military in politics*. London: Pall Mall.
First, Ruth
   1972   Jonathan Steele and Christabel Gurney, *The South African connection; Western
          investment in apartheid*. London: Temple Smith.
Fitzgibbon, Russell H.
   1956a A statistical evaluation of Latin American democracy. *Western Political Quarterly*,
          9.
   1956b Revolutions: Western hemisphere. *South Atlantic Quarterly*, **55.**
   1963   Revolution in Latin America: A tentative prognosis. *Virginia Quarterly Review*,
          39, Spring.
Fletcher, Arnold
   1965   *Afghanistan, highway of conquest*. Ithaca, New York: Cornell Univ. Press.
Fluharty, Lee Vernon
   1957   *Dance of the millions: Military rule and the social revolution in Columbia, 1930–
          1956*. Pittsburgh: Univ of Pittsburgh Press.
Foot, M. R. D.
   1961   *Men in uniform: Military manpower in modern industrial societies*. London:
          Weidenfeld and Nicolson.
Fossum, Egil
   1967   Factors influencing the occurrence of military coups d'etat in Latin America. *Journal
          of Peace Research*, **3.**
Fraser-Tytler, William Kerr
   1967   *Afghanistan: A study of political developments in central and southern Asia*. 3rd ed.
          London: Oxford Univ. Press.
Freeman, Thomas (Pseud.)
   1963   *The crisis in Cuba*. Derby, Connecticut: Monarch Books.
Friedrich, Carl
   1954   (Editor) *Totalitarianism*. Cambridge, Massachusetts: Harvard Univ. Press.
   1966   (Editor) *Revolution*. New York: Atherton Press.
   1963   *Man and his government; An empirical theory of politics*. New York: McGraw-Hill.
Friedrich, Carl, and Z. Brzezinski
   1961   *Totalitarian dictatorship and autocracy*. New York: Praeger.
Friere, Paulo
   1968   *Pedagogy of the oppressed*. New York: Herder and Herder.
Fuller, J. F. C.
   1946   *Armament and history*. London: Eyre & Spottiswoode.

Galula, David
  1964   *Counterinsurgency warfare: Theory and practice.* New York: Praeger.
Gedye, George E. R.
  1939   *Fallen bastions; The central European tragedy.* London: Victor Gollancz.
Gerth, H. H., and Mills, C. Wright
  1958   *From Max Weber: Essays in sociology.* New York: Oxford Univ. Press.
Geschwender, James A.
  1968   Explorations in the theory of social movements and revolutions. *Social Forces,* **67,**
         December.
Giap, Vo-nguyen
  1962   *People's war, people's army: The Viet Cong insurrection manual for underdeveloped
         countries.* New York: Praeger.
Gittings, John
  1967   *The role of the Chinese army.* London: Oxford Univ. Press.
Gluckman, Max
  1963   Civil war and theories of power in Barotse-land: African and medieval analogies.
         Yale law journal, **72,** Summer.
Goldenberg, Boris
  1965   *The Cuban revolution and Latin America.* New York: Praeger.
Goode, William J.
  1972   Presidential address: The place of force in human society. *American sociological
         review,* **37,** October.
Goodspeed, Donald J.
  1962   *The conspirators: A study of the coup d'etat.* New York: Viking Press.
Gottschalk, Louis
  1944   Causes of revolution. *American journal of sociology,* **50,** July.
Graham, Hugh Davis and Gurr, Ted Robert, (Eds.)
  1969   *Violence in America: Historical and comparative perspectives.* Washington D.C.:
         National Commission of the Causes and Prevention of Violence.
Greene, T. N. (Ed.)
  1962   *The guerrilla and how to fight him.* New York: Praeger.
Gregory, John D.
  1935   *Dolfuss and his times.* London: Hutchinson and Co.
Griffith, Samuel B.
  1967   The Chinese people's liberation army. New York: McGraw-Hill.
Gross, Feliks
  1958   *The seizure of politics in a century of revolutions.* New York: Philosophical Library.
Gruening, Ernest
  1928   *Mexico and its heritage.* New York: Century.
Guevara, Che
  1968a *Reminiscences of the Cuban Revolutionary War.* Translated by V. Ortiz. New York:
         Monthly Review Press.
  1968b *Guerrilla warfare.* Translated by J. P. Morray. New York: Random House.
Guevara, Ernesto
  1961   *Che Guevara on guerrilla warfare.* Translated by Harries-Clichy Peterson. New York:
         Praeger.
  1968   *The diary of Che Guevara: Bolivia: Nov. 7, 1966–Oct 7, 1967.* Bantam. New York:
         Grosset & Dunlap.

Bibliography

Gulick, Charles A.
1948 *Austria from Hapsburg to Hitler,* Vol. II. Berkeley. California, Univ. of California Press.
Gurr, Ted Robert
1965 The genesis of violence; A multivariate theory of the pre-conditions for civil strife. Unpublished Ph.D dissertation, New York University.
1966 *New error-compensated measures for comparing nations: Some correlates of civil strife.* Princeton, New Jersey: Center of International Studies, Princeton University, Research Monograph No. 25.
1968 Psychological factors in civil violence. *World politics,* **20,** January.
1970a Sources of rebellion in western societies: Some quantitative evidence. *Annals of the American academy of political and social science,* **391,** September.
1970b *Why men rebel.* Princeton, New Jersey: Princeton Univ. Press.
Gurr, Ted Robert, and Ruttenberg, Charles
1967 *The conditions of civil violence: First tests of a causal model.* Princeton University, Research Monograph No. 28.
Gutteridge, William
1962 *Armed forces in new states.* London: Oxford Univ. Press.
Hall, Daniel G. E.
1960 *Burma.* 3rd ed. London: Hutchinson and Co.
Harris, Chester W. (Ed.)
1963 *Problems in measuring change.* Madison, Wisconsin: Univ. of Wisconsin Press.
Hartz, Louis
1964 *The founding of new societies.* New York: Harcourt, Brace and World.
Hasluck, Eugene L.
1938 *Foreign Affairs,* 1919–1937. Cambridge, England: Cambridge Univ. Press.
Hatto, Arthur
1949 Revolution, an enquiry into the usefulness of an historical term. *Mind.* **68.**
Hayden, Tom
1970 *Trial.* New York, Holt, Rinehart and Winston.
Heberle, Rudolph
1951 *Social movements: An introduction to political sociology.* New York: Appleton-Century-Crofts.
Hill, Christopher
1964 *Puritanism and revolution.* New York: Schocken.
Hobsbawm, Eric J.
1959 *Primitive rebels.* Manchester: Manchester Univ. Press.
1965 Pentagon's dilemma; Goliath and the guerilla. *The nation,* **20 1,** July 19.
Hoffer, Eric
1951 *The true believer.* New York: New American Library of World Literature.
Hoover, C. B.
1960 Revolutions and Tyranny. *The Virginia quarterly review,* **36.**
Hopkins, P.
1938 *The psychology of social movements; A psychoanalytic view of society.* London: Allen and Unwin.
Hopper, Rex D.
1950 The revolutionary process, a frame of reference for the study of revolutionary movements. *Social forces,* **28,** March.

Horowitz, Ralph
1967   *The political economy of South Africa.* New York: Praeger.
Horrell, Muriel
   Annual   *A survey of race relations in South Africa.* Johannesburg: South African Institute of Race Relations.
   1966   *Legislation and race relations: A summary of the main South African laws which affect race relationships.* Johannesburg: South African Institute of Race Relations.
   1968   *Terrorism in South Africa.* Johannesburg: South African Institute of Race Relations.
Houghton, D. Hobart
   1964   *The South African economy.* Cape Town: Oxford University Press.

Howard, Michael (Ed.)
   1957   *Soldiers and governments: Nine studies in civil-military relations.* London: Eyre & Spottiswoode.
Huberman, Leo, and Paul M. Sweezy
   1960   *Cuba: Anatomy of a Revolution* (2nd edition); New York: Monthly Review Press.
Huntington, Samuel P.
   1952   *The soldier and the state; The theory and politics of civil-military relations.* Cambridge, Massachusetts: Harvard Univ. Press.
   1961   Patterns of violence in world politics. In Samuel P. Huntington (Ed.) *Changing patterns of military politics.* New York: Free Press.
   1965   Political development and political decay. *World politics,* **17,** April.
Isaacs, Harold
   1961   *The tragedy of the Chinese revolution.* Stanford: Stanford Univ. Press.
Janne, Henri
   1960   Un modele théorique du phénomène revolutionnaire. *Annales,* **15,** November–December.
Janos, Andrew C.
   1963   Unconventional warfare: Framework and analysis. *World politics,* **15,** July.
   1964   *The seizure of power: A study of force and popular consent.* Princeton, New Jersey: Center of International Studies, Princeton University, Research Monograph No. 16.
Janowitz, Morris
   1960   *The professional soldier.* New York: Free Press.
   1964a   (Editor) *The new military: Changing patterns of organization.* New York: Wiley.
   1964b   *The military in the political development of new nations; An essay in comparative analysis.* Chicago: Univ. of Chicago Press.
   1965   *Sociology and the military establishment.* Revised edition. New York: Russell Sage Foundation.
   1968   Armed forces and society: A world perspective. *Armed forces and society: Sociological essays.* Edited by Jacques van Doorn. The Hague: Mouton.
Johnson, Chalmers A.
   1962   Civilian loyalties and guerrilla conflict. *World politics,* **14,** July.
   1964   *Revolution and the social system.* Stanford, California: Stanford University Press, Hoover Institute of War, Revolution and Peace.
   1966   *Revolutionary change.* Boston: Little, Brown and Co.
Johnson, John J. (Ed.)
   1962   *The role of the military in underdeveloped countries.* Princeton: Princeton Univ. Press.

Jureidini, Paul A., Norman A. La Charité, Bert H. Cooper, and William A. Lybrand
    1962   *Casebook on insurgency and revolutionary warfare: 23 summary accounts.*
           Washington D.C.: Special Operations Research Office.
Kaplan, Morton A. (Ed.)
    1962   *The revolution in world politics.* New York: Wiley.
Kecskemeti, Paul
    1958   *Strategic surrender: The politics of victory and defeat.* Stanford, California: Stanford
           Univ. Press.
    1961   *The unexpected revolution.* Stanford, California: Stanford Univ. Press.
Kiernan, B.
    1962   Limitations of U.S. policy toward the underdeveloped world; A note on the soci-
           ology of revolution. *American scholar,* **31.**
Killian, L. M.
    1964   Social movements. In R. E. L. Faris (Ed.) *Handbook of modern sociology.* Chicago:
           Rand McNally and Co.
Kirchheimer, Otto
    1965   Confining conditions and revolutionary breakthroughs. *American Political Science
           Review,* **59,** December.
Knorr, Klaus
    1956   *The war potential of nations.* Princeton: Princeton Univ. Press.

    1962   Unconventional warfare: Strategy and tactics in internal political strife. *The annals
           of the American academy of political and social science,* **346,** May.
Kornhauser, William
    1959   The politics of mass society. New York: Free Press.
    1966   Rebellion and political development. In Harry Eckstein (Ed.), *Internal war: Problems
           and approaches.* New York: Free Press.
Kuper, Leo
    1960 . *Passive resistance in South Africa.* New Haven, Connecticut: Yale Univ. Press.
    1969   *Pluralism in Africa.* Berkeley: Univ. of California Press.

    1971   Theories of revolution and race relations. *Comparative study of society and history,*
           13, January.
Kilpatrick, Ivone
    1964   *Mussolini; A study in power.* New York: Hawthorn Books, p. 55.
Lanternari, Vittorio
    1963   *The religions of the oppressed: A study of modern messianic cults.* New York: Knopf.
Laquer, Walter
    1968   Revolution. *International encyclopedia of the social sciences,* Vol. **13.**
Lasswell, Harold, and Daniel Lerner (Eds.)
    1965   *World revolutionary elites; Studies in coercive ideological movements.* Cambridge,
           Massachusetts: M.I.T. Press.
Lasswell, Harold D., Daniel Lerner, and Abraham Kaplan
    1950   *Power and society: A framework for political inquiry.* New Haven: Yale Univ. Press.

Leach, Edmund R.
    1964   *Political systems of highland Burma: A study of Kachin social structure.* London:
           G. Bell and Sons.
League of Nations
    1924–1939/40. *Armaments yearbook.*

Le Bon, Gustave
    1913   *The psychology of revolution.* New York: Putnam's.
    1960   *The crowd; A study of the popular mind.* New York: Viking Press.

Legget, J. C.
  1963   Uprootedness and working-class consciousness. *American Journal of Sociology,* **68.**
Legum, Colin, and Margaret Legum
  1964   South Africa: *Crisis of the West.* New York: Praeger.
Leiden, Carl, and Karl M. Schmitt.
  1968   *The politics of violence: Revolution in the modern world.* Englewood Cliffs, New Jersey: Prentice-Hall.
Leites, Nathan, and Charles Wolf
  1970   *Rebellion and authority: An analytic essay on insurgent conflicts.* Chicago: Markham.
Lieuwen, Edwin
  1958   *Arms and politics in America.* New York: Praeger.
  1961a *Arms and politics in Latin America.* Revised ed. New York: Praeger.
  1961b The military: A revolutionary force. *The annals of the American academy of political and social science,* **334,** March.
  1964   *Generals vs. presidents; Neo-militarism in Latin America.* New York: Praeger.
Lipset, Seymour Martin
  1960   *Political man: The social bases of politics.* Garden City: Doubleday.
  1963   *The first new nation.* London: Heinemann.
  1968   *Revolution and counterrevolution; Change and persistence in social structures.* New York: Basic Books.
Liu, Frederick F.
  1956   *A military history of modern China: 1924–1949.* Princeton, New Jersey: Princeton Univ. Press.
Luttwak, Edward
  1969   *Coup d'etat.* Greenwich, Connecticut: Fawcett Publications.
Macgaffey, Wyatt, and Barnett, Clifford
  1965   *Twentieth century Cuba: The background of the Castro revolution.* Garden City, New York: Doubleday and Company.
Malaparte, Curzio
  1932   *Coup d'etat, the technique of revolution.* Translated by Sylvia Saunders. New York: E. P. Dutton.
Malloy, James M.
  1970   *Bolivia; The uncompleted revolution.* Pittsburgh: Univ. of Pittsburgh Press.
Marcuse, Herbert
  1954   *Reason and revolution; Hegel and the rise of social theory.* 2nd ed. New York: Humanities Press.
  1969   *An essay on liberation.* Boston: Beacon Press.
Marquard, Leo
  1969   *The peoples and policies of South Africa.* London: Oxford Univ. Press.
Martz, John D.
  1962   *Colombia; A contemporary political survey.* Chapel Hill: Univ. of North Carolina Press.
Marx, Karl
  1906   *Capital.* New York: Random House.
Marx, Karl, and Friedrich Engels
  1896   In Eleanor Marx Aveling (Ed.), *Revolution and counter-revolution.* New York: C. Scribner's Sons.
Marx, Karl, and Engels, Friedrich
  1959   *Manifesto of the communist party.* Moscow: Foreign Languages Publishing House.
Masotti, Louis H., and Don R. Bowen (Eds.)
  1968   *Riots and rebellion: Civil violence in the urban community.* Beverly Hills: Sage Publications.

MacAlister, Lyle N.
   1957   The "fuero militar" in new Spain. Gainseville: Univ. of Florida Press.
Meadows, Paul
   1941   Sequence in revolution. American Sociological review, **6,** October.
Meisel, James H.
   1966   Counterrevolution: How revolutions die. New York: Atherton Press.
Merriman, Robert B.
   1938   Six contemporaneous revolutions. Oxford: Clarendon Press.
Michels, Robert
   1915   Political parties: A sociological study of the oligarchical tendencies of modern de-
          mocracy. New York: Hearst International Library.
Midlarsky, Manus, and Tanter, Raymond
   1967   Toward a theory of political instability in Latin America. Journal of peace research, **3.**
Miksche, F. O.
   n.d.   Secret forces: The technique of underground movements. London: Faber and Faber.
Mills, C. Wright
   1960   Listen Yankee! The revolution in Cuba. New York: McGraw-Hill.
Modelski, George
   1964   International settlement of internal war. In James N. Rosenau (Ed.), International
          aspects of civil strife. Princeton, New Jersey: Princeton Univ. Press.
Moore, Barrington M., Jr.
   1954   Terror and progress in the USSR. Cambrige, Massachusetts: Harvard Univ. Press.
   1962   On the notions of progress, revolution, and freedom. Ethics, **72,** January.
   1966   Social origins of dictatorship and democracy. Boston: Beacon Press.
   1968   Thoughts on violence and democracy. In Robert M. Connery (Ed.) Urban riots:
          Violence and social change. Proceedings of the Academy of Political Science, Vol.
          29, No. 1. New York: The Academy of Political Science.
   1969   Revolution in America? New York review of books, **13,** January, 30.
Moreno, José A.
   1970   Che Guevara on guerrilla warfare: Doctrine, practice and evaluation. Comparative
          studies in society and history, **12,** April.
Mosca, Gaetano
   1939   The ruling class. In Arthur Livingston (Ed. and revised). Translated by Hannah D.
          Kahn. New York: McGraw-Hill.
Mousset, Albert
   1930   L'Albanie devant l'Europe, 1912–1929. Paris: Delagrave.
Neumann, Frantz
   1957   In Herbert Marcuse (Ed.), The democratic and the authoritarian state: Essays in
          political and legal theory. New York: Free Press.
Neumann, Sigmund
   1942   Permanent revolution. New York: Harper and Brothers.
   1949   The structure and strategy of revolutions: 1848 and 1948. Journal of politics, **2.**
Nieburg, H. L.
   1969   Political violence: The behavioral process. New York: St. Martin's Press.
Nomad, Max
   1959   Aspects of revolt; A study in revolutionary theories and techniques. New York:
          Noonday Press.
Novack, George
   1971   Democracy and revolution. New York: Pathfinder Press.

O'Ballance, Edgar
  1962   *The red army of China.* London: Faber and Faber.
Olson, Mancur, Jr.
  1963   Rapid economic growth as a destabilizing force. *Journal of economic history,* **23,** December.
  1965   *The logic of collective action.* Cambridge, Massachusetts: Harvard Univ. Press.
Oppenheimer, Martin
  1969   *The urban guerrilla.* Chicago: Quadrangle Books.
Ortega y Gasset, Jose'
  1960   *The revolt of the masses.* New York: W. W. Norton and Company.
Osanka, Franklin M. (Ed.)
  1962   *Modern guerrilla warfare: Fighting communist guerrilla movements, 1941–1961.* New York: Free Press.
Osborne, Harold
  1944   *Bolivia: A land divided.* 3rd ed. London and New York: Oxford Univ. Press.
Paret, Peter, and John W. Shy
  1962   *Guerrillas in the 1960's.* Revised ed. New York: Praeger.
Pareto, Vilfredo
  1935   *The mind and society.* Vols. **3** and **4.** New York: Harcourt, Brace and Co.
Parkes, H. B.
  1960   *A history of Mexico.* 3rd ed.; Boston: Houghton Mifflin.
Peers, Edgar A.
  1936   *The Spanish tragedy, 1930–1936.* New York: Oxford Univ. Press.
Pettee, George
  1938   *The process of revolution.* New York: Harper.
Phillips, Ruby Hart
  1960   *Cuba: Island of paradox.* New York: McGraw-Hill.
  1969   Political conflict: Perspectives on revolution. *Journal international affairs,* **23.**
Pomeroy, William J. (Ed.)
  1968   *Guerrilla warfare and Marxism.* New York: International Publishers.
Prewitt, Virginia
  1941   The Mexican army, *Foreign affairs,* Vol. XIX. April.
Pustay, John S.
  1965   *Counterinsurgency warfare.* New York: Free Press.
Pye, Lucien W.
  1956   *Guerrilla communism in Malaya: Its social and political meaning.* Princeton, New Jersey: Princeton Univ. Press.
  1964   The roots of insurgency and commencement of rebellions. In Harry Eckstein (Ed.) *Internal war: Problems and approaches.* New York: Free Press.
Rhyne, Russel
  1962   Unconventional warfare—problems and questions. *The annals of the American academy of political and social science.* **34,** May.
Richardson, Lewis F.
  1952   Is it possible to prove any general statements about historical fact? *British journal of sociology,* **3,** March.
  1960   *Statistics of deadly quarrels.* Pittsburgh, Pennsylvania: Boxwood Press.
Ridker, Ronald G.
  1962   Discontent and economic growth. *Economic development and cultural change.* **15,** October.

Riezler, Kurt
  1943   On the psychology of modern revolution. *Social research.* **10.**
Rogers, Barbara
  1971   *The Standard of living of Africans in South Africa.* Notes and documents, No. 45/71, Unit on Apartheid, United Nations, November.
  1972   *South Africa: The Bantu Homelands.* London: International Defense and Aid Fund.
Ropp, Theodore
  1962   *War in the modern world.* revised ed. New York: Collier Books.
Rosenau, James N. (Ed.)
  1964   *International aspects of civil strife.* Princeton, New Jersey: Princeton Univ. Press.
Ross, Stanley R.
  1956   Some observations on military coups in the Caribbean. In A. Curtis Wilgus (Ed.) *The Caribbean: Its political problems.* Gainsville, Florida: University of Florida, School of Inter-American Affairs.
Rothman, Stanley
  1970   Barrington Moore and the dialectics of revolution: An essay review. *American Political Science Review,* **66,** March.
Roux, Edward
  1964   *Time longer than rope: A history of the black man's struggle for freedom in South Africa.* Madison: Univ. of Wisconsin Press.
Rudé, George
  1959   *The crowd in the French revolution.* London: Oxford Univ. Press.
  1964   *The crowd in history, 1730–1884.* New York: Wiley.
Rummel, Rudolph J.
  1963   Testing some possible predictors of conflict behavior within and between nations. *Peace research society papers,* **1.**
  1966a   A foreign conflict behavior code sheet. *World politics,* **18,** January.
  1966b   Dimensions of conflict behavior within nations 1946–1959. *Journal of Conflict Resolution,* **10.**
Russell Ekman, Diana
  1970   A comparative study of the relation between the loyalty of armed forces and the outcome of mass rebellion in the twentieth century. Unpublished Ph.d dissertation, Harvard University.
Russett, Bruce M.
  1964a   Inequality and instability; The relation of land tenure to politics. *World politics,* **16,** April.
  1964b   Measures of military effort. *American Behavioral Scientist,* **7,** February.
Russett, Bruce M., Hayward H. Alker, Karl Deutsch, and Harold Lasswell
  1964c   *World handbook of political and social indicators.* New Haven: Yale Univ. Press.
Sacks, A.
  1970   *The violence of Apartheid.* 2nd ed. London: International Defense & Aid Fund.
Salvemini, Gaetano
  1939   *Historian and scientist: An essay on the nature of history and the social sciences.* Cambridge, Massachusetts: Harvard Univ. Press.
Sandor (Pseud.)
  1963   *The coming struggle for South Africa.* London: The Fabian Society.
Sartre, Jean-Paul
  1961   *Sartre on Cuba.* New York: Ballentine Books.

Sathyamurthy, T. V.
   1965   Revolutions and revolutionaries. *Transition.* 5, No. 2.
Schöffer, I.
   1961   The Dutch revolt anatomized; Some comments. *Comparative studies in society and history,* **3.**
Schwartz, David C.
   1968   Toward a new knowledge-base for military development operations during insurgencies. *Orbis,* **12,** Spring.
Seton-Watson, Hugh
   1951   Twentieth century revolutions. *The Political Quarterly.* **22.**
Shah, Sirdar Ikbal Ali
   1933   *The tragedy of Amanullah.* London: Alexander-Ouseley Ltd.
Sharabi, Hisham B.
   1966   *Nationalism and revolution in the Arab world.* Princeton: Van Nostrand.
Sharp, Gene
   1959   The meaning of non-violent resistance: A typology. *Journal of Conflict Resolution.* **3,** March.
Silvert, Kalman H.
   1961   *Reaction and revolution in Latin America.* New Orleans: Hauser Press.
Simons, H. J., and Simons, R. E.
   1969   *Class and colour in South Africa 1850–1950.* Harmondsworth: Penguin.
Singer, J. David, and Melvin Small
   1966   The composition and status ordering of the international system: 1815–1940. *World politics.* **18,** January.
Smelser, Neil J.
   1959   *Social change in the industrial revolution.* Chicago: Univ. of Chicago Press.
   1963   *Theory of collective behavior.* New York: Free Press.
Snyder, David, and Charles Tilly
   1972   Hardship and collective violence in France, 1830 to 1960. *American Sociological Review.* **37,** October.
Sorel, Georges
   1961   *Reflections on violence.* New York: Collier Books.
Sorokin, Pitirim A.
   1925   *The sociology of revolution.* Philadelphia: Lippincott.
   1962a   *Society, culture and personality.* New York: Cooper Square Publishers.
   1962b   *Social and cultural dynamics.* Vol. 3. New York: Bedminster Press.
Southwood, Ken
   1967   Riot and revolt: Sociological theories of political violence. *Peace Research Reviews.* **1,** June.
Stinchcombe, Arthur L.
   1965   Social structure and organization. *Handbook of organizations.* Edited by James G. March. Chicago: Rand McNally.
Stone, Lawrence
   1965   *Social change and revolution in England 1540–1640.* London: Longmans, Green and Co.
   1966   Theories of revolution. *World politics.* **18,** January.
Swire, Joseph
   1929   *Albania: The rise of a kingdom.* London: Unwin Brothers Ltd.
Sykes, Percy
   1940   *A history of Afghanistan,* Vol. 2. London: Macmillan and Co.

Taber, Robert
  1970   *The war of the flea.* New York: Citadel Press.
Talmon, J. L.
  1952   *The rise of totalitarian democracy.* Boston: Beacon Press.
Tannenbaum, Frank
  1960   The Mexican and Cuban Revolutions. In D. L. B. Hamlin (Ed.), *The Latin Americas,
          the Couchiching Conference.* Toronto: The Canadian Institute on Public Affairs,
          Univ. of Toronto Press.
  1962   *Ten keys to Latin America.* New York: Knopf.
Tanter, Raymond
  1966   Dimensions of conflict behavior within and between nations, 1958–1960. *Journal of
          conflict resolution,* **10,** March.
Tanter, Raymond, and Manus Midlarsky
  1967   A theory of revolution. *Journal of Conflict Resolution.* **11,** September.
Thomas, Hugh
  1971   *Cuba: The pursuit of freedom.* New York: Harper.
Thrupp, Sylvia L. (Ed.)
  1962   *Millennial dreams in action.* The Hague: Mouton.
Tilly, Charles
  1963   The analysis of a counter-revolution. *History and theory,* **3.**
  1964a Reflections on the revolutions of Paris. *Social problems,* **12.**
  1964b *The Vendee.* Cambridge, Massachusetts: Harvard Univ. Press.
  1969   Collective violence in European perspective. In Hugh Davis Graham and Ted Robert
          Gurr (Ed.), *Violence in America; Historical and comparative perspectives.* Wash-
          ington D.C.; National Commission on the Causes and Prevention of violence.
  1974   Revolutions   and   collective   violence.   In Fred I. Greenstein and Nelson
          Polsby (Ed.), *Handbook of political science.* Reading, Massachusetts: Addison-
          Wesley.
Tilly, Charles, and James Rule
  1965   *Measuring political upheaval.* Princeton: Center of International Studies, Princeton
          Univ. Research Monograph No. **19.**
Timasheff, Nicholas S.
  1965   *War and revolution.* New York: Sheed and Ward.
Toch, Hans
  1965   *The social psychology of social movements.* Indianapolis: Bobbs-Merrill Co.
Trotsky, Leon
  1959   In F. W. Dupee (Ed.), *The Russian revolution.* Garden City, New York: Doubleday.
Tse-tung, Mao
  1954   *Selected works.* **1–4,** New York: International Publishers Co.
  1963   *Selected military writings.* Peking: Foreign Language Press.
  1967   In Stuart R. Schram, *Quotations from Chairman Mao Tse-tung.* Bantam. New York:
          Grosset & Dunlap.
Tucker, Robert C.
  1961   Towards a comparative politics of movement regimes. *American political science
          review,* **55,** June.
  1968   *Paths of communist revolution.* Princeton: Center of International Studies, Princeton
          University, Research Monograph No. 29.
Turner, Ralph H., and Killian, L. M.
  1957   *Collective Behavior.* Englewood Cliffs, New Jersey: Prentice-Hall.
Ulam, Adam B.
  1960   *The unfinished revolution.* Cambridge, Massachusetts: Harvard Univ. Press.

Vagts, Alfred
1959   *A history of militarism, civilian and military.* London: Hollis & Carter.
Váli, Ferene Albert
1961   *Rift and revolt in Hungary: Nationalism versus communism.* Cambridge, Massachusetts: Harvard Univ. Press.
van den Berghe, Pierre L.
1965   *South Africa: A study in conflict.* Middletown: Weslegan Univ. Press.
Van Doorn, Jacques (Ed.)
1968   *Armed forces and society: Sociological essays.* The Hague, Netherlands: Mouton.
Venturi, Franco
1966   *Roots of revolution.* New York: Grosset & Dunlap.
Wada, George, and James Davies
1957   Riots and rioters. *Western Political Quarterly.* **10,** December.
Waelder, Robert
1967   *Progress and revolution.* New York: International Univ. Press.
Wallace, Anthony F. C.
1956   Revitalization movements. *American Anthropologists.* **58,** April.
Walter, E. V.
1964a   Violence and the process of terror. *American Sociological Review.* **29,** April.
1964b   Power and violence. *American political science review.* **58,** June.
1969   *Terror and resistance.* New York: Oxford Univ. Press.
Walzer, Michael
1963   Revolutionary ideology: The case of the Marian exiles. *American Political Science Review.* **57,** September.
1965   *The revolution of the saints; A study in the origins of radical politics.* Cambridge, Massachusetts: Harvard Univ. Press.
Weber, Max
1947   In A. M. Henderson and Talcott Parsons (Trans. and Ed.), *The theory of social and economic organization.* New York: Oxford Univ. Press.
1964   What indicates what? World handbook of political and social indicators. *American Behavioral Scientist.* **8,** December.
Wigdil, W.
1912   Addition without division = revolution, *Independent.* **72,** June 20.
Wild, Roland
1933   *Amanullah, ex-king of Afghanistan.* London: Hurst and Blackett.
Willer, David, and George K. Zollschan
1964   Prolegomena to a theory of revolutions. In George K. Zollschan and Walter Hirsch (Eds.), *Explorations in social change.* Boston: Houghton Mifflin.
Wilson, Francis
1970   *Information service manual on Southern Africa.* London: International Defense and Aid Fund.
Wintringham, Thomas Henry
1936   *Mutiny: Being a survey of mutinies from Spartacus to Invergordon.* London: Stanley Nott.
Woddis, Jack
1972   *New theories of revolution.* New York: International Publishers.
Wolf, Kurt H. (Ed.)
1950   *The sociology of Georg Simmel.* New York: Free Press.

Wolf, Eric R.
   1969a   On peasant rebellions. *International Social Science Journal.* **21.**
   1969b   *Peasant wars of the twentieth century.* New York: Harper.
Wolfe, J. N., and John Erickson (Eds.)
   n.d. *The armed services and society.* Edinburgh: Edinburgh Univ. Press.
Wolff, Robert Paul, Barrington Moore, Jr., and Herbert Marcuse
   1965   *A critique of pure tolerance.* Boston: Beacon Press.
Wolfenstein, E. Victor
   1967   *The revolutionary personality: Lenin, Trotsky, Gandhi.* Princeton, New Jersey:
          Princeton Univ. Press.
Worsley, Peter
   1961   The analysis of rebellion and revolution in modern British social anthropology.
          Science and Society. **25.**
   1968   *The trumpet shall sound: A study of "cargo" cults in Melanesia.* 2nd ed. New York:
          Schocken Books.
Wright, Quincy
   1965   *A study of war.* Vols. 1 and 2. Revised ed. Chicago: Univ. of Chicago Press.
Yoder, Dale
   1926   Current definitions of revolution. *American Journal of Sociology,* **32,** November.
Young, Jordan M.
   1967   *The Brazilian revolution of 1930 and the aftermath.* New Brunswick, New Jersey:
          Rutgers Univ. Press.
Zawodny, J. K.
   1962   Guerrilla and sabotage: Organization, operations, motivations, escalation. *Annals
          of the American academy of political and social science.* **341,** May.
Zinner, P. E.
   1962   *Revolution in Hungary.* New York: Columbia Univ. Press.

SOURCES USED FOR OBTAINING A UNIVERSE OF MASS REBELLIONS

Annual register of world events. 1907–1967.
Britannica book of the year. 1938–1967.
Encyclopedia britannica. 1967. Vols. I–XXIII.
Facts-on-file: Weekly world news digest with cumulative index. 1940–1967.
Hispanic American report. 1948–1967.
Keesing's contemporary archives. 1931–1967.
New international year book: A compendium of the world's affairs. 1907–1967.
Statesman's yearbook. 1907–1967.

CASE STUDY SOURCES

AFGHANISTAN

Castagne, Joseph A.
   1935   Soviet imperialism in Afghanistan. *Foreign affairs,* **13.**
Chokaiev, Mustafa
   1930   The situation in Afghanistan. *Asiatic Review,* **26.**
Fletcher, Arnold
   1965   *Afghanistan, highway of conquest.* Ithaca, New York: Cornell Univ. Press.

Fraser-Tytler, William Kerr
    1967   *Afghanistan: A study of political developments in central and southern Asia.* 3rd ed.
        London: Oxford Univ. Press.
Habibullah, Amir
    1930   *My life from brigand to king.* London: Sampson Low, Maiston and Co.
Shah, Sirdar Ikbal Ali
    1933a   *Modern Afghanistan.* London: Sampson Low, Maiston and Co.
    1933b   *The tragedy of Amanullah.* London: Alexander-Ouseley Ltd.
Sykes, Sir Percy
    1940   *A history of Afghanistan.* **2,** London: Macmillan.
Taillardat, C. F.
    1929   *Révolte Afghane.* Paris: L'Asie Française.
Viollis, Andrée (pseud.)
    1930   *Tourmente sur L'Afghanistan.* Paris: Libraire Valois.
Wilber, Donald N.
    1962   *Annotated bibliography of Afghanistan.* 2nd ed. New Haven: Human Relations
        Area Files Press.
Wild, Roland
    1933   *Amanullah, ex-king of Afghanistan.* London: Hurst and Blackett.

ALBANIA

Brooks, E. W.
    1962   A list of materials for the study of the history of Albania. Unpublished.
Federal Writer's Project
    1939   *The Albanian struggle in the old world and the new.* Boston: The Writer.
Mousset, Albert
    1930   *L'Albanie devant l'Europe, 1912–1929.* Paris: Delagrave.
Skendi, Stavro (Ed.)
    1957   *Albania.* London: Atlantic Press.
Swire, Joseph
    1929   *Albania: The rise of a kingdom.* London: Unwin Brothers Ltd.

AUSTRIA

Anon.
    1935   *The death of Dollfuss; An official history of the revolt of July, 1934 in Austria.* Trans-
        lated by J. Messinger. London: Denis Archer.
Bauer, Otto
    1924   *Austrian democracy under fire.* London: Labour Publications Dept.
Braunthal, Julius
    1945   *In search of the millennium.* London: Victor Gollancz.

    1948   *The tragedy of Austria.* London: Victor Gollancz.
Brook-Shepherd, Gordon
    1961   *Dollfuss.* London: Macmillan and Co.
Buttinger, Joseph
    1953   *In the twilight of socialism; A history of the revolutionary socialists in Austria.* New
        York: Praeger.

Deutsch, Julius
    1934   *The civil war in Austria.* D. P. Berenberg Trans. Chicago: Socialist Party National
        Headquarters.
Gedye, George E. R.
    1939   *Fallen bastions; The central European tragedy.* London: Victor Gollancz.
Gregory, John D.
    1935   *Dollfuss and his times.* London: Hutchinson and Co.
Gulick, Charles A.
    1948   *Austria from Hapsburg to Hitler.* Vol. 2. Berkeley, California: Univ. of California
        Press.
Hamilton, Cicely
    1935   *Modern Austria.* London: J. M. Dent and Sons.
Hasluck, Eugene L.
    1938   *Foreign affairs, 1919–1937.* Cambridge, England: Cambridge Univ. Press.
Sweet, Paul R.
    1950   Democracy and counter-revolution in Austria. *Journal of modern history,* **22,**
        March.

BOLIVIA

Alexander, Robert J.
    1958   *The Bolivian national revolution.* New Brunswick, New Jersey: Rutgers Univ. Press.
Barton, Robert
    1968   *A short history of Bolivia.* 2nd ed. La Paz: Editorial Los Amigos del Libro.
Malloy, James M.
    1970   *Bolivia: The uncompleted revolution.* Pittsburgh: Univ of Pittsburgh Press.
Osborne, Harold
    1944   *Bolivia; A land divided.* 3rd ed. New York: Oxford Univ. Press.
Patch, R. W.
    1961   Bolivia: The restrained revolution. *The annals of the American academy of political
        and social sciences,* **187,** March.
Zondag, Cornelius H.
    1966   *The Bolivian economy, 1952–1965; The revolution and its aftermath.* New York:
        Praeger.

BRAZIL

Bello, José M.
    1966   In J. L. Taylor (Translator); *A history of modern Brazil, 1889–1964.* Stanford,
        California: Stanford Univ. Press.
Camacho, Jorge Abel
    1952   *Brazil: An interim assessment.* London: Royal Institute of International Affairs.
Dulles, John W. F.
    1967   *Vargas of Brazil; A political biography.* Austin: Univ. of Texas Press.

Johnson, John J.
  1964   *The military and society in Latin America.* Stanford: Stanford Univ. Press.
Loewenstein, Karl
  1942   *Brazil under Vargas.* New York: Macmillan.
Poppino, Rollie Edward
  1968   *Brazil: The land and the people.* New York: Oxford Univ. Press.
Skidmore, Thomas E.
  1967   *Politics in Brazil; 1930–1964; An experiment in democracy.* New York: Oxford
         Univ. Press.
Young, Jordan M.
  1967   *The Brazilian revolution of 1930 and the aftermath.* New Brunswick, New Jersey:
         Rutgers Univ. Press.

BURMA

Cady, John F.
  1958   *A history of modern Burma.* Ithaca, New York: Cornell Univ. Press.
Hall, David G. E.
  1960   *Burma.* 3rd ed. London: Hutchinson.
Tinker, Hugh
  1967   *The union of Burma.* 4th ed. London: Oxford Univ. Press.
Trager, Frank N.
  1954   *Burma: Land of golden pagodas.* New York: Foreign Policy Association
  1966   *Burma: From kingdom to republic: A historical and political analysis.* New York:
         Praeger.

CHINA

Barnett, A. Doak
  1962   *Communist China in perspective.* New York: Praeger.
  1963   *China on the eve of communist takeover.* New York: Praeger.
Chassin, Lionel Max
  1965   *The communist conquest of China: A history of the civil war 1945–1949.* Cambridge,
         Massachusetts: Harvard Univ. Press.
Chen, Jerome
  1965   *Mao and the Chinese revolution.* New York: Oxford Univ. Press.
Chêng, Ch'êng-K'un
  1952   *The dragon sheds its scales.* New York: New Voices Publishing Co.
Fitzgerald, Charles Patrick
  1952   *Revolution in China.* New York: Praeger.
Gittings, John
  1967   *The role of the Chinese army.* London: Oxford Univ. Press.
Griffith, Samuel B., II
  1967   *The Chinese people's liberation army.* New York: McGraw-Hill.
Isaacs, Harold Robert
  1961   *The tragedy of the Chinese revolution.* Stanford: Stanford Univ. Press.

Johnson, Chalmers A.
   1962 *Peasant nationalism and communist power.* Stanford, California: Stanford Univ.
      Press.
Liu, Frederick Fu
   1956 *A military history of modern China: 1924–1949.* Princeton, New Jersey: Princeton
      Univ. Press.
North, Robert C.
   1963 *Moscow and Chinese communists.* (2nd Ed.) Stanford, California: Stanford Univ.
      Press.
O'Ballance, Edgar
   1962 *The red army of China.* London: Faber and Faber.
Rigg, Robert B.
   1951 *Red China's fighting hordes.* Harrisburg, Pensylvania: Military Service Publishing Co.
Schwartz, Ben I.
   1951 *Chinese communism and the rise of Mao.* Cambridge, Massachusetts: Harvard Univ.
      Press.
Snow, Edgar
   1961 *Red star over China.* New York: Grove Press.
United States Department of State
   1949 *United States relations with China, with special reference to the period 1944–1949.*
      Washington D.C.: U.S. Government Printing Office.
United States Department of War
   1952 Military Intelligence Division. *The Chinese communist movement,* 5 July 1949, in
      U.S. Senate, Committee on the Judiciary. *Institute of Pacific Relations, Hearings
      before the Subcommittee to Investigate the Administration of Internal Security Laws.*
      82nd Congress, 2nd Session, Part 7a, Appendix 2.

COLOMBIA

Anon.
   1948 Bogota beserk. *Newsweek,* April 19.
Beaulac, Willard L.
   1951 *Career Ambassador.* New York: Macmillan.
Bernstein, Harry
   1964 *Venezuela and Colombia.* New Jersey: Prentice-Hall.
Dix, Robert H.
   1967 Colombia: *The political dimensions of change.* New Haven: Yale Univ. Press.
Dubois, Jules
   1959 *Freedom is my beat.* New York, Bobbs-Merrill Co.
Fluharty, Vernon L.
   1957 *Dance of the millions; Military rule and the social revolution in Colombia, 1930–
      1956.* Pittsburgh, Pennsylvania: Univ. of Pittsburgh Press.
Galbraith, William O.
   1966 *Colombia: A general survey.* London: Oxford Univ. Press.
Hobsbawm, Eric J.
   1963 The revolutionary situation in Colombia. *World Today.* **19,** June.
Martz, John D.
   1962 *Colombia; A contemporary political survey.* Chapel Hill: Univ. of North Carolina
      Press.

CUBA 1912

Beals, Carleton
  1933 *The crime of Cuba.* Philadelphia: Lippincott Co.
Chapman, Charles E.
  1927 *A history of the Cuban republic.* New York: Macmillan Co.
Fitzgibbon, Russell H.
  1964 *Cuba and the United States 1900–1935.* New York: Russell & Russell.
Johnson, Willis F.
  1920 *The history of Cuba.* **4,** New York: B. F. Buck and Co.
Kennedy, W. M.
  1913 The revolution in Cuba. *Living Age.* **176,** February.
Rowland, Donald Winslow
  1926 The Cuban race war of 1912. Unpublished M.A. dissertation, Univ. of California, Berkeley.
Strode, Hudson
  1934 *The pageant of Cuba.* New York: Harrison Smith and Robert Haas.
Wigdil, W.
  1912 Addition without division = revolution. *Independent.* **72,** June 20.

CUBA 1958

Brennan, Ray
  1959 *Castro, Cuba, and justice.* Garden City, New York: Doubleday and Co.
Chapelle, Dickey
  1962 In Franklin M. Osanka (Ed.), How Castro won. *Modern guerrilla warfare: Fighting communist guerrilla movements, 1941–1961.* New York: Free Press.
Draper, Theodore
  1962 *Castro's revolution: Myths and realities.* New York: Praeger.
Dubois, Jules
  1959 *Fidel Castro.* New York: Bobbs-Merrill Co.
Du Four, J. M.
  1964 *Révolution: Capitale Cuba.* Paris: Tableronde.
Fagg, John Edwin
  1965 *Cuba, Haiti, and the Dominican Republic.* Englewood Cliffs, New Jersey: Prentice-Hall.
Fort, Gilberto V.
  1960 *The Cuban revolution of Fidel Castro viewed from abroad: An annotated bibliography.* Lawrence, Kansas: Univ. of Kansas Libraries.
Freeman, Thomas (pseud.)
  1963 *The crisis in Cuba.* Derby, Connecticut: Monarch Books.
Goldenberg, Boris
  1965 *The Cuban revolution and Latin America.* New York: Praeger.
Guevara, Ernesto C.
  1968 *Reminiscences of the Cuban revolutionary war.* New York: Monthly Review Press.
Huberman, Leo, and Paul M. Sweezy
  1960 *Cuba: Anatomy of a revolution.* 2nd ed. New York: Monthly Review Press.

International Commission of Jurists
    1962   *Cuba and the rule of law.* Geneva: International Commission of Jurists.
Kling, Merle
    1962   Cuba: A case study of a successful attempt to seize political power by the application
           of unconventional warfare. *Annals of the American academy of political and social
           science.* **391,** May.
Macgaffey, Wyatt, and Clifford R. Barnett
    1965   *Twentieth century Cuba; The background of the Castro revolution.* Garden City,
           New York: Doubleday and Co.
Matthews, Herbert L.
    1964   *Cuba.* New York: Macmillan.
Mesa-Lago, Carmelo (Ed.)
    1971   *Revolutionary change in Cuba.* Pittsburgh, Pennsylvania: Univ. of Pittsburgh Press.
Mills, C. Wright
    1960   *Listen, yankee! The revolution in Cuba.* New York: Ballentine Books.
Otero Echeverria, Rafael
    1959   *Reportaje a una revolución de Batista á* Fidel Castro. Santiago de Chile: Editorial
           del Pacifico.
Pflaum, Irving P.
    1964   *Arena of decision: Latin America in crisis.* Englewood Cliffs, New Jersey: Prentice-
           Hall.
Phillips, Ruby Hart
    1960   *Cuba: Island of paradox.* New York: McGraw-Hill.
Ruiz, Ramón
    1968   *Cuba: The making of revolution.* Amherst, Massachusetts: Univ of Massachusetts
           Press.
Sartre, Jean-Paul
    1961   *Sartre on Cuba.* New York: Ballantine Books.
Suárez, Andrés
    1967   *Cuba; Castroism and communism, 1950–1966.* Cambridge, Massachusetts:
           Massachusetts Institute of Technology Press.
Taber, Robert
    1961   *M-26, biography of a revolution.* New York: Lyle Stuart.
Thomas, Hugh
    1971   *Cuba: The pursuit of freedom.* New York: Harper & Row.

HONDURAS

Stokes, William S.
    1950   *Honduras: An area study in government.* Madison: Univ. of Wisconsin Press.

ITALY

Albrecht-Carrié, René
    1950   *Italy from Napoleon to Mussolini.* New York: Colombia Univ. Press.

Croce, Benedetto
    1963 In C. M. Ady (Trans.), *A history of Italy 1871–1915.* New York: Russell and Russell.
Finer, Herman
    c1935 *Mussolini's Italy.* New York: Holt.
Halperin, Samuel W.
    1964 *Mussolini and Italian Fascism.* Princeton, New Jersey: Van Nostrand Co.
Herder, H. and Waley, Daniel P. (Eds.)
    1963 *A short history of Italy.* Cambridge, England: Cambridge Univ. Press.
Horowitz, Daniel
    1963 *The Italian labor movement.* Cambridge, Massachusetts: Harvard Univ. Press.
Hughes, Serge
    1967 *The fall and rise of modern Italy.* New York: Macmillan Co.
Kirkpatrick, Ivone
    1964 *Mussolini; A study in power.* New York: Hawthorn Books.
McClellan, George B.
    1933 *Modern Italy; A short history.* Princeton, New Jersey: Princeton Univ. Press.
Mussolini, Benito
    1936 *My autobiography.* New York: Charles Scribner's Sons.
Salomone, Arcangelo W.
    1945 *Italian democracy in the making; The political scene in the Giolillian era 1900–1914.*
        Philadelphia: Univ. of Pennsylvania Press.
Salvadori, Masimo
    1965 *Italy.* Englewood Cliffs, New Jersey: Prentice-Hall.
Salvatorelli, Luigi
    1940 *A concise history of Italy.* London: Oxford Univ. Press.
Salvemini, Gaetano
    1936 *Under the axe of fascism.* New York: Viking Press.
Seton-Watson, Christopher
    1967 *Italy from liberalism to fascism; 1870–1925.* London; Methuen.
Smith, D. Mack
    1959 *Italy: A modern history.* Ann Arbor: Univ. of Michigan Press.
Sprigge, Cecil J. S.
    1944 *The development of modern Italy.* New Haven: Yale Univ. Press.
Surace, Samuel J.
    1966 *Ideology, economic change and the working classes; The case of Italy.* Berkeley,
        California: Univ. of California Press.
Thayer, John A.
    1964 *Italy and the great war; Politics and culture, 1870–1915.* Madison: Univ. of
        Wisconsin Press.
United States War Department, Office of the Chief of Staff.
    1916 *Strength and organization of France, Germany, Austria, Russia, England, Italy,
        Mexico and Japan.* Washington D. C.: Government Printing Office.
Villari, Luigi
    1929 *Italy.* London: Ernest Benn Ltd.
Wallace, William K.
    1917 *Greater Italy.* New York: Charles Scribner's Sons.
Whyte, Arthur J.
    1944 *The evolution of modern Italy.* Oxford: Basil Blackwell.
Zampaglione, Gerardo
    1956 *Italy.* New York: Praeger.

MEXICO

Beals, Carleton
   1932 *Porfirio Díaz.* Philadelphia: Lippincott.
Callcott, Wilfred H.
   1931 *Liberalism in Mexico, 1857–1929.* Stanford, California: Stanford Univ. Press.
Cline, Howard F.
   1953 *The United States and Mexico.* Cambridge, Massachusetts: Harvard Univ. Press.
Cline, Howard F.
   1962 *Mexico: Revolution to evolution 1940–1960.* London: Oxford Univ. Press.
Cumberland, Charles C.
   1952 *Mexican Revolution.* Austin: Univ. of Texas Press.
Gruening, Ernest
   1928 *Mexico and its heritage.* New York: Century.
Jones, Chester Lloyd
   1921 *Mexico and its reconstruction.* New York: D. Appleton and Co.
Parkes, Henry B.
   1960 *A history of Mexico.* 3rd ed. Boston: Houghton Mifflin.
Prewitt, Virginia
   1941 The Mexican army. *Foreign affairs,* **19,** April.
Quirk, Robert
   1960 *Mexican revolution, 1914–1915.* Bloomington: Indiana Univ. Press.
Ross, Stanley R.
   1955 *Francisco I. Madero; Apostle of Mexican democracy.* New York: Columbia Univ.
       Press.
Tannenbaum, Frank
   1933 *Peace by revolution: Mexico after 1910.* New York: Columbia Univ. Press.
   1950 *Mexico: The struggle for peace and bread.* New York: Knopf.
Womack, John, Jr.
   1969 *Zapata and the Mexican revolution.* New York: Knopf.

SPAIN

Anon.
   1934 *Bulletin of Spanish studies.*
Carr, Raymond
   1966 *Spain, 1808–1939.* Oxford: Clarendon Press.
de Madariaga, S.
   1958 *Spain.* New York: Praeger.
Jackson, Gabriel
   1965 *The Spanish republic and the civil war, 1931–1939.* Princeton, New Jersey: Prince-
       ton Univ. Press.
Manuel, Frank E.
   1938 *The politics of modern Spain.* New York: McGraw-Hill.
Peers, Edgar A.
   1936 *The Spanish tragedy, 1930–1936.* New York: Oxford Univ. Press.
Petrie, Sir Charles
   1952 *The history of Spain.* Part 2. (2nd Ed.) London: Eyre and Spottiswoode.

Smith, Rhea M.
    1965   *Spain; A modern history.* Ann Arbor: Univ. of Michigan Press.
Thomas, Hugh
    1961   *The Spanish civil war.* New York: Harper.

SOUTH AFRICA

Adam, Heribert
    1971a *Modernizing racial domination.* Berkeley, California: Univ. of California Press.
    1971b (Ed.) *South Africa: Sociological perspectives.* London: Oxford Univ. Press.
Benson, Mary
    1966   *South Africa: The struggle for a birthright.* London: Penguin.
Bunting, Brian
    1964   *The rise of the South African reich.* London: Penguin.
Carstens, Kenneth
    1973   Economic conditions of Africans in South Africa. Unpublished paper, Harvard
           Divinity School, January.
Carter, Gwendolen M.
    1962   *The politics of inequality: South Africa since 1948.* New York: Praeger.
De Kiewiet, C. W.
    1965   South Africa's gamble with history. *The Virginia Quarterly Review.* **40,** Winter.
Duncan, Patrick
    1964   *South Africa's rule of violence.* London: Methuen.
First, Ruth, Steele, Jonathan, and Gurney, Christabel
    1972   *The South African connection; Western investment in apartheid.* London: Temple
           Smith.
Horowitz, Ralph
    1967   *The political economy of South Africa.* New York: Praeger.
Horrell, Muriel
    Annual   *A Survey of Race Relations in South Africa.* Johannesburg: South African Institute of
           Race Relations.
    1966   *Legislation and race relations: A summary of the main South African laws which*
           affect race relationships. Johannesburg: South African Institute of Race Relations.
    1968   *Terrorism in South Africa.* Johannesburg: South African Institute of Race Relations.
Houghton, D. Hobart
    1964   *The South African economy.* Cape Town: Oxford Univ. Press.
Kuper, Leo
    1960   *Passive resistance in South Africa.* New Haven: Yale Univ. Press.
    1967   *An African bourgeoisie: Race, class, and politics in South Africa.* New Haven,
           Connecticut: Yale Univ. Press.
    1969a Conflict and the plural society: Ideologies of violence among subordinate groups.
           In Leo Kuper and M. G. Smith (Eds.), *Pluralism in Africa.* Berkeley, California:
           Univ. of California Press.
    1969b Political change in white settler societies: The possibility of peaceful democratiza-
           tion. In Leo Kuper and M. G. Smith (Eds.), *Pluralism in Africa.* Berkeley,
           California: Univ. of California Press.

1970   Nonviolence revisited. In R. J. Rotberg and Ali A. Mazrui (Eds.), *Protest and power in black Africa*. New York: Oxford Univ. Press.

1971   African nationalism in South Africa, 1910–1964. *The Oxford history of South Africa. Vol. 2. South Africa 1870–1966*. Edited by Monica Wilson and Leonard Thompson. Oxford: Clarendon Press.

Lawrence, John
1968   *The seeds of disaster*. New York: Taplinger.

Legum, Colin, and Margaret Legum
1964   *South Africa: Crisis of the west*. New York: Praeger.

Mandela, Nelson
1965   *No easy walk to freedom*. London: Heinemann.

Marquard, Leo
1969   *The peoples and policies of South Africa*. London: Oxford Univ. Press.

Mbeki, Govan A. M.
1964   *South Africa: The peasant's revolt*. Baltimore: Penguin.

Ngubane, Jordan K.
1963   *An African explains apartheid*. New York: Praeger.

Rogers, Barbara
1971   *The standard of living of Africans in South Africa*. Notes and Documents, No. 45/71. Unit on Apartheid, United Nations, November.

1972   *South Africa: The "Bantu homelands."* London: International Defence & Aid Fund.

Rotberg, R. J. and Mazrui, Ali A. (Eds.)
1970   *Protest and power in black Africa*. New York: Oxford University Press.

Roux, Edward
1964   *Time longer than rope: A history of the black man's struggle for freedom in South Africa*. Madison: Univ. of Wisconsin Press.

Sachs, A.
1970   *South Africa: The violence of apartheid*. (2nd Ed.) London: International Defence & Aid Fund.

Sandor (pseud.)
1963   *The coming struggle for South Africa*. London: The Fabian Society.

Simons, H. J., and R. E. Simons
1969   *Class and colour in Africa 1850–1950*. Harmondsworth: Penguin.

Tomlinson, F. R., et al.
1956   *Report submitted by the commission on the socio-economic development of the Bantu areas within the Union of South Africa*. Pretoria, South Africa: Government Printers.

van den Berghe, Pierre L.
1965   *South Africa: A study in conflict*. Middletown: Wesleyan Univ. Press.

van der Horst, Sheila
1965   The effects of industrialization on race relations in South Africa. In G. Hunter (Ed.). *Industrialization and race relations*. London: Oxford Univ. Press.

Wilson, Monica, and Leonard Thompson (Eds.)
1971   *The Oxford history of South Africa. 2, South Africa 1870–1966*. Oxford: Clarendon Press.

Index